Fiscal Limits of Absolutism

Fiscal Limits
of Absolutism

Direct Taxation in Early
Seventeenth-Century France

James B. Collins

University of California Press

Berkeley / Los Angeles / London

University of California Press
Berkeley and Los Angeles, California

University of California Press, Ltd.
London, England

© 1988 by
The Regents of the University of California

Library of Congress Cataloging-in-Publication Data

Collins, James B.
    Fiscal limits of absolutism.

    Bibliography: p.
    Includes index.
        1. Taxation—France—History—17th century.   2. Tax
administration and procedure—History—17th century.
3. France—Politics and government—17th century.
4. Elite (Social sciences)—France—History—17th century.
5. Despotism—History—17th century.   I. Title.
HJ2648.C65   1987   336.2'00944   87-19090
ISBN 0-520-05911-5 (alk. paper)

Printed in the United States of America

1   2   3   4   5   6   7   8   9

Contents

List of Tables

Appendix

Abbreviations

AD	Archives départementales
AM	Archives municipales
AN	Archives Nationales
Annales E.S.C.	*Annales Economies. Sociétés. Civilisations.*
BN	Bibliothèque Nationale
d.	*denier* (penny) 240 pence = 20 shillings = 1 pound
l.	*livre tournois* (French pound)
l.m.	*livre monnaie* (Breton pound)
Ms.	Manuscrits
Ms. Fr.	Manuscrits Français
NAF	Nouvelles Acquisitions Françaises
ob.	*obolle* (half-penny)
Ordonnances	*Ordonnances des rois de France de la troisième race.* 14 vols. Paris, 1722–1848.
s.	*sou* (shilling)

Acknowledgments

Nancy and I set out for great adventure in France in March 1975, hoping to enjoy the delights of French life while I toiled away in various archives. It was not quite the idyll we had anticipated, but it was the start of an adventure that has taken us to more parts of France than we had ever imagined. I still marvel that she has survived the various hardships of our travels, as well as the mountain of clutter the research has produced. She has been a bulwark of strength and support throughout the research, writing, and living of the past eleven years.

The moral support so essential for this work has come also from others, most of all from my mother, sisters, and daughters. Straddling the line between personal and professional among my friends are my Lafayette colleagues, especially Bob Weiner and Don Miller, and the old China Jocks at Columbia. Reaching further back, to my first mentors, I have not forgotten that Al Beebe and Nathan Rosen helped a young man when he needed it most. Lastly, I would like to thank our old friend, Stewart Galanor, who shared one of our most delightful trips to France and whose well-timed bottles of champagne made this process seem worth it when I wasn't sure if it was.

The professional debts one accumulates in years of research and writing are too numerous to repay in a few sentences. This work owes much to my teachers, to Allan Wise and George Adams of the Loomis School, to Bob Kreiser of the University of Rochester, under whom I first studied early modern France, and to Marc Raeff at Columbia, from whom I learned so much of the historian's craft. Two of my Columbia mentors are also good friends: I would like to thank Gene Rice and Andrzej Kaminski in both respects. Lastly, there is Wim Smit, under whose direction I wrote my thesis. Were it not for his constant editorial discipline, I would probably still be at it. Thanks, Wim.

Other colleagues, at home and abroad, have offered helpful suggestions and have pointed out some of the shortcomings of earlier drafts. In France, I owe special debts to Jean Bart, Françoise Bayard, Bernard Barbiche, the late Georges de Braux, Emmanuel Le Roy Ladurie, Jean Meyer, Michel Morineau, and, especially, to Jean Tanguy (and his family). Closer to home, Orest Ranum, Jim Riley, Peg Brown, Hilton Root, and Bill Beik have all offered important suggestions about the manuscript, while Jon Dewald gave special encouragement when it was needed. There is no room to mention the many archivists and their staffs who have been so patient, helpful, and good-humored in the face of my many requests. I would, nonetheless, like to give special thanks to the personnel of the Departmental Archives of the Loire-Atlantique, Ille-et-Vilaine, the Côte-d'Or, and the Cher, as well as to those of the Municipal Archives of Nantes. At the University of California Press, Sheila Levine, Barbara Ras, Jonas Weisel, and the anonymous readers all made very helpful suggestions. I thank them all for their help and absolve them for the remaining shortcomings.

My subsequent trips to France have been far easier than our first foray. Much of the credit for that goes to the various organizations who have lifted the burden of economic worry. I would like to thank the Ecole des Hautes Etudes en Sciences Sociales, the Lane Cooper Foundation, the American Council for Learned Societies, the Economic History Association, the Society of Fellows in the Humanities of Columbia University, the National Endowment for the Humanities, Lafayette College, and Georgetown University for their kind support for trips and for writing and study.

The one person most responsible for my undertaking and completing this project, however, was my father, my first and best teacher as a historian. From him I got my love of history and my first inkling that there was more to it than the famous battles that fascinated a little boy. He was the finest man I have ever known. How hard it is that I can share this with him only in spirit. This book is dedicated to him. If I might, though, I would like to mention another special person. Not long ago, Dad's oldest friend, Vinnie Rogers, also died. "Uncle Vinnie" was like a second father to me, and I'm sure Dad would be happy to be reunited once again with his old friend. So, this is for Big Jim and the Eagle, the biggest of the Little Giants.

Introduction

In *The Discourses* Machiavelli credits Quintus Curtius with the original affirmation that money is the sinews of war. Disagreeing with Quintus Curtius, Machiavelli noted that "this opinion is constantly quoted, and is acted upon by princes who are unwise enough to follow it."[1] Machiavelli held that good troops, not money, are the sinews of war, for while gold will not always provide good troops, good troops will always procure gold.

Writing to Cardinal Richelieu in 1639, the superintendent of finances, Claude le Bouthillier, fell into the old trap, stating that "les finances sont les nerfs de la guerre."[2] Richelieu, perhaps because of his different perspective on the situation, perhaps because of his greater astuteness, would change this maxim in his *Testament politique:* "On a toujours dit que les finances sont les nerfs de l'état."[3] But in fact, people had not always drawn this connection; they had echoed the sentiments of Quintus Curtius and of Bouthillier on the relationship between money and war, not that between money and the state itself. The remark sums up Richelieu's own capacity for innovating in the (often self-proclaimed) guise of following tradition. It also neatly sums up the Crown's ambivalent attitude to both change and tradition.

My central purpose in this work is to address the new issue raised by the Cardinal. The ability to raise and spend money is one of the attributes that makes a state a state. The manner in which the state chooses to do so, therefore, tells us a great deal not only about the nature of that state but also about the nature of the political society that state represents.

The early modern French political system was a series of compromises among various corporate groups, of which the Crown

---

1. N. Machiavelli, *The Prince and the Discourses* (New York, 1950), 308–9.
2. O. Ranum, *Richelieu and the Councillors of Louis XIII* (Oxford, 1963), 120.
3. A. Richelieu, *Testament politique* (Paris, 1958), 427, following Jean Bodin.

was the most powerful. From the midfourteenth century to the seventeenth century the administrative apparatus of the French state evolved in response to the constantly shifting balance of power among these groups.

There was a notable centralization of the financial administration of the kingdom in the period from 1360 to 1660, yet the financial system never became either a willing or an able tool of absolutism. Its apparent inability to enforce its decisions or its inefficiency (when viewed with modern eyes) was one of the strongest limitations on absolutism. The contradiction here is that those elements we would view as inefficient—localism, high costs of collection, privileges—were precisely those that enabled the system to work at all. One of the greatest dangers in any analysis of the tax system of seventeenth-century France is the anachronistic application of terms such as *efficiency* (or *net revenue*) to the realities of a different age. As for the system's willingness to do the king's bidding, that, too, depended on the consonance of interests between the king and the officers who had to carry out his wishes.

The tax system and taxation itself are central to any understanding of the early modern French state and of early modern French society. Although the ability to tax and spend at will (*à volonté*) has long been held to be a key attribute of the absolute state,[4] in fact, the king of France neither taxed nor spent at will, and local elites retained a great deal of control over the practical workings of the system. The limits of the seventeenth-century French state were set by its ability to raise money to pay for its projects.

Our concern here is not simply the tax system and the level of taxation but also French government and society as a whole. To understand how Henry IV and Louis XIII governed France, we must know the limits they faced. Nowhere were those limits more evident than in their efforts to raise and spend money. If we are to see these limits, we must look at the system from two directions: from Paris outward to the provinces and from the provinces to Paris. We must examine both how the money was raised and how it was spent.

The tax system presents a mixture of the obvious and the not-so-obvious. On the one hand, we are familiar with the administra-

---

4. A rare exception to this view can be found in V. Tapié, *France in the Age of Louis XIII and Richelieu* (New York, 1975), 54–60.

tive diversity of early modern France, the localism against which the king so often fought. On the other, we have long believed that this localism and diversity were anachronistic remnants of a feudal past. Nothing could be further from the truth. The elaborate system of privileges and administrative diversity represented genuine socioeconomic and political interests, often camouflaged behind a smokescreen of appeal to inviolable past contracts. For example, the bourgeoisie were often exempt from direct taxation, not only for their urban property but for their rural holdings as well. While this privilege usually dated back to the Middle Ages and had specific historical roots, one would nonetheless be hard put to argue that such a privilege did not meet the social and economic interests of an increasingly important group of French landlords.

Local elites had powerful institutions with which to protect their interests: judicial institutions, such as the Parlements; representative bodies, such as the provincial Estates; military structures, such as the garrison network; and financial offices, such as the *élus* or even the parish officers (*commissaires des tailles*) charged with drawing up the village tax rolls. One of the most important aspects about the resistance of these local elites is that it varied from one period to the next. The collapse of certain methods of resistance to the king, such as provincial Estates, did not mean that resistance had ceased, merely that its form had changed. Provincial Estates usually collapsed because they were ineffective, because they failed to serve adequately either the needs of the local elites or those of the king. We must consider not only the king's short-term interest— that is, the assembly's vote of a given sum of money. We must also remember that the king needed provincial Estates to ensure the co-operation of the local elites. When the Estates ceased to provide the king with such cooperation, they quickly lost their ability to influence him and, therefore, their chief purpose for the local elites. The elites could then turn to alternative methods of exerting leverage, such as the political patronage system.[5]

France was a collection of local economies and local political societies dominated by local elites. Absolutism was strictly limited in practice; the king could do little without the cooperation of local notables. One of the most important means of obtaining such co-

---

5. S. Kettering, *Patrons, Brokers, and Clients in Seventeenth-Century France* (New York, Oxford, 1986).

operation was the tax system. The king could share the proceeds with notables directly, through the budgets of the provincial Estates or through royal offices, or indirectly, through the royal pension system. He could further enroll their support by selling them liens on the royal taxes. All these mechanisms tied the king and the elites together.[6]

Peasant revolts, landholding patterns, economic development, and local sociopolitical structure were closely related to taxation. The revolts were usually aimed at taxation, while grievances could result from inequities between tax distribution and land distribution. Economic development could be stifled by overtaxation, as happened in the Loire valley wine trade.[7] The dominance of one group at the local level could be solidified or undermined by changes in the tax structure. Taxes touched every aspect of life.

To analyze the relationship between the tax system and French society, we must first go back to the origins and early development of the system. The peculiarities of the seventeenth-century French tax system responded to specific historical developments. Certain periods between 1300 and 1598 have received outstanding historiographical treatment (notably the fourteenth century), but there is no overall narrative of the development of the tax system from its origins in the fourteenth century to the seventeenth century. Much of what happened under Henry IV and Louis XIII can be traced back to the sixteenth century, especially the initiatives of Henry III: the extension of *élections* into the *pays d'Etats*, the centralization of the tax farms, major increases in direct taxation, and, perhaps most interesting for our purposes here, the use of forced loans (of one variety or another) on the royal officers to fund the debt.

The French tax system was not the irrational hodgepodge it is so often held to be. The traditional distinctions used by historians—*pays d'élection, pays d'Etats*, area within the *aides*, area outside the *aides*—are limited in their applicability to any given period. In the early seventeenth century, three of the official *pays d'Etats*—Guyenne, Normandy and Dauphiné—lost their privi-

6. My doctoral dissertation, "Taxation in Bretagne, 1598–1648," (Columbia University, 1978), studies this process in one province. Chapters 6 and 8 treat the issue of the king's relationship with the local elites.

7. J. Collins, "Les impôts et le commerce du vin en Bretagne au XVIIe siècle," *Actes du 107e Congrès National des Sociétés Savantes* 1 (1982): 155–68.

leges, so the *élections/Etats* dichotomy would not do us much good. The basic split in the kingdom dated from the middle of the fourteenth century—that is, from the origins of unlimited-term taxation. Those areas covered by the Estates General of Languedoil in the 1350s and 1360s, together with some of the conquests from the English, made up the central core of both the direct and indirect tax systems.

When consequently kings added either indirect or direct taxes to the existing system of levies, they could collect them in a broader area. Thus while the king could not levy the *taille* or its adjuncts in Brittany, because Brittany had not been part of the original area within which the *taille* had been levied, he could levy the *taillon* (created by Henry II, when Brittany was part of the kingdom) in Brittany. Modern observers are often struck by the extremely complicated nature of early modern French taxation, but we must remember that custom severely limited the king's freedom of action. The French monarchy was very assiduous in its adherence to custom; the trick was to circumvent the spirit of the custom without violating the letter.

One cannot take lightly the pattern of respect for local customs. The process of greater accumulation of central power was quite a gradual one, and it evolved within a very traditional framework. The many tax exceptions within the system made sense on an individual basis. While one can call such a system irrational and overly fragmented, one can certainly make similar arguments with respect to the rather arbitrary (yet politically intelligible) deduction categories of the current American income tax system. The deductions of our current system respond to specific needs, and we recognize that taxation is not only a means of raising money but also an expression of political and social policy. The French government of the Valois and Bourbons operated under similar assumptions.

Their policy responded to their own needs; the general principles on which it was based, however, were quite similar. The necessity of compromise with local elites was critical to any success the monarchy might have in the fifteenth as in the seventeenth century. The local elites might be defined as a combination of the landlords (noble, nonnoble, Church), officers, and the greater bourgeoisie, such as important merchants and lawyers. The tax system had to respond to the needs of these people or it would not succeed, just as the tax system must protect the interests of the middle class in twentieth-century America in order to be politically palatable. The needs of early modern French elites changed over time, so the tax system changed as well. The Crown usually instigated these changes to suit its needs, but it always had to consider local reaction to the proposed changes if they were to be effective.

Chapter 1 provides a brief survey of developments prior to the sixteenth century and an analysis of what happened to the tax system in the period from 1523 to 1598. Chapter 2 picks up with the system as it existed in 1596—that is, at the time of Henry IV's summoning of the Assembly of Notables of Rouen. The chapter has three parts: in the first I look at the issues facing Henry in 1596; in the second I analyze his reforms in the period 1596–1604 and the system they created; in the last I examine the collapse of that system in 1634.

In Chapter 2, I will look at the relationship between the Crown and the local elites in the first half of the seventeenth century. We must remember that while the local elites had definite objections to expansion of royal power and to royal taxation, they nonetheless derived considerable benefits from both the royal government as a whole and the tax system itself. The middle class, or rather that section of it George Huppert has called the "bourgeois gentilshommes," bought royal offices. Officers were usually members of powerful local bourgeois families and they were often clients of major regional noble families. Most officers were landlords, which gave them another common interest with fellow members of the local elite. As officers, however, they sought to enhance the power of the royal bureaucracy and thereby their own influence in society. The conflict of interest for the officers was clear: when the power of the king increased, by means of the increase of the power of his bureaucracy, it could threaten the power of local elites, whose members included these same royal bureaucrats. A truly felicitous compromise, though, would enhance the positions of *both* the local elites and the Crown.

The argument that the interests of these local elites and those of the Crown were antithetical must be revised. The place of taxation in this complex relationship was absolutely central, because the king used tax monies to help solidify his ties to local elites, just as he used royal offices (military, judicial, and financial) to do so. To argue that the basic situation of seventeenth-century political life was that of "monarchy against the aristocracy" (to borrow the title of one of Roland Mousnier's articles on this subject) ignores the great congruity of interest of the two sides.

To take but one example, at the Estates of Brittany in 1636, Pierre de Cambout, baron of Pontchâteau, held second rank in the order of the nobility; on those days (quite frequent) when the duke de la Trémoille was absent, Pontchâteau presided over the Second Estate. Yet he was also the *lieutenant particulier* for the king in Lower Brittany and, as such, one of the *commissaires du roi*. At the opening of the Estates, he had asked the *greffier* of the Estates not to read his separate letter of convocation as *commissaire du roi*. He was one of the deputies of the nobility selected to sign the contract with the king; he was later designated as one of the deputies to Court of the Estates. In recognition of his services to the province, the Estates voted him a gift of 12,000 l. (a gift that had to be approved by the king).[8] Pontchâteau had arrived at the Estates with a retinue of more than one hundred gentlemen. He relied on his position in the royal military bureaucracy to run a patronage network that could provide for these individuals. The views on direct taxation held by Pontchâteau and his retinue differed from those of the king. The trick of the tax system was to work out a compromise that would satisfy the king's need for money without, at the same time, alienating Pontchâteau and his followers.

The king's compromise with local elites was remarkably simple. The king determined what his needs were: he set the amount to be raised (within limits, as we shall see). The elites decided how the taxes would be raised. In the *pays d'Etats* they decided on the actual form the taxes would take. In the towns they also influenced the selection of the form of taxation. In the countryside the parishioners themselves assessed the taxes in the village, so that the tax system did not threaten the elites' control of the socioeconomic situation. The king further sweetened the pot by coopting the elites into a vested interest in the functioning of the tax system. The nobility got pensions and military wages, and, in the case of major families, their clients were able to buy royal offices. The bourgeoisie bought offices, *rentes,* and, later, *droits.* While the king often forced them to buy, nonetheless, the fact of possession gave the bourgeoi-

8. F.-N. Baudot, Dubuisson-Aubenay, "Journal des Estats de Bretagne Commencé à Nantes en Décembre 1636," in *Bulletin de la Société Archéologique de Nantes,* ed. A. Bourdaut (1927): 339–99. The *assises* (papers) of the Estates are in AD Ille-et-Vilaine, C 2770. Cambout was also Richelieu's cousin.

sie a vested interest in full collection of direct taxes, so that they could be paid their *gages* and liens.

When we discuss the relationship between the king and the royal bureaucracy, we must remember that royal officers footed most of the cost of three major (and one minor) bankruptcies between 1602 and 1654. The two largest segments of the budget were debt service and the military; in times of war the brunt of any budgetary cutbacks had to be borne by the former. The great problem with such a policy was that the holders of the debt were precisely those people charged with collecting the taxes to pay it. The king greatly increased the nominal amounts the officers were supposed to collect. At the same time he asked them to obtain this money from an uncooperative population, while foregoing payment of both their own *gages* and their share of the debt service. As we shall see in Chapters 2 through 4, this combination proved as unlikely as it sounds. The officers did not perform their duties; the collection of direct taxes declined sharply in most areas outside the army's sphere of intervention.

It was a revolution in government. The changes of 1634 interrupted nearly 300 years of continuous development in French financial administration. The bankruptcy at the expense of the tax officers forced the Crown into a drastic administrative change—the widespread introduction of the intendants. The king now had to circumvent his own local officers in order to collect his taxes. The new system coopted some members of the old, but it proved to be a failure in its first configuration. It was Colbert who effectively blended the new system and the old.[9]

Chapter 3 covers this decline in revenues from direct taxation, in the 1630s and 1640s, and provides both a technical explanation of why the figures currently used by historians are inadequate and a new set of figures for the period 1597–1640. There are two basic questions to answer here: (1) How much money did the system collect? and (2) How much money did the king receive? The current understanding of these questions derives essentially from the figures provided by J. R. Mallet, a clerk in the Controller General's office in the early eighteenth century. While Mallet understood the limitations of the figures he gave, the historians who have used these figures often have not.

9. This synthesis is now brilliantly described in D. Dessert, *Argent, pouvoir et société au Grand Siècle* (Paris, 1984). A special thanks here to Ran Halévy for helping me to get a copy of this work on very short notice.

As the technical points in this matter have some bearing on Chapters 1 and 2, and as they are a matter of importance with respect to the general issue of taxation and the state, we must briefly review them here. The key issue is the nature of the Central Treasury budget—that is, the manner in which the state defined its revenues and expenses. This problem is clearest with respect to regional and local expenses. Mallet noted that these expenses were not included in the figures he cited for the period prior to 1661. He explained the nature of these expenses but said nothing about their size or about their substantial modification under Louis XIII. Historians using these figures have misrepresented both the total direct tax levy and the amount from that sum at the king's disposal. In addition, there was a considerable district-to-district variation in such charges; Mallet's figures, therefore, distort the relationship between areas.

The importance of this problem becomes clearer if one considers recent work on seventeenth-century French taxation, such as that of Alain Guéry.[10] Guéry analyzed the evolution of the French budget from 1600 to 1789, using the figures of Mallet for the first half of the seventeenth century. Guéry's approach ignores revenue disappearance at the local and regional levels and thus distorts both income and expenses. If we confine ourselves to the figures of Mallet (that is, the figures from the *bordereau de l'Epargne*), what do they represent? For Guéry, the answer is simple: "C'est l'ensemble de ces fonds appartenant au roi, qui forme le Trésor de l'Epargne, où n'est compté que le 'revenant bon', ou 'deniers revenant bon', c'est-à-dire, le revenu net."[11]

The money coming into the Central Treasury (*Epargne*) was precisely *not* net revenue. The modern concept of net revenue is totally alien to the system of early modern France. What do we mean by net revenue? Just because the money was at the direct disposition of the Central Treasurer, does that make it net revenue? Precious little cash actually went to Paris: in 1609, for example, only 3 million l. of 10 million l. in direct taxes owed to the Central Treasurer, itself part of a levy of some 16.5 million l., was shipped to Paris. The Central Treasury paid its bills with paper money—that is, with *mandements* and *rescriptions* of the Central Treasury, not with

10. A. Guéry, "Les finances de la monarchie française sous l'ancien régime," *Annales E.S.C.* 33 (1978): 216–39. The source of all these figures is J. R. Mallet, *Comptes rendus de l'administration financière de la France* (London, 1789).
11. Guéry, "Les finances."

cash. Local and regional expenses consisted primarily (and increasingly, after 1616) of the same type of expenses as those carried on the Central Treasury records: military costs and debt service.

Some regional and local expenses, such as the costs of the financial administration and the cost of parish collection, should be deducted from gross revenues. The costs of the parish collection were 7.5 to 8.33 percent; the upkeep of the local and regional financial bureaus was about 11 percent. If we define net revenue as gross revenue minus the costs of collecting that revenue, we would say that net revenue from direct taxation was about 80 percent of gross revenue. Any other procedure is overly prone to semantic difficulties.

If we consider the *taillon* (roughly 1.2 million l. under Henry IV), we find it was always listed as a regional charge, yet its proceeds went to pay royal men-at-arms. Should we deduct the *taillon* from gross revenue, while we keep the garrison tax in our figures for net revenue? Each went to pay soldiers. Why is one company of men-at-arms to be counted as a central government expense and another to be counted a regional expense? Such distinctions make a mockery of the terms *net* and *gross revenue*. The situation with respect to judicial institutions was equally unclear. All courts were paid from resources other than those of the Central Treasury budget, as that budget appeared in the *bordereau de l'Epargne*. I believe the *gages* of the Parlement of Paris were a legitimate expense of the *central* government. While those *gages* were paid by the *gabelle* farmers, I would argue that they should be assessed against the net revenue of the state.

The way in which the French government accounted for various expenses makes it quite difficult to determine net revenues, especially for indirect taxes. After 1616, the legitimate costs of collection became closely intertwined with royal debt service. Fortunately, the *droits aliénés* for the direct taxes were usually listed as separate from the regular levies, so we know the amounts. By 1633, the last year in which they were fully paid, the *droits* (surtaxes sold to royal officers) were over 40 percent of the total collection. If we exclude the *droits* from net revenue, net revenue by 1633 would have been only about a third of the total collection. The *droits*, however, represented a substantial portion of royal debt service and, as the king proved in 1634, he could get his hands on this money if he really wanted to. The *droits* should not be deducted from the gross revenues, but they, along with other debt service expenses, should be excluded at the point at which we determine the disposable income of the government.

In fact, the accounting procedures represented by the *bordereau de l'Epargne* (Mallet's source) reflected the manner in which the French government conceived of its budget. Known, fixed expenses were not carried on the *bordereau*. The Central Treasurer accounted for such expenses—costs of Parlements, the *taillon*, costs of the royal tax bureaucracy, *rentes*—on the general preliminary budget (the *état du roi*) and then on the final budget statements (*états au vrai*) of each jurisdiction and of each tax farmer. These budgets carried a distinct amount as the *partie de l'Epargne*, and the total of such amounts was what appeared as revenue on the *bordereau*.

On the expense side the *bordereau* covered outlays whose size varied from year to year: the royal household, certain military costs, and most pensions.

Some revenue and expenses did not fit neatly into either of these traditional categories—that is, fixed or variable costs—and they created havoc with the budgetary process. A third shadow budget came to dominate the other two. Its resources (the *parties extraordinaires*) came from the *traités* or *partis* signed, in the king's council, with financiers. The king sold them the right to sell new offices and *droits*, to levy new taxes, and to provide various services, such as sutlering troops. In 1642, he even sold them the right to collect the *tailles*. While the king received a portion of the money as an advance, full payment was spread out over several years. In the 1630s and 1640s, the king was using these projected future payments to cover expenses current in the year of the *traité* itself— that is, he was setting off current expenses against promised future revenues (thus Richelieu's lament that the king had already spent not only the current year's revenue but that of the next two years as well).[12] It is this third budget that makes virtually impossible the reconstruction of the overall budget of the later 1630s and 1640s.

In rejecting the figures of Mallet and those who have followed him, we need a new data base from which to reconstruct the revenues of the system. We must confine ourselves largely to revenues from direct taxation because those from indirect taxation fell in-

12. The king made the same complaint to the Estates of Brittany in 1641.

creasingly into the third budget and thus cannot be reconstructed on a year-to-year basis. Chapter 3 will confine itself to revenues from direct taxation; however, total revenues are discussed in Appendix B.

The sources for these new figures are central documents from the Bibliothèque Nationale and the Archives Nationales and a much broader selection of regional and local material from the departmental archives. These latter documents originated with the regional *bureaux des finances, élection* officers, parish communities, regional Chambers of Accounts and Courts of Aides, and various groups concerned with financial matters (the Estates of Brittany, municipalities, private individuals). The most useful materials on revenues come from the regional and local records of the *généralités* of Rouen, Caen, Châlons, Bordeaux, Bourges, Lyon, Nantes, Dijon, and Limoges.[13]

These documents provide information on a battery of questions: How much was supposed to be levied? How much was really paid? How many officers were there? How was the money spent? By what mechanism did it change hands? What effect did the financial system have on the country at the local level? Who paid the taxes?

While Chapter 3 deals with the amount of money levied in direct taxes from the 1590s to the 1640s in the *pays d'élection*, its main focus is on the period 1597–1633. Little can be said about the period 1634 to 1648 because, while there are a great many central documents, they cannot be trusted. Richard Bonney, Julian Dent, and Daniel Dessert have all shown that the king borrowed heavily in this period, and that he declared bankruptcy in 1648. As Bonney rightly points out, the king could not raise enough money through taxation to pay his debts. The budgets of the 1640s (and late 1630s) were, therefore, almost always fraudulent.

Our emphasis must remain with the period 1597–1633. The figures from this period are reasonably exact. Taken from central documents and local archives, the consonance of the sources from all levels of French taxation, from the parish to the royal council, is so

13. Several *départements* have nothing in the archives from this period (financial records)—those held in Tours, Orléans, Poitiers, and Soissons. I have looked at those of Amiens, but they yielded little. The only three missing from the *pays d'élection* are Paris (there is apparently not much, based on the secondary literature), Riom, and Moulins. I have used all five Breton depositories, as well as the archives at Niort and Evreux.

strong that I feel confident in presenting these figures as an alternative to Mallet. Even these figures, however, have significant limitations. For instance, they leave out local surtaxes such as *étapes* (troop victualing) and the small levies made by individual parishes for their own needs (church repair, levees, small bridges, roads, and lawsuits).

The issue of the amounts of money being raised (both for the central government and for others) brings us to the heart of direct tax system: the parish. There has been virtually no discussion of how much the peasantry paid (everyone simply says they paid too much), nor has there been any analysis of tax rolls to determine who within the parishes paid the taxes. The only province for which historians have used tax rolls and cadastral registers is Languedoc, and there the *taille* was *réelle* (based on the status of the land), not *personnelle* (based on the status of the individual).[14] Using a total figure and dividing by the number of hearths, as has been done for Lower Normandy, is of some use, but it ignores too many variables, such as the relative richness of the land, and the distribution of the tax burden within the parish itself.[15]

The only way to describe the tax distribution accurately is to look at village tax rolls. We will see that the top quartile of the taxpayers (as defined by their assessments) paid two-thirds or more of the taxes, while the bottom quartile paid about 1 or 2 percent. In the one case for which we have both the tax assessments and the land distribution—St-Ouen-de-Breuil, in Normandy—the eleven people (of seventy-eight assessed) assessed for over 100 l. accounted for 54.5 percent of the proposed total taxes. But these same people controlled 67 percent of the land. As much as they paid, they seem to have paid too little.

If the tax rolls are an accurate indicator of the income distribution of the taxpayers, they show a very skewed pattern. Moreover, they leave out the richest members of society, almost all of whom were tax exempt. At St-Ouen, for example, 78 percent of the land on the roll was owned by people not listed on it. While such figures varied sharply from parish to parish in the areas where we know the land distribution, we must still realize that tax-exempt individuals dominated the possession of the land.

14. E. Le Roy Ladurie, *Les Paysans de Languedoc* (Paris, 1966).
15. In *Cahiers des Annales de Normandie*, 1963, this was done for Lower Normandy (Caen) under the direction of P. Chaunu.

We must also begin to think a bit more seriously about the group of peasants so often left out (or rather left on the fringes) of the great *thèses* on rural society: the poor. Studies such as those by Goubert and Jacquart have shown that a few peasants dominated each village and that most of the peasants owned (or rented) little land. The tax rolls confirm this view in every case and demonstrate the numerical strength of the very poor. It is hard to do research on those who rented little land. Nonetheless, when we find, as at St-Ouen, that the bottom quartile of the population controlled less than 1 percent of the land (and the bottom half less than 8 percent), it is time to take this issue more seriously in our view of French agriculture and society in the seventeenth century.

The rolls indicate a society in motion. In every case of rolls close together in time, there was an annual average loss of 5 to 7 percent of the taxpayers, *excluding* those who died and were succeeded by heirs listed on the roll. Virtually all of the disappeared ones were poor; at Dournazac, six of the seven *bordiers* of 1623 were gone in 1630. Women, who made up 15 percent of the taxpayers in an average village, were overrepresented both in the bottom quartiles and among these apparent migrants.

This image of constant migration contradicts most of what is said about this question in the available monographic literature. Goubert and the Annalistes insist that the villages were fairly static and that there was relatively little migration in this period. The available evidence from the tax rolls would seem to contradict this view of a static society, so a bit of clarification is in order. For instance, in Dournazac over 40 percent of the taxpayers of 1623 left no record in 1630 (either of themselves or of heirs). The pattern was the same elsewhere.

What happened to these people? I would hypothesize that most of them migrated from one village to the next within the same (fairly small) region. The missing taxpayers were overwhelmingly from the bottom quartile in every village. If the situation at St-Ouen-de-Breuil was at all typical, these people would likely have had no land to farm or, as in the case of the *bordiers,* a very tiny plot rented on an annual basis (one too small to provide for a family).

I believe these relatively rootless individuals wandered the countryside in search of work and of a tiny plot (and cottage). Given the highly localized nature of French customs, agricultural practices, and language, the migrants probably confined themselves to a relatively small area. One would expect such people, especially the women, returned to their native village to get married, which would provide the endogomy figures used by demographic historians to demonstrate their static society.[16]

Many of these poor migrants were women, just as many of those in the bottom quartile of the tax distributions were women. The tax rolls also demonstrate another little examined facet of French rural history: the role of women as heads of households. The rolls indicate that women headed from 10 to 20 percent of the households in any given parish. The single women were invariably clustered at the bottom of the roll, but the widows could be found scattered throughout it (albeit disproportionately in the bottom half). While these widows were often caretakers, in the sense that a fully grown son would take over the holding when he reached his majority, nonetheless we should not overlook the importance of such a role. Most peasant families could expect to have the male adult die before the majority of the eldest son at some point in a two- or three-generation period, and a capable woman partner was essential for the maintenance of the integrity of the family holding during the interim period. Many leases foresaw this eventuality by listing both the man and the woman as lessees. The tax rolls indicate that women were a significant economic force in the French countryside, not merely within two-adult peasant households, but as heads of households in their own right. It is also worth noting that widows held a substantial portion of the royal and urban debt in this period, usually 15 to 30 percent.[17]

16. P. Goubert, *Beauvais et le Beauvaisis* (Paris, 1960), 65, explains his method for reaching this conclusion about sedentarism (a method followed by most others): "Rien de plus aisé que de noter les paroisses d'origine des époux, de les identifier, de les porter sur les cartes, d'en dresser des tableaux de fréquences. . . . En Beauvaisis, ces élémentaires comptables donnent des résultats d'une grande netteté. Au XVIIe siècle, les déplacements effectués pour se marier étaient extrèmement rares. . . . Il semble qu'on ait fortement exageré, même lors des périodes de grandes crises, l'importance des groupes d'errants, mendiants ou vagabonds qui auraient sillonné les chemins français." The tax rolls paint a different picture, one of a society in motion, although that motion might well have been within a very restricted area. One could easily (especially in the age group 15–25 years, before one could lease land) move about from village to village, selling one's labor, and then return to the home village to marry (particularly given the role of parents in arranging marriages). High endogamy rates say little about this kind of migration.

17. At Morlaix, for example, in 1673, women held 20.2 percent of the town's debts (AD Finistère, 2 E 1505).

The key issues related to taxation and its impact on French society can be understood only if we analyze the situation in the villages. We know little of the parish repartition process or of the actual collection of indirect taxes. The tax system was the largest employer in France, giving work to at least 75,000 people for the collection of the indirect taxes alone. For the direct tax system, there were thousands of sergeants, the universally despised enforcers of royal will at the village level. The peasant collectors themselves should also be counted among the employees of the system; this would add another 80 to 100,000 people to our total. If we count these collectors, something like 2 or 3 percent of the adult male French population worked for the tax system each year.

Literally everyone in France knew someone who worked for the tax system. They were likely to know not only those who collected the village's direct taxes but also the employees of the indirect tax syndicates, especially those who collected wine taxes. In Brittany one in every hundred people in the bishopric of Nantes sold wine. Every one of these tavernkeepers had to be visited by the clerks of the wine tax farmers. The Breton records show that the inspectors also visited the producers.

This day-to-day contact with the tax system must have been of capital importance. The position within the community of the tax agent must have had a great influence on the community's perception of the tax system as a whole. Within the direct tax system the influence of the notables, defending their tenants and putting pressure on day laborers, must have been enormous. Such patterns of dependency, so clear in the eighteenth and nineteenth centuries, were no doubt as strong or stronger in the seventeenth.

We will never understand the system without further local research. I have left out major elements of the overall tax system, such as the *pays d'Etats*, the indirect taxes, and the levies of the towns. A large city like Nantes had a budget that could run to more than 40,000 l. a year; even small towns, those of five or six thousand people, raised close to 10,000 l. each year. There is little discussion of that money here, but any true picture of the weight of taxation should take it into account, particularly since a large portion of the town budgets went to debt service on loans contracted to pay royal troops in times of war (notably the 1590s and the 1630s and 1640s).

The tax system was an integral part of day-to-day French life.

Its particularism accurately reflected the particularism of French society, just as its distribution of the tax burden illustrated both political realities, in terms of who was exempt, and economic realities, in terms of who among the nonexempt paid the taxes. We must also view the question of exemption, not in terms of complete evasion of tax liability, but rather in terms of underassessment. The landlords contributed indirectly through their tenants, who paid the bulk of the direct taxation. In some cases landlords even shared the costs of the *tailles* with their *métayers*. The bourgeoisie, often tax exempt, in fact paid taxes through its contribution to financing the royal debt. The three major bankruptcies of this period make the taxation aspect of the bourgeoisie's contribution to the debt all the more clear.

The central flaw of the system was that these two groups (and the clergy) paid far less than their share. The political realities of getting the cooperation of local elites made it impossible for the king to broaden the French tax base sufficiently. When war forced periods of high expenditure (the 1590s, the 1620s through 1640s, the war periods of Louis XIV or Louis XVI), the French monarchy responded with dubious fiscal expedients and large-scale borrowing, precisely because it could not reach the resources of those who held the capital by any other means.

The tax base was never large enough to permit repayment of these loans when peace returned, although it was larger in the eighteenth century than in the seventeenth, and the monarchy's finances were therefore more resilient. Each war cycle ended in bankruptcy: 1602, 1634, 1648, 1721, and 1789. In the long run this fundamental flaw in the structure of the French monarchy led to its collapse.

1. The Creation of a Direct Tax System, circa 1300 to 1598

Overview

The creation of the French tax system of the seventeenth century was not the work of a series of innovators but an incremental process of increasing central control over widely divergent local conditions. There were few abrupt changes prior to 1598; each stage was closely related to some prior situation. Nonetheless, certain events, such as the unilateral creation of King John's ransom aids in 1360, and certain periods, such as the second half of Charles VII's reign, were of particular importance in the constant process of reevaluating the contracts between the Crown and the groups constituting the nation.

Early modern French society was contractual. As Roger Doucet has put it: "The monarchy reposed, in reality, on a set of contracts concluded with the groups constituting the nation: provinces, towns, economic groupings, ecclesiastical establishments, classes of the society." [1] The monarchy's central problem was the inapplicability of one area or group's contracts to another area or group. This problem was particularly acute in two aspects of government: the financial system and the judicial system.

To the present-day historian, these two systems often appear to be an irrational vestige of an earlier time. The judicial system was a thicket of overlapping and interweaving jurisdictions: royal courts of various kinds, special courts for specific offenses (such as woodland crimes), ecclesiastical courts, and municipal tribunals. [2] The financial system was also extremely diverse and localized, both

1. R. Doucet, *Les institutions de la France au XVIe siècle* (Paris, 1948), 35–36.
2. R. Mousnier, *Les institutions de la France sous la monarchie absolue* (Paris, 1974, 1980), vol. 2, chap. 4.

in its fundamental administrative structure (including the variety of taxes in a given area) and in its own judicial structure.

In its efforts to standardize and centralize the administration of the kingdom, the government had to compromise with various powerful groups. At the beginning of the seventeenth century the five most powerful such groups were the Catholic church, the Huguenots, the nobility, the royal officers, and local, quasi-independent political bodies (Estates and town councils). These groups overlapped and shared many common interests, but they also had corporate interests that were frequently at odds with the interests of the other groups.[3] The old debate about whether the king allied with the nobility against the bourgeoisie, or allied with the bourgeoisie against the nobility is a remarkably sterile one.[4] Rather we must understand the process as one of constantly shifting alignments, based on the perception of corporate interests (here including the Crown as one of the corporations) on the given question.

The tax system was a central element in this pattern of changing loyalties, not only because the king's efforts to raise money touched the interests of all members of society, but because the royal bureaucracy was such an important connector between the elements of the local elites. Officers were often clients of powerful nobles: as late as 1650, the advocate general of Burgundy claimed that every official in Burgundy—whether military, judicial, or financial—was a client of the Condé family. Even the very effective intendant of the 1660s and 1670s, Claude Bouchu, was a client of the Condés.[5]

3. J. Collins, "Provincial Power in Early-Modern France: The Estates of Brittany as a Mechanism for Local Control" (Paper delivered at the American Historical Association Annual Meeting, 1984, session 104). See J. Collins, "Taxation in Bretagne, 1598–1648" (Ph.D. dissertation, Columbia University, 1978) on one province; and W. Beik, *Absolutism and Society in Seventeenth-Century France* (Cambridge, England, 1984) on another (Languedoc).

4. The Pagès-Mousnier school has long argued for the Crown-bourgeoisie alliance; the Russian school (Porshnev, Lublinskaya) has argued for various nuances of the Crown-nobility alliance against the bourgeoisie. The general lines of the debate are well summarized in Beik, *Absolutism and Society,* "Introduction."

5. N. A. Millotet, *Mémoires des choses qui se sont passées en Bourgogne depuis 1650 jusqu'à 1668* (Dijon, 1864), 3–4. Speaking of the Great Condé in 1651, Millotet wrote: "No one entered into an office [charge], either at the Parlement or other jurisdictions, other than by his mediation or that of Monsieur his father." Millotet went on to say that Condé also controlled access to all benefices and military offices in Burgundy. In Burgundy, the "frondeurs" were those who supported Mazarin.

The royal officers, while often clients of powerful nobles and while usually substantial landowners themselves, had a basic conflict of interest in matters involving the royal bureaucracy's extension of power. On the one hand, as members of the local elite, they opposed the extension of the king's power vis-à-vis that elite. On the other hand, as royal officials, their power increased when that of the king expanded. One of the most confusing aspects of seventeenth-century French history is that the king both attacked the royal officials and utilized them to attack other privileged groups. As we shall see, the king's 1634 decision to abandon the royal officials (notably the tax officials) drove many of them into the camp of local resisters. Yet the government continued to rely on *some* of these officials, just as it forged alliances with some members of the other powerful groups. The Fronde was a confused muddle precisely because it did not pit one group against another but rather pitted members from each group in an overall alliance against other members from the same groups in a conflicting alliance. Because these alliances were essentially issue-oriented (the *paulette* is a good example), when the issues changed, alliances oftentimes shifted as well.

The key background element of the shifting alliances of the Fronde was the failure of the *élection-généralité* system in 1634. This failure was essentially the same as that of the Parlements in the eighteenth century: neither could be an effective agent for reform and modernization. The conflict between intransigent, particularist local officers and a modernizing, centralizing government was a central thread in the fabric of the Ancien Régime. It had to remain the key point of difficulty because the underlying assumptions of the two sides were inalterably opposed.

The monarchy sought to standardize in order to be more efficient and more effective. The underlying assumption of standardization, by definition, is that everyone or everything should be treated the same way. But the opposition believed that everyone should be treated differently, because everyone belonged to a contracting group (or corporation) that had a unique status within the kingdom. The various royal institutions, while trying to enforce some kind of standardization on the kingdom, at the same time, represented the very diversity of the contracts they were trying to subvert. The *élections* and *greniers* of the financial system and the

Parlements of the judiciary—the privileged groups of all sorts—had a vested interest in defeating standardization.

The same process was evident in the evolution of political theory, in which the Bodinian sovereign came to treat his subjects as a mass (in one sense). Yet this same theory allows a special place for the king's contracts, which he, like any other individual, is bound to respect.[6] There was a fundamental conflict here on every level, from the practical to the theoretical, and nowhere was that conflict more acute than in the field of taxation.

The three major aspects to the direct tax system of 1598 were the taxes themselves, the tax administration, and the revenues from taxation. This third element actually had two parts—the total revenue collected in direct taxation and the portion of that revenue that got to the king. The problems in the execution of these two functions must lead us to another element: borrowing. The direct tax system always produced money too slowly to allow for efficient cash flow; the king made up the short-term difference by borrowing, often from the tax bureaucracy itself. Since there was no really efficacious means for handling the debt, this short-term debt quickly turned into long-term debt. The king also contracted long-term debt by means of alienations and borrowing because revenues did not keep pace with outlays during periods of high (war) expenses.

To understand this process, we need to break down the system into its constituent elements. For our purposes, we need to begin with the sixteenth-century system, because its problems (particularly its borrowing) left a dangerous legacy to the seventeenth-century system. The direct tax system of 1523 (or of 1598) had its roots in the fourteenth century. We may say that fourteenth-century tax practices became a system in the late 1360s and 1370s, and that this system was effectively codified between 1439 and 1452. Before we treat the direct tax system of the sixteenth and seventeenth centuries, therefore, we must briefly analyze the evolution of the system in the fourteenth and fifteenth centuries. We can then come back to the four major elements of the sixteenth-century system with a better understanding of why it functioned as it did.

6. J. Bodin, *Les Six Livres de la République* (Paris, 1576). This issue is discussed in greater detail in J. Collins, "Was There a Renaissance Monarchy in France?" (Paper delivered at the Columbia University Seminar on the Renaissance).

The Evolution of the French Direct Tax System to 1523

In the fourteenth century the king of France sought to transform services due him as suzerain into obligations that could be interpreted as being due to him as sovereign. These services or obligations fell into three main areas: justice, military affairs, and taxation. The first two were closely related to taxation, and we will treat them here in terms of their relationship to it. As for taxation itself, we must concentrate on direct, rather than indirect, levies. When reviewing the development of the system up to 1598, however, we will see that the interrelationship of the two forms of taxation must play its part.

Most early taxes represented the necessity of paying for troops. While it was in the interest of vassals to be able to commute their military service into money payments, it also gave the king new financial and military independence. By the middle of the thirteenth century France had established fixed commutation rates for vassals and had codified the military obligations of the peasants.[7]

These payments in lieu of military service for commoners led to two forms of taxation: hearth taxes in the countryside and some towns, and sales taxes in large towns such as Rouen, Paris and Arras, in the 1270s and 1280s.[8] Philip IV (1285–1314) tried to systematize these taxes and to levy them himself. To that end, he sought the approval and assistance of local, regional, and national Estates. Philip had no success in establishing long-term taxation, but his efforts to create a tax system set a number of precedents that would have a lasting effect.

The most important legacy of these early efforts to establish national taxation was particularism, the respect for local conditions. This particularism took several forms. In order to get the approval of major nobles for royal taxation on their serfs, Philip agreed to share the proceeds of royal hearth taxes with many landlords. He extended the same privilege to major towns, such as Arras or

7. R. Fawtier, *The Capetian Kings of France* (London, 1960), 195; J. Strayer, *The Administration of Normandy under St. Louis* (Cambridge, Mass., 1932), 139.

8. J. Strayer, *Philip the Fair* (Princeton, 1980), chap. 3; J. Strayer, "Consent to Taxation under Philip the Fair," in *Studies in Early French Taxation* (Cambridge, Mass., 1939), 95–97; Strayer, *The Administration of Normandy*, 87 and 90; G. Besnier, "Les finances d'Arras, 1282–1407," in *Recueil de Travaux Offerts à M. C. Brunel* (Paris, 1955), 139.

Rouen.[9] Throughout the next four centuries local elites would continue to feel that they had a right to a share of the proceeds of taxation. As we shall see, the manner in which they shared the money changed over time, but some members of the elites would always get part of the tax money. Philip and his sons also established the principles of consent to taxation and *cessante causa* (when the cause ceases, the effect ceases).[10] These principles, too, helped to promote particularism.

Respect for local conditions meant, in practice, that local or regional bodies decided on the form of taxation.[11] The king and local elites would continue to use this system through the early seventeenth century in those areas, such as Brittany, that maintained powerful Estates.[12] The great difficulty with establishing some form of national taxation was that local and regional Estates invariably defined their needs as local or regional. How was one to get Languedoc to contribute to a campaign in Flanders? The solution to this problem proved to be twofold. In 1347, an Estates General of Languedoil voted a tax package to pay for men-at-arms, with the taxes to be apportioned by province in the same ratio as the men-at-arms. The soldiers were to serve in the local areas.[13] Although the plague of 1348 disrupted this effort at national taxation, Charles V used this method in 1363 when he established a national hearth tax.[14] The Estates General of Languedoil, meeting at

9. Strayer, *Philip the Fair*, 149; A. Vuitry, *Etudes sur le régime financier de la France avant la Révolution de 1789* (Paris, 1883), 2 vols.

10. Among the broad literature on this subject, see first two articles by E. A. R. Brown, "Cessante Causa and the Taxes of the Last Capetians: The Political Applications of a Philosophical Maxim," *Studia Gratiana* 15 (1972): 565–87 and "Philip the Fair, Plena Potestas and the Aide pur fille Marier," *Studies Presented to the International Commission for the History of Representative and Parliamentary Institutions* 39 (1970): 1–28.

11. J. B. Henneman, *Royal Taxation in Fourteenth-Century France* (Princeton, 1971) and his many articles detail this process.

12. Collins, "Taxation in Bretagne," chaps. 6 and 8.

13. J. B. Henneman, "The Black Death and Royal Taxation in France, 1347–1351," *Speculum* 43 (1968): 405–28.

14. P. Contamine, *Guerre, Etat et Société à la fin du Moyen Age* (Paris, 1972), 137, gives the figure of 6,000 men-at-arms for Languedoil. Contamine has some excellent remarks on the thinking behind Charles V's organization of both the army and the financial system. C. M. Radding, "The Administration of the Aids in Normandy, 1360–80," in *Order and Innovation in the Middle Ages: Essays in Honor of Joseph R. Strayer*, ed. W. Jordan, B. McNab, and T. Ruiz (Princeton, 1976), 41–53, is by far the best discussion of how these taxes were collected and who collected them.

Amiens, voted that "there will be paid one gold franc for the four months beginning the first of January past and finishing the coming first of May; and it will be thus every four months *until the end of the need.*" [15]

This arrangement was a brilliant tactical maneuver by the king. He created a standing army and the means to pay it without overriding local privileges. It was part of a regionalization policy pursued by Charles V. He apportioned the army on a regional basis, with expenses and receipts administered at a regional rather than a national level. A permanent standing army in each area responded to the need to demonstrate to local assemblies that their taxes were spent on *their* needs. In time of war, the standing army also turned the doctrine of *cessante causa* on its head: a standing army was a standing cause for taxation, thus the absence of any chronological limitation in the grant of 1363.

The second half of the solution to permanent taxation was more fortuitous: the creation of King John's ransom aids in 1360. The size of the ransom was so large (3 million crowns) that long-term taxation was essential to pay it. The king opted for a package of indirect taxes: a 5 percent sales tax; a tax of one-thirteenth on wine sold wholesale; and a 25 percent tax on salt (the *gabelle*).[16] The first two taxes later became known together as the *aides;* they also gave rise, in 1369, to the first export-import duties levied by the state (earlier ones were seigneurial): the *imposition foraine.*[17] Except for a brief period after Charles V's death in 1380, the *aides* and the *gabelle* lasted until 1789.[18]

The combination of direct and indirect taxes levied by Charles V brings us to the problem of particularism. While these taxes were national in some sense, in that they took in a major portion of the

---

15. P. Varin, *Archives administratives de la ville de Reims* (Paris, 1848), 3 vols. See 3: 273–82 on ordinance creating taxes in 1363, postscript to the instructions.

16. *Ordonnances,* 3: 433–39. A. Coville, *Les Etats de Normandie au XIVe siècle* (Paris, 1895), 107, notes that the feudal *aide* of 1360 was the first regular tax of more than one year's duration. M. Rey has cast new light on these early taxes: "Aux origines de l'impôt: les premiers comptes des Aides dans l'élection de Langres," in *Economies et Sociétés au Moyen Age: Mélanges offerts à Edouard Perroy* (Paris, 1973), 498–518. There is also a new synthesis by J. B. Henneman, *Royal Taxation in Fourteenth-Century France: The Captivity and Ransom of John II, 1356–1370* (Philadelphia, 1976).

17. *Ordonnances,* 6:206–10.

18. *Ordonnances,* 6: 527, on abolition. See Collins, "Taxation in Bretagne," chap. 1, for a discussion of the historiography on this question.

kingdom, they were not universal within the realm. The direct taxes approved at Amiens in 1363 were binding only on those who had voted them—that is, the areas within the jurisdiction of the Estates General of Languedoil: north-central France. The other parts of the kingdom made separate agreements with the king. The largest such area was Languedoc, which had also drawn up a separate agreement in 1360 with respect to the ransom aids. Thus Languedoc paid a hearth tax in lieu of the aid of 1360 and a package of indirect taxes in lieu of the hearth tax of 1363. This distinct system lasted until the Revolution.[19]

The system of Charles V continued the tradition of Philip IV with respect to compromise with local elites. Thus Charles V had separate agreements with Languedoc, the Rethelois, the viscounty of Turenne, and many other enclaves.[20] He continued to share the direct tax receipts with both nobles and towns: most major towns kept one-third of the taxes collected within their jurisdiction; major nobles kept a similar share of hearth tax receipts on their lands; members of the royal family usually pocketed the entire collection in their appanages.[21]

This tradition of respect for local privileges and conditions remained standard practice for the French monarchy. The king long respected the separate tax systems of the provinces and enclaves not represented at the Estates General of Languedoil in the 1350s and 1360s. Provinces such as Brittany, Burgundy, Dauphiné, and Provence maintained completely autonomous tax systems into the seventeenth century. Even areas such as the Southwest, which eventually had to pay the regular royal direct taxes, kept separate systems for salt taxes and indirect taxes. On the one hand, these systems represented the powerful position of local elites both at the time of the creation of royal taxes or of absorption into the kingdom and later when the given province was well established as part of the realm. On the other hand, these particularist tax systems

19. *Ordonnances*, 3: 618. See Doms Devic and Vaissette, *Histoire de Languedoc* (Toulouse, 1889) and the accompanying documents. In addition, on this period, see P. Dognon, *Les institutions politiques et administratives du pays de Languedoc du XIIIe siècle aux Guerres de Réligion* (Toulouse, 1895).

20. *Ordonnances*, 3, on exceptions for Lille (p. 503), Artois (690–92); Ibid., 5, on Ponthieu (689).

21. Varin, *Archives de Reims*, vol. 3: 217, 338 (1370). M. Rey, *Le domaine du roi sous Charles VI* (Paris, 1965), 180 n. 6, and 199 n. 1. See also Rey, *Les finances royales*, 269–70.

represented genuine social and economic interests in the given provinces. For example, in Brittany there was no tax on salt (a major local product), and local landlords kept direct taxation at an absurdly low level (in a province that usually exported large amounts of grain).[22]

If the particularism of the tax system was firmly established in the fourteenth century, its administrative framework came into being in the 1360s and 1370s. Charles V modified some earlier practices, such as changing the name of the chief oversight officials from *généraux-élus* to *généraux-conseillers*. The original name denoted a distinction between local overseers, *élus,* and general ones. The element *élu* signified their election to the respective position and their responsibility to those who had elected them (various bodies of Estates). The new name, with the element *conseiller,* meant that these officials would be named by the king, because all recognized his fundamental right to name his councillors.

After consolidating his control over the general overseers, Charles V turned his attention to local officials. By means of the *généraux*, Charles began to take over local administration. Thus, in 1372: "The *généraux* will have decision-making power on the number of *élus*, receivers and other officers of the aids in each diocese; and by great consideration, will limit and moderate them to the best of their ability, to the profit of the king."[23] A year later the king took the next step, acting "because of the ignorance, negligence or fault" of certain officers and because of "the griefs, wrongs and oppression to the people," to "throw out of their offices" all of the "*élus,* receivers, *grenetiers,* controllers, viscounts, commissioners, sergeants and others deputized by them for the said fact (of the aids)."[24]

The king had made the local officials responsible to him (by means of his officers) rather than to Estates, and he then made these local officers into royal officials, holding commission directly from him. This distinction was all the more clear in that many of the officers kept their posts in the 1373 "reform."[25]

This standardization of the system was also evident in the level of specialization at its center. The *généraux* evolved into a group

22. Collins, "Taxation in Bretagne," chaps. 4 and 5.
23. *Ordonnances,* 5: 537–41.
24. Ibid.: 645–51.
25. Radding, "Administration of the Aids."

running the tax system on behalf of the king. They lost their judicial functions, which were transferred to a new body, the *Cour des Aides*.[26] The *Cour des Aides* judged all cases related to taxation. A Chamber of Accounts, greatly strengthened in the last quarter of the fourteenth century, now audited all accounts. All these elements of the administration of the direct taxes—the *élus*, receivers, *généraux, Cour des Aides,* Chamber of Accounts—lasted until the Revolution, performing duties relatively similar to those they had carried out in the fourteenth century.

As with the taxes themselves, so too with their administration, we see the persistence of particularism. From the late fourteenth century until the beginning of the seventeenth century, the jurisdiction of these royal tax administrators remained about the same. The *élus* remained confined to the area in which the national taxes of Charles V were levied, and the jurisdictions of the *Cour des Aides* and the Chamber of Accounts of Paris extended beyond this area only in rare cases (notably in areas of questionable jurisdiction in the 1360s). The later-arriving provinces, such as Provence or Brittany, did not have *élus,* but they had their own *général* and their own Chambers of Accounts and *Cours des Aides,* where the latter were applicable. One of the most enduring legacies of fourteenth-century France was its complex network of jurisdictions, yet this network precisely paralleled the taxes themselves. The parts of the kingdom in which the king levied the national taxes (*aides, gabelle,* hearth tax, later *tailles*) were those that had the jurisdiction of the Paris courts and that had the basic royal financial bureaucracy (*élus* and *généraux*).

The direct tax system of seventeenth-century France was largely in place by 1379. The basic administrative and judicial framework was there, as was a direct tax that fell largely on the peasantry. The nature of this latter tax changed at the end of the fourteenth century, from a hearth tax (*fouage*) based on a given contribution per hearth, to a *taille,* based on a given share for each jurisdictional unit: *généralité, élection,* parish. The jurisdictional units were as they would remain for centuries: large districts under the oversight of a *général,* taking their name from the official—the *généralités;*

26. G. Dupont-Ferrier, *Etudes sur les institutions financières de la France à la fin du Moyen Age,* vol. 2, *Les finances extraordinaires et leur mécanisme* (Paris, 1932) and *Nouvelles études sur les institutions financières de la France à la fin du Moyen Age* (Paris, f1371933), which is concerned primarily with the Cour des Comptes.

local districts under the oversight of the *élu* (or *élus*), again taking their name from the official—the *élections*.[27]

The next period of significant change in the direct tax system began in 1439 and lasted until 1452 (perhaps 1459). Charles VII institutionalized all three elements of the system: the taxes themselves, the officers, and the jurisdictions. The most significant change was in the taxes themselves. Charles created a permanent *taille* to pay for the *compagnies d'ordonnance*, the standing army. He followed the precedent of Charles V, dividing the army among the provinces and then apportioning the *taille* on the same basis as the army.[28] Charles VII also abolished royal authorization for any levies of direct taxation other than regular royal taxation; this outlawed both seigneurial *tailles* and illegal requisitions and surtaxes levied by royal military captains.[29] The royal *taille* created in this period became the centerpiece of the direct tax system for the next 150 years.

Charles VII codified the entire royal system of taxation in the period from 1439 to 1452. By prohibiting seigneurial *tailles*, even on serfs, on pain of forfeit of the estate on which such taxes were levied, the king reduced the extent of the interposition of local seigneurs between the Crown and the mass of the population. The king was now recognized as being solely responsible for the protection of the kingdom and its inhabitants.[30] Peasants still looked to their landlords for some protection, especially protection *from* the king, but protection in the larger sense now meant the royal army.

Charles also extended the responsibilities of royal tax officials. In 1445, he gave *élus* all jurisdiction in both criminal and civil cases relating to "aydes, gabelles, tailles ou aultres subventions."[31] This jurisdiction extended even to the lands of high justiciars. Charles

27. On the early *élections*, vol. 1 of the *Etudes* of Dupont-Ferrier, *Les élections et leur personnel* (Paris, 1930).

28. M. Wolfe, *The Fiscal System of Renaissance France* (New Haven, 1972), mentions 2,000 lances (pp. 36–39), but the original figure was 1,500 modified to 2,000 by the addition of Normandy, in 1450. The *taille* would have been 744,000 l. for 2,000 lances at 31 l./month/lance. J.-J. Clamageran, *Histoire de l'impôt en France* (Paris, 1888), 2: 3, gives a *taille* of 1.2 million l., later raised to 1.7–1.8 million l. On Normandy, see H. Prentout, *Les Etats de Normandie* (Rouen, 1925), 3 vols.

29. *Ordonnances*, 13: 311–13.

30. F. Lane, "The Economic Meaning of War and Protection," in *Venice and History* (Baltimore, 1966), has some interesting observations on this matter. Professor Richard Lowenthal was also kind enough to share some of his thoughts on this matter with me.

31. *Ordonnances*, 13: 428 and ff.

also forced receivers to render accounts each year, accompanied by the *état du roi* for their jurisdiction. The *état du roi,* the official preliminary account issued at the beginning of the year, now became a mandatory list of authorized spending.[32] All expenses not listed on the *état du roi* had to be justified through written, royally sanctioned authorization for the given expense.

Charles also expanded the system of *élections* by creating new jurisdictions and by creating more *élections particulières;* he did not expand the *élection* system into new areas, he merely fleshed out the system where it already existed. Charles also systematized the subsidiary systems, such as that of Languedoc. He codified the particularism of these systems (thus ruling that the *taille* in Languedoc was *réelle*—on the status of the land—not *personnelle*—on the status of the individual—as in the north).[33] As part of this process, Charles created new courts to oversee these subsystems, and to help his local officials make more accurate rulings, he sought to have the law codified by bailiwick throughout the kingdom.[34]

The last great ordinance of the reform period 1439–52 was issued in August 1452. It outlined the *élection* system that would be the backbone of the French direct tax system until the seventeenth century.[35] Its preamble said that seigneurial judges had been eliminated from the system because of their ignorance and partiality. The ignorance of these judges with respect to financial matters must have been a matter of some concern, but the second accusation, that they favored the *fermiers* and *métayers* of the nobility, was much more serious. As we shall see in Chapter 4, the tenants of the nobility paid a substantial portion of the direct taxes, and a constant goal of the Second Estate was to have its tenants exempted from the *taille* for their income from noble-owned property.

This ordinance brings us to a system that would last for almost seventy-five years with little modification and whose essence would endure far longer. Charles VII broke the kingdom into a number of subsystems, responding to the needs of areas such as Languedoc or, later, Brittany, to have taxation tailored to their political and socioeconomic realities. Far from being the beginning of a decentralized "Renaissance Monarchy," these reforms were a geographic and so-

32. Ibid.: 414 and ff.
33. Ibid.: 493–94.
34. The results of this effort are discussed in W. Church, *Constitutional Thought in Sixteenth-Century France* (Cambridge, Mass., 1941).
35. *Ordonnances,* 14: 239–40.

cial expansion of the king's power. They were geographic in that they enabled the Crown to enforce its decisions (modified by local input) in a larger area, and they were social in that they created a strong tie between local elites and the Crown, giving them a mutual interest in the expansion of the authority of the given system or subsystem.

The political situation of the midfifteenth century made it impossible for Charles VII to have done otherwise. Even the *compagnies d'ordonnance* were often paid in kind; they, too, were organized along regional lines, both to facilitate recruitment and to make their payment easier.[36] Charles VII created a national army and national taxation, but both of them had to be adapted to local conditions. This adaptation meant local quartering of the men-at-arms and local tax systems for those areas not bound by the fourteenth-century agreements.

The system of Charles VII lasted, with minor modification, until 1523, when Francis I instituted important central reforms. Those reforms altered the overall system in some areas, but they did not change its basic structure in others. The basic outline of Charles VII's system was as follows: in administrative matters, the direct tax burden was apportioned first within the king's Council, although it relied on the apportionment among the *généralités* and *élections* done by the *généraux*. In theory the *général* of each district acted by himself to divide the tax burden in that district; in practice, the *généraux* ignored royal prohibitions and acted collegially to divide the tax burden. At the local level the *élu* or *élus* split the amount demanded of their *élection* among the parishes; the parishioners themselves divided the burden within the parish. Charles VII also established the incidence rules: in the North, all nobles and inhabitants of many towns were tax exempt; in the South, noble land was exempt and personal status had no bearing. The greater incidence of urban exemption seems to date from the

---

36. T. Basin, *Histoire de Charles VII* (Paris, 1944), 2: 21. A. Vallet Viriville, "Notes et extraits de chartes et de manuscrits appartenant au British Museum de Londrès," *Bibliothèque de l'Ecole des Chartes* (1846): 129. P. Solon, "Valois Military Administration on the Norman frontier," *Speculum* 51 (1976): 93. "La Compagnie d'ordonnance du Sénéchal du Poitou en 1470," *Archives Historiques de Poitou*, 2: 300–11. On p. 311, the anonymous author states that a man-at-arms received 15 l. per month, an archer 7.5 l.: the 96 men-at-arms and 190 archers of the company received 8,595 l. for the first quarter of 1470, paid to them at a muster held on 5 May 1470.

midfifteenth century.[37] By the end of Charles VII's reign the *taille* had become essentially a tax on the peasantry, which it would remain until the end.

Charles VII also established or reinforced the basic administrative structure of the tax system. He instituted a central core system for the area of the old Estates of Languedoil and buttressed it with a series of individualized subsystems for the outlying provinces. His successors followed this policy of localized subsystems for the three great additions of the late fifteenth century: Burgundy, Provence, and Brittany. Charles VII's tax bureaucracy had full jurisdiction, both administrative and judicial, throughout the kingdom. In the central area this administration included the *élections* and *greniers,* as well as the Paris *Cour des Aides* and Chamber of Accounts. In the subsystems, the king relied on the adaptation of preexisting local bodies. The king did, however, introduce a *général* for each new province.

The reforms begun in 1523 mark a convenient dividing point in the evolution of this tax system. They allow us to consider four aspects of that system: its administration, its taxes, the revenues from the taxes, and the borrowing necessitated by the shortcomings of the tax collection process. We will begin with the administration and then treat the others in turn. We must bear in mind, however, that the system produced substantial income (through the sale of its offices) and that, as we discuss the royal bureaucracy, we are also discussing those who held a large portion of the royal debt. This relationship between royal tax officers and the royal debt takes us, in fact, to the heart of the reforms of 1523 and to Francis I's creation of three key institutions: the Central Treasury, the *rentes sur l'Hôtel de Ville de Paris,* and the official venality of offices.

The Administration of Direct Taxes, 1523–98

The changes begun in 1523 and gradually worked out over the next four decades involved the creation of a more effective receiving

37. P. Solon, "Popular response to standing military forces in fifteenth-century France," *Studies in the Renaissance* 19 (1972): 78–111. Solon notes, p. 84, that contributions of towns in Basse-Auvergne dropped from 32 percent of the total in 1445 to 14 percent in 1458 and to 11 percent in 1459.

system and of a regional organizational level. A fiscal crisis in
1522–23 led Francis I to alter the traditional system, in which the
généraux oversaw all receipts and in which the receivers general
and the *changeur du Trésor* (the king's private treasurer) divided
responsibilities for disbursement of funds. The first step was the
creation of a single receiver for all revenues: the Central Treasurer
(*trésorier de l'Epargne*). Francis quickly added two controllers general to keep an eye on the Central Treasurer.[38]

The new system represented the final recognition that tax revenues were not merely an extension of the king's personal treasure
but a necessary sum raised to pay for the costs of government.
Francis I also ended the traditional distinction between ordinary
revenues, those from the demesne, and extraordinary revenues,
those from the tax system. The old system allowed the *généraux* to
run the kingdom's finances with little interference. They acted collegially to administer the taxes and they also functioned as the
king's chief bankers, borrowing money in his name or, more frequently, in their own.[39] The collective nature of their work was
reinforced by close family ties: most of the *généraux* (and treasurers
of France, in charge of the demesnes) were related by blood or marriage.

The position of the *généraux* was further strengthened by the
antiquated system of receiving money. The receivers general were
responsible for all money collected in their *généralité*, but this
money was spent (and accounted for) in three ways: (1) on local
and regional expenses, such as the cost of the financial administration itself; (2) on the obligations of the *changeur du Trésor* for the
king's private needs; and (3) on central expenses assigned to the
receipts of a given *généralité*.

This method of collecting and disbursing money had many important inconveniences. First, the king did not get money on a pre-
dictable basis. When expenses were low, this unpredictability was
not a problem; but when, under Francis I, expenses rose sharply,
the king was not able to obtain needed ready cash. This problem
remained a critical flaw in the system until the Revolution. The

38. R. Doucet, "L'état des finances de 1523," *Bulletin Philologique et Historique* (1920): 5–123, and *Les Institutions de la France au XVIe siècle* (Paris, 1948),
2 vols.
39. A. de Boislisle, "Semblançay et la Surintendance des Finances," *Annuaire-
Bulletin de la Société de l'Histoire de France* 18 (1881): 248–50.

early-sixteenth-century solution was to borrow money from the *généraux,* or to have them borrow money from merchants and from Italian bankers both in the king's name and in their own (their credit was usually better than his). For example, at the time of his disgrace, the most powerful *général,* Jacques de Beaune (Semblançay), had liens of over 1.1 million l. on the king.[40]

The *généraux* had the king in an extremely difficult position. He borrowed money from or through them, in return for which he gave (or sometimes merely promised) them liens on tax revenues; yet only the *généraux* knew how much given taxes produced because there was no royal financial council or Central Treasurer. The possibilities for irregularities and peculation in such a system were staggering.[41]

The continued abandonment of substantial tax revenues to members of the royal family and to powerful nobles and favorites greatly complicated the situation. It was precisely the question of accountability of funds given to the Queen Mother, Louise of Savoy, that led to the disgrace of Semblançay in 1523.[42]

Francis upset this system by creating the Central Treasurer, to whom all receipts had to be delivered or, barring direct delivery, from whom written orders to disburse funds had to be obtained. The only exceptions were the local and regional costs ordered at the beginning of the year by the king's council: such charges were never included in the share of the Central Treasury (the so-called *partie de l'Epargne*). This distinction on the accounts remained very important, and it explains a great deal of the problem with the misuse of the figures emanating from the Central Treasury (such as those of Jean-Roland Mallet for the seventeenth century). At their origin the figures for the share of the Central Treasury were very much like net revenue: the total revenue minus the costs of collecting said revenue. Many of the expenses added during the sixteenth century, such as the *rentes* or the *taillon,* came to be listed as regional or local expenses, thus altering the relationship between the share of the Central Treasury and the collection as a whole. By the

40. Doucet, "L'état des finances de 1523," and P. Clément, *Trois drames historiques* (Paris, 1878).
41. The de Beaune and Bohier families, heavily intermarried, amassed very large fortunes while running the king's finances. The chateau of Chenonceau was only one example of their wealth.
42. Doucet, "L'état des finances de 1523."

seventeenth century the share of the Central Treasury no longer bore a relation to any conception of net revenue (see Chapters 2 and 3 for a discussion of this issue).

Francis I's creation of the Central Treasurer deprived the *généraux* of much of their powers of oversight. Francis purged the *généraux* in the 1520s and executed Semblançay. The royal council now divided the tax burden, while the Central Treasurer, in theory, accounted for all the money. In fact the continued presence in Paris of the receivers general made the situation far more complicated. Francis ordered the receivers general, the *généraux,* and the treasurers to reside at the seats of their jurisdictions, but the constant reiteration of such edicts was a clear sign of their ineffectiveness.

Francis finally acted to rectify the situation in 1542, when he created sixteen *recettes générales* to act as regional receiving districts. As he put it:

> In order to put and establish a good order in the matter of our finances . . . we have . . . sent our letters of ordinance, containing, among other things, that there will be sixteen *recettes générales* of our finances in our towns of Paris, Châlons-s-Marne, Amiens, Rouen, Caen, Bourges, Tours, Poitiers, Issoire, Agen, Toulouse, Montpellier, Lyon, Aix, Grenoble and Dijon.[43]

Francis ordered the receivers general to these seats to supervise the collection of funds by *élection* receivers and to collect and spend the receipts from the *généralité.*

The administrative responsibilities of the *général* were obscure after 1523. As with the receivers general, the king found little for them to do in Paris (other than confuse matters). Francis ordered them to their regional seats in 1546, but this arrangement proved impractical because there were not enough *généraux* for all of the *recettes générales.* Henry II corrected the problem in 1552, when he established one *général* for each *recette générale.* Henry also combined the offices of *général* and treasurer (noting that the demesne produced little or no revenue) and ordered the *généraux* to their seats. The *recettes générales* now included Nantes, while Riom had replaced Issoire and Bordeaux, Agen.[44] At this time Henry II also changed the central administration, creating first the controller

---

43. Fontanon, *Les édits et ordonnances* (Paris, 1581), 2: 1278–82.
44. Ibid.: 885–90.

general and then the *intendants des finances*.[45] The central reforms, depriving the *généraux* of all oversight power, culminated in the creation of the royal financial council, early in the reign of Charles IX.

The new regional *généraux* supervised the receivers general, checking their accounts and those of the local receivers, and ordering them to make specific disbursements. Yet the change was more than administrative; the king also had financial motives. The cost of an office of *général* was 25,000 l. (at *gages* of 2,500 l.), those of receiver general the same. Henry II was desperate for money at this time: one estimate of August 1553 showed him needing 700,000 l. for the month of September, solely for the armies in Champagne and Picardy. He expected to get 50,000 l. of this sum from the sale of offices of receivers general.[46]

Regular financial crises arose throughout the next half century, but the system changed very little. With respect to the system, the king took a number of actions, such as separating the functions of the treasurers and *généraux* (thereby creating seventeen new offices to sell, for 425,000 l.), creating and abolishing districts, and making *comptable* offices *alternative* (Henry II)—that is, held by two men, functioning in alternate years. The permanent additions of the second half of the sixteenth century, aside from new *élections* (see below), were four *généralités:* Orléans (1573), Limoges (1586), Moulins (1587), and Soissons (1595). Most of these measures were taken several times; for example, the *généralité* of Limoges was created and abolished twice before the definitive action of 1586.[47]

From a theoretical perspective the overall structure of the French direct tax system did not change in the fifteenth and sixteenth centuries. The system of Henry II represented the same tripartite relationship used by Charles V in the 1370s. Charles V made the dioceses the local units, the provinces or bailiwicks the regional units, and the group of *généraux* and the two financial sovereign

---

45. Doucet, *Les institutions.* M. Antoine, "L'administration centrale des finances de France du XVIe au XVIIIe siècle," in *Histoire comparée de l'administration (IVe-XVIIIe siècles)* [Actes du XIVe colloque historique franco-allemand, Tours, 1977] (Munich, 1980), 511–33.
46. BN, Ms. Fr. 3127, fols. 75–76.
47. J.-P. Charmeil, *Les trésoriers de France à l'époque de la Fronde* (Paris, 1963), 6–9. For Moulins, see also F. Dumont, *Le bureau des finances de la généralité de Moulins* (Moulins, 1929).

courts the central unit. The new system of the sixteenth century also consisted of three levels: (1) the *élections;* (2) the *généralités;* and (3) the royal financial council and the sovereign courts. The third level had two elements because of the judicial and administrative responsibilities of the local officers (*élus* and *grenetiers*). The judicial superstructure included the various *Cours des Aides* and Chambers of Accounts and, to a lesser extent, the Parlements. By the seventeenth century the royal council evoked to its jurisdiction many financial cases, particularly those involving powerful financiers or, after 1634, the intendants. While the principle of a tripartite division remained the same throughout this long period, the enormous increase in the number of personnel after 1550 or so had far-reaching practical consequences.

The sixteenth-century tax system was more centralized than it had been in the time of Charles V or even Charles VII. The dioceses of Charles V's time were far larger than the *élections* of Henry II's reign, and the intermediate level of the sixteenth century, the *généralité,* was an important step in better communications between the center and local areas. The principle of establishing several levels of communication between the local areas and the government, and of involving the local elites in the process, remained the same. The *généralité* system also covered all of France, whereas the *élections* did not. One of the primary goals of the period 1572 to 1632 was to extend the *élections* throughout the kingdom. The Crown's failure to do so forced a fundamental change in the manner in which it governed France, as we shall see in Chapter 2.

George Pagès saw the series of changes in the sixteenth century as an effort to reconcile local interests and those of the king through the interposition of regional bodies. He felt that the *élections* and the *généralités* were independent local and regional bodies, respectively. In both cases venality (officers owned their offices) and collegiality helped assure individual officers a great deal of independence.

Pagès further argued that it was precisely this venality and the ease of advancement within the system that gave the monarchy such solid support within the middle reaches of French society. By allowing the bourgeoisie to take over the various levels of the administration, starting with the towns and moving up to the *généralités* and Chambers of Accounts, the Crown made the increase in

power of the royal bureaucracy in the interest of part of the bourgeoisie, too.[48]

The king accommodated the nobility through the army, pensions, and some judicial offices. In addition, the king chose his officers from among the clients of the nobility. Jonathan Dewald has
shown that the magistrates of the Parlement of Rouen, for example,
were often clients of major Norman noble families. Many of the
Parlementaires were lawyers or administrators for such families as
the Longuevilles or the Aumales: "What was critical to most robe
careers at Rouen was not loyalty to the crown but patronage from
members of the great aristocracy."[49] The same situation applied to
the financial officers. Robert Harding has demonstrated the substantial powers of sixteenth- and seventeenth-century governors in
the constitution of the local royal bureaucracy. Those who held
appanages from the king or grants of certain demesne revenues
even collected the transmission fees (resignation taxes or the price
of a new office) on all offices within their appanage or grant area.[50]

This conflict between the central government and the centrifugal
forces in French society came to a head under Henry III. As we
have seen in the evolution of the tax system up to the middle of the
sixteenth century, French kings moved with great circumspection
when it came to introducing any new methods or usages into their
system of administration. The system may have appeared to be an
irrational hodgepodge at any given moment, but the various exceptions and privileges responded to very real regional differences in
social, economic, political, and legal matters. Following his father's
example, Henry III sought to eliminate much of the regionalism in
government. His urgent need for money made reform of the tax
system doubly attractive as a means to attack local and regional
opposition to centralization, because a more consistent system
could produce more money and because the sale of the offices
needed to staff such a system would also raise substantial sums.

The centripetal forces concentrated around the king grew

48. G. Pagès, "Essai sur l'évolution des institutions administratives en France du
XVIe à la fin du XVIIe siècle," *Revue d'Histoire Moderne* 7 (1935): 8–57, 113–38.

49. J. Dewald, *The Formation of a Provincial Nobility, The Magistrates of the
Parlement of Rouen, 1499–1610* (Princeton, 1980), 86.

50. R. Harding, *Anatomy of a Power Elite: The Provincial Governors of Early
Modern France* (New Haven, 1978). In Brittany, for example, Marie de Medicis
collected transfer taxes on certain offices.

stronger in the sixteenth century, and one of the most important
areas in which the king sought to centralize was the tax system. Administrative financial reform was a recurrent theme from
Henry II to Henry III. Henry II sought to create a more unified
gabelle system (following the initiative of his father); he created the
controllers-general; he established the oversight officials (*intendants des finances*) at the Central Treasury; he added new direct
taxes; he simplified the transit duties; he created alternative service
in *comptable* offices; and he created the permanent *généralités*.
Francis II and Charles IX made few moves, but their younger
brother tried an extensive series of reforms.

Henry III was not the worst of French kings, yet it was his mis-
fortune to be king at a time when his shortcomings—indecisive-
ness, a short attention span, and an image of weakness—were precisely those that could prove most harmful. The religious problems
of the late sixteenth century were a serious threat to public order,
especially after 1572, but other stresses in French society were
equally divisive. There were three major threats to royal power in
Henry III's time: the Huguenots, the great nobles, and the centrifugal forces represented by the Estates of the outlying provinces.
The tax administration was a key weapon in the struggle with all
three groups, not only under Henry III, but under Henry IV and
Louis XIII as well.

From a purely administrative point of view Henry III's reign was
an important one. He tried many reforms that his successors
brought to fruition in the next century. In 1577, Henry perma-
nently combined the functions of the treasurers and *généraux* (here-
inafter referred to as treasurers), created a fifth treasurer in each
district, institutionalized collegiality in their meetings, and gave
these colleges the principle of majority vote. As Pagès pointed out,
collegiality and majority vote allowed individuals to hide behind
the collective decision, thus making it more difficult to discipline
them.[51]

Henry III's great design was to centralize and standardize the tax
system. He combined the export-import duties into the *Cinq
Grosses Fermes* (CGF) in 1581, and he also centralized the *gabelle*
and *aides* farms. In each case the increased centralization was necessary in order for the king to use the taxes as security for loans

51. Pagès, "Essai," 17 and 26.

from major international, mostly Italian, bankers. The earlier failure of the *Grand Parti de Lyon* made the international financiers unwilling to accept any other arrangement. Thus the Gondis, Sebastien Zamet, and André Ruiz were all tax farmers in addition to being bankers for the king.

The effort to obtain a greater degree of control and centralization can best be seen, however, in the methods used by Charles IX and Henry III to break the power of the provincial Estates and to extend the number and scope of the *élections* and *généralités*. While financial concerns influenced the creation of many of these offices and jurisdictions (a new *généralité* would have generated some 250,000 l. from the sale of its offices in 1580), political factors were also very important. The new *généralités* of the late sixteenth century were all in areas where royal control was weak: the Orléans appanage lands—Orléans and Moulins; the Southwest—Limoges, and, following the same principle in the seventeenth century, Montauban (1634); the Flemish frontier—Soissons.[52]

These new jurisdictions weakened the authority of all the groups threatening the king, but they created a fourth group—the officers themselves. The attack on provincial privileges was clearest in the *pays d'Etats,* first, in the sixteenth century, in Normandy, and then, in the seventeenth, in Guyenne, Dauphiné, Provence, and Burgundy. Since the Norman case is ideal for examining the king's techniques in such matters, we will discuss it in detail.

Normandy had the dubious distinction of being both a *pays d'Etats* and a *pays d'élection,* which made it a particularly inviting target for the king. It was also an extremely important target because it paid between one-fourth and one-fifth of the total direct taxes of the *pays d'élection*. The province had fifteen *élections* in 1500; by 1554, the two Norman *généralités*—Rouen and Caen— had seventeen *élections*.[53] The great change began in the 1560s, with complaints about the Estates losing their role in apportioning the tax burden. In 1572, Charles IX accelerated the assault by creating eleven new *élections*.[54] After a long and bitter dispute with

52. A *généralité* would have had five treasurers (25,000 l. each), two receivers, two controllers, and an array of lesser personnel in 1580. After 1586, it would have had ten treasurers.

53. E. Esmonin, *La taille en Normandie au temps de Colbert* (Paris, 1913), 1–10.

54. C. de Robillard de Beaurepaire, *Cahiers des Etats de Normandie* (Rouen, 1873–99). *Règne* Charles IX, vol. 1, *cahiers* of 1573.

the king, the Estates of Normandy bought the suppression of these *élections* in 1581. Yet Henry III changed his mind two years later, exempting four of the new *élections* from the edict of suppression. In 1586, he reactivated all of the *élections* created in 1572.[55]

The king had not neglected the old *élections* in this period, apparently adding an *élu* to each one in 1572. Henry III followed the same double game with these new offices, abolishing them in 1581 and reestablishing them in 1586. He also doubled the number of both *élus* and treasurers in 1586.[56] Each Norman *élection* had only one or two *élus* until 1572 but five to seven by 1587.[57]

The king attacked Norman privileges with great circumspection and patience. He began by excluding the Estates of Normandy from the apportionment of the *tailles* in the 1560s and then created new offices to carry out the greater apportionment responsibilities.[58] The *cahiers* of 1569 asked that the delegates to the viscounty (local judicial and electoral unit) assemblies assist at the apportionment of the *tailles* among the parishes; the king refused. The king later restored this right, in 1580, and confirmed the right in 1593, 1618, and 1642. This last confirmation granted a 1622 petition of the city of Rouen to respect this right even in years in which the Estates of Normandy did not meet.[59]

The creation of the new offices and of the new *élections* was accomplished with a respect for precedent. All of the new *élections* were in the *généralité* of Rouen. Charles IX applied the system used in the *généralité* of Caen, where the viscounties were also the *élections*, to that of Rouen. The king could claim that the viscounties were the geographic subdivisions for the Estates because both the Second and Third Estates held their elections at that level. While there were a few exceptions to this strict duality, they could easily be explained on practical geographic grounds, and the king relied exclusively on indigenous Norman jurisdictional units.[60]

The king was trying to break the fiscal power of the Estates of

55. Ibid., *règne* Henri III, vol. 2, *cahiers* of 1587, arts. 17 and 18.
56. This doubling was done all over France, making service alternative (that is, five treasurers sitting in alternate years in each *généralité*, for a total of ten).
57. J. Vannier, *Le bureau des finances de Rouen* (Rouen, 1927), 19–20.
58. De Beaurepaire, *Cahiers*, *règne* Charles IX, vol. 1: 39–40. Prentout, *Etats de Normandie*, 2: 179.
59. Prentout, *Etats de Normandie*, 2: 179–82.
60. J.-B. Voysin de la Noiraye, *Mémoire sur la généralité de Rouen en 1665*, ed. E. Esmonin (Paris, 1913).

Normandy by extending the system of *élections*, but he nonetheless paid proper respect to local customs. In the end the Estates failed because the *élections* were already there and because the *taille* was levied in Normandy much as it was elsewhere. (It is worth noting that the Norman portion of the total direct tax levy did not go up as a result of the changes.) The weakness of the Norman position was summed up in the response of Henry IV's commissioners to the Estates, when the latter refused to vote the full sum asked of them: "in order not to leave the king's service behind, that, by provisional action, a division and apportionment (of the *taille*) shall be done." Henri Prentout rightly stated of this doctrine: "The formula of the Commissioners which ordered the integral levying of the sum demanded, in spite of the refusal of the Estates, suppressed, in reality, their rights."[61]

Henry III used the creation of these *élections* as one weapon in the destruction of Norman privileges. He also called small special meetings of the Estates of Normandy and of the Estates in the other *pays d'Etats*, hoping to have more success with them than with the full-scale meetings. This use of extraordinary meetings of provincial Estates was, in part, prompted by the contentious mood of the various regular provincial assemblies in 1578 and 1579. For example, the Estates of Normandy proposed the elimination of the *élus* and the entire direct taxation system. They offered repartition among the viscounties by the Estates, within the viscounty by the local meetings of the electoral Estates, and collection by a bourgeois of the major town of the viscounty.[62] The king refused, noting that he could not enter into "such a change and new order."

Henry had constant recourse to the smaller bodies of Estates in this period. In Burgundy, where the Estates normally met every third year, he called them each year from 1578 to 1581.[63] In Brittany several sessions met each year.[64] But he was no more successful with the smaller meetings than he was with the larger ones. The main problem he faced was that confronted by medieval kings: the

---

61. Prentout, *Etats de Normandie*, 2: 154.

62. De Beaurepaire, *Cahiers, règne* Henri III, vol. 1; Prentout, *Etats de Normandie*, 1: 39–40.

63. G. Weill, "Les Etats de Bourgogne sous Henri III," *Mémoires de la Société Bourguignonne de Géographie et d'Histoire* 9 (1893): 130. J.-L. Gay, "Fiscalité royale et Etats Généraux de Bourgogne, 1477–1589," in *Etudes sur l'histoire des Assemblées d'Etats*, ed. F. Dumont (Paris, 1966), 179–210.

64. Collins, "Taxation in Bretagne," chap. 4.

lack of authority given to representatives sent to Paris. For example, in April 1579, Henry wrote to the Estates of Normandy:

> we find it good . . . that those who will be named to bring the *cahier* to us and make remonstrances for the said *pays* will have the power and authority to solicit, procure, manage and negotiate, together with the *procureur* of the Estates, the affairs of the said province, until the next meeting of the Estates, in which they will answer for their negotiation, just as is practiced in the other provinces of this kingdom that have regular Estates.[65]

Henry was lying about this last part. He made similar demands (also unsuccessful) of the Burgundians; it was much easier to intimidate a few deputies in Paris than an entire body in Rouen or Dijon.

Henry III found that the extensive use of local assemblies would not work; indeed his efforts led to communication between the Burgundians, Normans, and Bretons as to how best to oppose him. Nonetheless, Henry III did seek to reform the kingdom by traditional means: first, in 1576, through an Estates General; then, from 1578 to 1581, through extensive use of local and provincial Estates. This was the method followed since the fourteenth century: get agreement on general principles from an Estates General and then move to provincial Estates to work out the local details. Henry III did, in fact, issue an important series of ordinances related to taxation between 1577 and 1579, such as that creating the *bureaux des finances* (colleges of treasurers). Henry also changed the money of account, from the *livre tournois*, a purely theoretical denomination, to the *écu*, an actual coin.[66]

After failing with the traditional Estates General-provincial Estates mechanism, Henry shifted to a more centralized approach. In 1581, he acted unilaterally to centralize the transit taxes (the major ones) into the *Cinq Grosses Fermes*. He also granted new leases on lesser farms, such as the wine taxes of Brittany, to major financiers, such as André Ruiz. Henry decided to use an Assembly of Notables, whose participants he could select, to reform the kingdom. The Assembly met at St-Germain-en-Laye, in 1583—that is, immediately after Henry's disillusionment with frequent meetings of provincial Estates.

---

65. De Beaurepaire, *Cahiers, règne* Henri III, 1: 348–49.
66. On prices, J. Meuvret and M. Baulant, *Les prix des céréales extraits du mercuriale de Paris* (Paris, 1960–61); on currency, F. Spooner, *L'économie mondiale et les frappes monétaires en France, 1493–1680* (Paris, 1956).

This 1583 attempt at reform was a serious one. The royal bureaucracy produced a broad series of memoirs on the situation in the kingdom, particularly the financial problems. The famous 1581 estimate of the king's finances, which gives an historical background going back into the fifteenth century, was probably drawn up for the 1583 Assembly of Notables. The treasurers of France also produced a series of memoirs on each of the *généralités*. These memoires provided detailed information on every aspect of the financial and judicial administration of each area, including the names of all royal officers and the various petty feudal rents owed to the king for both rural landholdings and urban houses.

These memoires must have been used to draw up the reform proposals for the meeting. The report on Brittany was so detailed and so exact that it was used as the basis for all future commissions dealing both with finances and with the royal demesne.[67] For the rural demesne holdings, the Breton memoir listed, not only the amounts due in cash and in kind, but, in order to evaluate the value of the latter, price estimates of all goods received, based on recent market prices in the locality. The memoir explained the Breton tax farms and listed all royal officials and their salaries. In a separate document, apparently drawn up as background material, the treasurers gave a detailed analysis of hearth counts for each parish.[68] Another background document listed *rente* holders, with the amount of their *rente* and its year of purchase. The report on the *généralité* of Rouen was also quite detailed.[69]

These reports, and the 1583 Assembly itself, are evidence of an entirely new conception of royal government. There does not seem to have been any earlier effort to establish so broad a documentary base for a royal analysis of the kingdom's financial situation. We cannot be certain whether Henry III's predecessors had a clear picture of their financial situation, but we do know that Henry was aware of exactly where he stood and why. One of the prerequisites of modern, effective government is the ability to gather and analyze detailed information, as a necessary precondition for effective government action. It was indicative of Henry III's reign that he planned such an extensive reform of the kingdom, and that he obtained such detailed information—only to allow the opportunity

67. AD Loire-Atlantique, B 12871.
68. AD Loire-Atlantique, B 12871, separate document.
69. AD Seine-Maritime, C 1272.

to slip away. Nonetheless, as we shall see, Henry III's use of the
Assembly of Notables of 1583 would prove an important precedent
for Henry IV.[70]

By 1585, Henry III was back to the old ways: creating offices in
each *élection*, making *élus* and treasurers alternative, mortaging the
indirect taxes (and perhaps the *taille* as well), selling *rentes* on all
sorts of revenues. In 1589, Henry left his successors a disorganized
and fragmented financial system—that is, a financial system in
much the same state as the kingdom itself.

Still, the possibilities of the financial system, and those of the
kingdom, were considerable. By the end of Henry III's reign, all of
France was covered by the *généralité* system and the number of
élections had risen sharply. The royal bureaucracy was several
times larger than it had been under Francis I. This size made the
king's authority more effective in outlying areas, when he had phys-
ical control of them. Local elites had developed powerful bastions
of authority in the offices of the *généralités* and *élections*, as well as
in the provincial sovereign courts. These officers were a key element
in the ongoing struggle between local particularism and royal centralization. While they represented local, particularist interests,
they also represented the king; it was never entirely clear which role
was the key one in any given situation. In the late sixteenth century,
with the period's semipermanent civil wars, the royal bureaucracy
faced less pressure from the center. After 1596, however, the king
would be able to use the bureaucracy already in place to try to
govern, and to tax, more effectively.

By 1589, the indirect tax farms were now quite large. Henry III
successfully created the CGF, as well as a single *gabelle* farm for
the North (the *pays des grandes gabelles*) in 1578, devised a more
centralized system for the *aides* (paving the way for the *Aides Générales* farm under Henry IV), and increased pressure for single
farms in the *gabelles* of the South (consolidated into four large
farms under Henry IV).

The direct tax system was far more coherent and centralized
than it had been in 1574. Twice as many officers were working for
it in 1589 than had been doing so in 1574. Henry III had extended
the *généralité* system into new areas and created a large number of

70. A. Karch, "L'assemblée des notables de St-Germain-en-Laye," *Bibliothèque
de l'Ecole des Chartes* (1956): 115–62.

new *élections*. He also raised the level of direct taxation very sharply, although much of the increase merely compensated for inflation. Lastly, in his preparations for the Assembly of Notables of 1583, Henry III had amassed a detailed body of information on the state of his finances.

The French tax system of 1598 was more centralized than ever before, and the king was using the system to attack local privileges with more and more effectiveness. Had Henry III ruled in more tranquil times, his effort at reform in 1583 might have succeeded. As it was, he left a legacy of failed initiatives. Yet this legacy of failure was important, because it helped prepare the custom-bound mentality of the period for the changes that were to come under Henry IV and Louis XIII. Henry III was also responsible for major innovations: the creation of collegiality in the *généralités,* the centralization of the indirect tax farms, and the enormous expansion of the royal bureaucracy. These innovations helped keep the system that had evolved from the time of Charles V more responsive to the needs of the times, and gave it new life. They also showed that this system could be adapted to circumstances and gave promise—a promise not fulfilled, as we shall see—of using the *élection-généralité* system to make France into a more centralized state. The failure of this system in the early seventeenth century is the subject of the next three chapters.

Direct Taxes in Sixteenth-Century France

The basic direct tax throughout the sixteenth century was the *taille,* the continuation of Charles VII's levy for the men-at-arms. The king levied the *taille* only in the areas within the jurisdiction of the old Estates of Languedoil of the fourteenth century; the outlying provinces were all exempt. Some areas, such as the Southwest and Normandy, had somewhat irregular arrangements with the king. In each case the king levied the *taille,* but he did so only with the consent of Estates. Nonetheless, such Estates had little impact on the size of the province's contribution, which remained set at a relatively fixed portion of the levy for the kingdom as a whole.[71] This constancy of proportion was a direct reflection of the *taille*'s

71. Prentout, *Etats de Normandie.*

original correspondence to a given number of men-at-arms for each province.

Francis I augmented the *taille* with a *crue* of 600,000 l. (3 *sous/l.* or 15 percent). He paid for his ransom by means of taxes on everyone's income—taxes to which the nobility and clergy contributed. Francis also introduced the tax for 50,000 infantrymen: it was originally a "forced loan" but soon dropped this pretense. The tax records of the city of Nantes indicate that the king levied this tax in 1524, 1536, 1544, 1547, 1550, 1551, 1574–76, and 1578, while the Paris records show that he raised it there in 1564 and 1566. This tax, which Henry II expanded to cover the entire country, appears to have been levied without interruption from the 1540s on.[72]

Francis I also created a tax of 20 l./belfry; this tax was levied sporadically for the next fifty years. Both the tax on belfries and the wages of the 50,000 infantrymen seem to have died out under Henry III, and there is no record of them in the seventeenth century. The levy for the 50,000 infantrymen may have been the forerunner of the *grande crue* (or *crue des garnisons*) instituted by Henry IV.[73]

Henry II added two new taxes, the *taillon* (tax for men-at-arms) and the mounted constabulary tax (*crue des prévôts des maréchaussées*).[74] Charles IX created another *crue*, of 300,000 l. All of the late Valois levied public service taxes, such as those for postal service, dike and levee repairs, and roads and bridges.[75]

These taxes appeared as separate amounts on the seventeenth-century records, but it is unclear when this practice began. All such levies were counted as regional expenses—that is, the money spent with the proceeds of these taxes was carried on the budget of the *généralité*. None of this money was listed on the part of the Central Treasury. Two other taxes were also subsumed within the *taille*, although, again, they bore separate listings on the seventeenth-century records. The two taxes, the *subvention des villes* and the *équivalent des aides*, each of 125,000 l., were levied only in certain *généralités*. The *équivalent*, established at the time of Louis XI's

72. AM de Nantes, AA 23; CC 72, 74, 75, 76, 77.

73. Doucet, *Institutions*. G. Zeller, *Les institutions de la France au XVIe siècle* (Paris, 1948).

74. The mounted constabulary tax existed already at the local level; Henry II systematized it into a national levy.

75. BN, Ms. Fr. 16622, 16623, 16624 show the taxes broken down by category in 1620. There are also many examples in provincial archives.

abolition of the *aides* on all but a few goods, was levied only in those areas that paid the *aides*.[76]

Henry IV seems to have added another tax to this list: the *grande crue*. The earliest mentions of this tax come from the 1590s: 1594 in Champagne, 1598 in Brittany and Languedoc, and 1597 in the *pays d'élection*. The ostensible purpose of the *grande crue* was to allow Henry to disband his armies and to keep a certain number of fixed garrison troops throughout the country: for example, in Brittany there were 300 officers and men in such garrisons, costing 75,000 l.[77] The *crue* was extremely large, in some provinces as large or larger than the *taille* itself. We will consider the *crue* in detail in Chapter 2, but we will note here that the *crue* was far more flexible than the *taille* and that most fluctuation in direct taxation after 1597 did not involve the *taille* itself.

In contrast to the *taille*, the *crue* and the taxes created under Henry II were levied throughout the kingdom, even in the new provinces, such as Brittany or Provence. They were a perfect illustration of the flexibility of the monarchy; the king did not levy the *taille* in the provinces in question because they had not been part of the original area within which the *taille* had been created. Without some authorization from the inhabitants, however indirect or limited, the *taille* or other tax would have been a violation of privileges. It would have been illegitimate for the king to extend retroactively a preexisting royal tax, such as the *taille*, into a new province. He had every right to assess the entire kingdom of the moment for a *new* tax, although he often bargained with provincial Estates in some areas to collect it. While provincial Estates did purchase exemption from some of the new indirect taxes created after 1547, the king did not grant such exemptions for the new direct taxes.

At the end of the sixteenth century, therefore, the main body of direct taxes, usually referred to by historians with the indiscriminate label "*taille*," was, in fact, an amalgam of various taxes. The "taille et crues y joint," which included the *taille*, the roads and bridges levy, the two sixteenth-century *crues*, a special levy for officers' *gages*, and the postal tax, were levied exclusively in the jurisdiction of the old Estates of Languedoil: the *généralités* of Paris, Soissons, Amiens, Châlons, Rouen, Caen, Bourges, Orléans, Tours,

---

76. Doucet, *Institutions;* Zeller, *Institutions.* See below, chap. 3, for details.
77. BN, Ms. Fr. 22311, fols. 111–14, account rendered 1604.

Riom, Bordeaux, Poitiers, Limoges, and Moulins. (Areas that had been under English control in the mid-fourteenth century were included, even though they had not been part of the Estates' meetings.) The king levied the *taillon,* the *grande crue* (usually known in the *pays d'Etats* as the garrison tax), and the mounted constabulary tax throughout the kingdom in 1598 (with the exception that Amiens was exempt from the *crue*). Although we often speak of various provinces, such as Brittany, as being "exempt from the *taille,*" in fact this exemption covered only the "taille et crues y joint," not the direct taxes created in the sixteenth century.

The outlying provinces had their own local direct taxes: in Provence and Brittany, the *fouage;* in Languedoc, a package of taxes levied in the form of a *taille* (but not part of the royal *taille*); in Dauphiné, the *octroi;* in Burgundy, an *octroi* or *don gratuit*. In Provence and Dauphiné, the chief royal taxes were, in fact, direct levies for troops, usually for supplies (*étapes*). In the late sixteenth century such levies for troops were also very high both in Brittany and Languedoc.[78]

Revenues from Sixteenth-Century Taxation

The documentary evidence for the revenues of the French monarchy before Henry IV is both spotty and scanty; if not used with extreme caution, it is also misleading. There is little point in embroiling ourselves here in the controversies over royal revenues during the late Middle Ages. A brief summary, concentrating on the sixteenth century, is more in order.

Charles V's revenue seems to have been about 2 million l. per year; the *fouage* was his most important source of income. Under Charles VI, the *tailles* were quite irregular, and their size ranged from 0.6 to 1.4 million l. Royal income remained in the same 2 million l. range. Charles VII raised some 1.2 to 1.5 million l. per year from the *tailles* in the late 1440s and the 1450s, and perhaps half as much in other ways. Louis XI increased the *taille* to about

---

78. Devic and Vaissette, *Histoire de Languedoc;* Collins, "Taxation in Bretagne"; L. S. Van Doren, "The Royal *Taille* in Dauphiné, 1560–1610," *Proceedings of the Third Western Conference for French History* 3 (1975): 35–53.

4.4 million l. by 1483, but it declined sharply after his death, to 2.1 million l. in 1487.[79]

In the sixteenth century both the rate of taxation and the revenue from taxation went up sharply. Direct taxes rose a bit more than general prices until the 1550s, but they did not keep pace with the rampant inflation of the 1550–85 period. Indirect sales taxes, transit taxes, and, most especially, the *gabelle* rose far more sharply than direct taxes.

Francis I listed an income of about 8 million l. in the early 1520s: 4.8 million l. in direct taxes, 825,000 l. in *aides,* and 460,000 l. in *gabelles.* The tenth on the clergy (*décime*) added another 1.1 million l., while the remainder came from the sale of offices, the demesne, and other sources.[80] The figure of 8 million l., however, excluded demesnes and taxes given to royal favorites and family members, as well as the local and regional charges, 825,000 l. on the direct taxes (about 15 percent of the total, a proportion similar to that of later periods).[81] It also excluded those taxes, such as the *gabelle* levied for the *gages* of the Parlement of Paris, raised for a specific expense.

Francis I's regular income remained some 8 to 10 million l., but extraordinary levies of many kinds supplemented it greatly, particularly during wartime. In the 1520s, the chief supplemental levy was that for the king's ransom, which was paid by everyone— clergy, nobles, townsmen, and peasants.[82] Francis also introduced the "forced loan" on closed towns to pay the wages of the infantry. This tax appeared in 1524, when the towns of Brittany paid 12,000 l.; since Brittany usually supported one-twentieth of the troops, this figure would mean 240,000 l. for the kingdom. The most extensive

79. Rey, *Le domaine du roi,* 262. This information is backed up by *Ordonnances,* 5: 537–41, art. 4, 18–21. See also, Rey, *Le domaine du roi,* 371–77. A new effort at synthesis is C. Radding, "Royal Tax Revenues in Late Fourteenth-Century France," *Traditio* 32 (1976): 361–68. Radding, "Aids in Normandy," also has some figures. On Charles VI, see Rey, *Le domaine du roi,* 404, and *Les finances royales sous Charles VI: Les causes du déficit, 1388–1413* (Paris, 1965). On Charles VII, see Clamageran, *Histoire de l'impôt,* vol. II, pp. 1–20, backed up by Prentout, *Etats de Normandie,* vol. 3, and by P. de Commynes, *Memoirs* (Columbia, S.C., 1969), 360. Commynes claims Charles VII's maximum was 1.8 million *francs,* that of Louis XI, 4.7 million l., plus an artillery surtax, in 1483. In 1484, the levies were only 2.5 million l.

80. Doucet, "L'état des finances de 1523."

81. BN, Ms. Dupuy 848, fols. 60 and ff., extracts of the "comptes de l'Epargne."

82. AM de Nantes, AA 68, on contribution of Nantes (10,000 l.).

records concerning this tax are those of Nantes, which indicate that it was levied with great regularity; indeed, the tax may have been collected every year. The Breton contribution ranged from 15,000 l. in 1547 to 60,000 l. in 1536, 1551, and 1577.[83] Two of the indirect taxes of Paris bore liens of 63,125 l. for the infantry. These liens alert us to the constant problem of distinguishing direct from indirect taxation, because the towns in question could, as Paris did, raise their contribution as they saw fit.[84]

There are two series of documents concerning the king's revenues through the sixteenth century: a brief history of French taxation from Philip Augustus to Henry III, drawn up for the Assembly of Notables of 1583; and extracts from the *comptes de l'Epargne* for twelve years between 1522 and 1599.[85] We also have isolated documents, such as the list of revenues and expenses for 1549 (Table 1) or the occasional estimates of military costs.[86]

The 1549 estimate, which is the most complete for the middle of the century, has substantial gaps. For example, direct taxes alone in Dauphiné were 91,700 l., while Breton regular taxation was about 650,000 l. The listings for the *aides* and *gabelles* are clearly incomplete, particularly with respect to indirect taxes in the *pays d'Etats*, and the revenue from the sale of offices was below normal. This listing also ignores the *taillon*, which took effect the following year, and which added 1.2 million l. to the direct tax burden.

The regular direct tax burden can be estimated at some 8 to 9 million l.: 4 million l. for the *taille*, 600,000 l. for the *crue* added by Francis I, 1.2 million l. for the *taillon*, about 400,000 l. for the mounted constabulary, close to a million for local and regional costs, and another 1 to 1.5 million in the *pays d'Etats*.[87] Charles IX added another *crue* of 300,000 l.

83. AM de Nantes, AA 23 and CC 72, 74–77. The king also levied the *francs fiefs* in 1539 (BN, Ms. Fr. 22342, fols. 193v and ff. on levy in Brittany) and 1566 (AD Loire-Atlantique, B 3023).

84. BN, 500 Colbert 41, fols. 51–62.

85. BN, Ms. Dupuy 848, fols. 60 and ff.; BN, Ms Dupuy 41, fols. 62 and ff. (among many copies) for the 1583 estimate done for the Assembly. The extracts are from 1522–25 (unspecified year), 1530, 1540, 1545, 1550, 1563, 1570, 1576, 1581, 1587, 1590, 1599, and 1604. The document prepared for the 1583 assembly lists revenues from 1497, 1514, 1547, 1560, 1574, and 1581. (BN, Ms. Fr. 21479, fols. 31v and ff.) It also has a brief history of French taxation, beginning with Philip Augustus.

86. BN, Ms. Fr. 3127, fols. 91 and ff.

87. In Brittany, about 350–400,000 l., with perhaps an equal amount in Lan-

Table 1. *French Royal Income and Spending, 1549 (in 000 l.)*

Income Source	Amount	Expenses	Amount
Tailles	4,466	Military	4,483
Gabelles	852	Household	664
Aides	700	Embassies	200
Décimes (2)	700	Pensions	800
Parties casuelles	100	Courts	118
Demesne	100	Interest, Lyon	388
Wood sales	200	Loans due	2,422
1548 carryover	577	*Gages* and *non-valeurs*	1,200
Brittany	514	Others	1,157
Dauphiné	32		
Burgundy	38		
Provence	27		
Total	8,302[a]	Total	11,432

Source: BN, Ms. Dupuy 3127, fols. 91 and ff.
[a] The sums listed total 8,306,000 l.; the cited figure is the total given by the document.

These regular taxes were only the framework on which the king levied the "extraordinary" amounts. We have seen that the tax for the 50,000 infantrymen usually ran to 1.2 million l. a year. From Francis I on, the king also levied an occasional tax of 20 l./belfry; in 1574 he raised such a tax whose value must have approached 600,000 l.[88] There were periodic levies on the "rich," such as the 100,000 l. the Bretons claimed to have paid in 1575.[89] The king also raised money from the Church, from towns, and from the sale of offices and by alienating revenues. He created new indirect taxes or expanded old ones. Most of these activities have left some records: for example, we know that the *parties casuelles* (primarily the revenue from office sales) ranged from a low of 275,000 l. in 1563

guedoc. In the Southeast, most direct taxes were military. See Van Doren, "The Royal *Taille*," and "War Taxation, Institutional Change, and Social Conflict in Provincial France—The Royal *Taille* in Dauphiné, 1494–1559," *Proceedings of the American Philosophical Society* 121 (1977): 71–96. In the 1530s, for example, direct taxation in Dauphiné ranged from 30,000 l. (1531) to 382,100 l. in 1538.

88. Parish counts from BN, Ms. Fr. 7736 (from the 1640s) as well as in Ms. Fr. 21479, fols. 37–39. The latter are less accurate, since they are given as estimates by *généralité*. The figures in Ms. Fr. 7736 are given by *élection*.

89. AD Loire-Atlantique, C 414, pp. 695 and ff.

to a high of 10.6 million l. in 1581.[90] The clergy paid about 1.6 million l. a year after their agreement with the king in 1561.[91]

The largest source of missing revenue, however, was the military levies. L. S. Van Doren has shown that direct taxation for the armies ranged as high as 382,100 l. (1538) in Dauphiné. In the 1550s, it averaged some 130,000 l. a year. Under Henry III and in the first part of Henry IV's reign, it surpassed a million l. a year.[92] In Brittany, where we have more complete records than in many other areas, the Estates claimed, in 1578, that the king had levied more than 4 million l. in extraordinary taxation since 1561.[93] The Estates included in this sum the 160,000 l. that the troops of the duke d'Etampes had levied in 1562, as well as the 300,000 l. levied by the count of Martigues in 1567–68 for troops brought to Paris.[94]

War was extremely expensive. In July 1573, the city of Vannes raised 7,764 l. (by borrowing from local merchants) to outfit four ships to send to La Rochelle. This sum included 1,800 l. for biscuit, 583 l. for 30 tons of red wine from Nantes, and 1,603 l. for the pay of the soldiers for one month.[95] Land armies were a much larger expense. Several documents from Henry II's reign show us how expensive. War cost him 1.4 million l. between August and November 1553, and he frequently had trouble raising the money. In August, for example, he needed 700,000 l. for the September campaigns in Champagne and Picardy. He proposed to raise this sum by money from regular receipts (77,000 l.), by selling demesnes and *rentes* (180,000 l.), and by selling offices (192,000 l.).[96]

A document from 1550 shows that Henry had 3,520 active lances in the *compagnies d'ordonnance*, costing him about 3 million l. a year. He proposed at that time to cut 1,100 lances, thus saving 848,000 l.[97] The annual cost of a lance, therefore, was about

90. BN, Ms. Dupuy 848, fols. 60 and ff.

91. BN, Ms. Fr. 21479, fols. 18–20v, has a breakdown of the 1.615 million l. by bishopric, done in 1574.

92. Van Doren, "The Royal *Taille*."

93. AD Loire-Atlantique, C 414, pp. 858 and ff.

94. Ibid., pp. 150 and ff.

95. AM de Nantes, EE 221. One of the merchants was André Ruiz. The accounting dates from February 1574, for outfitting in July 1573.

96. BN, Ms. Fr. 3127, fols. 75–76. He expected the 700,000 l. for October to come from the receipts of the *généralités* of Paris (70,000 l.), Châlons (30,000 l.), the *parties casuelles* (200,000 l.), old debts (200,000 l.), *rentes* (100,000 l.), and odd sources.

97. Ibid., fols. 3–4v.

850 l. At the end of the century, a French foot soldier could receive 12 l. a month, a Swiss one even more. Men-at-arms got 480 l. a year.[98] The heaviest expenses, however, were for the officers. The duke of Brissac, for example, received 300 l. a month as lieutenant general of Upper and Lower Brittany, as well as 10,000 l. for his *état* as marshal of France. In his company of men-at-arms, Brissac and the staff of four received 16 percent of the total paid to the company of 96 men, excluding any money they might get for pensions or *états*.[99]

The most detailed estimate of total revenues from the late sixteenth century is that done for 1581 to present to the Assembly of Notables of 1583 (see Table 2). Even this document is subject to some revision, however, because it leaves out many revenues. It excludes some 4.5 million l. in local and regional charges in the listings for the *généralités*. There are also enormous listings for highly irregular revenues and expenses: the *parties extraordinaires* listing includes all revenue from indirect taxes (but also includes money from loans), while the 3.9 million *écus* under "comptants ès mains du Roi" is a sixteenth-century record.[100] The local records in Lyon and Bourges indicate that this 1581 estimate may be very misleading, since, for Lyon, the indirect tax revenues were lumped

98. BN, Ms. Fr. 22311, fols. 111–14. The cost of soldiers was extremely high in the late sixteenth and early seventeenth centuries. For example, the cost of one hundred men staying in Guérande in 1628 for one month was 2,649 l. (plus 250 l. of other costs, such as raising the money to pay them). Soldiers got 5 shillings a day as a housing allowance (they were boarded with various families, in groups of two or four). In a similar case in St-Brieuc, the town spent nearly 3,000 l. to pay for the cost of two companies staying there for eight days. They spent heavily on delegations to the commanders to convince them to board the troops elsewhere (with some success, as the original plan specified four companies). Three deputations to the commanders, for example, cost 450 l. The account also specified money for planks (to make beds), for various workers and for the town sergeant (to help keep order) (AD Loire-Atlantique, C 3672). Many subsidiary costs such as these are often forgotten in estimates of the "cost of war" that focus exclusively on the armies themselves. The money spent on these occasions was not listed on central revenue accounts.

99. BN, Ms. Fr. 22311, fols. 6–10, muster of Brissac's company in 1612.

100. The Chamber of Accounts, in the margin notes of the document, "dit que lad. somme excedde de beaucoup les comptes préceddens, la chambre ordonne qu'il sera faict très humble remonstrances au Roy." Henry IV used some 12.5 million in 1594 to bribe the League leaders, but his normal range was 2–3 million l. a year. No year between 1595 and 1610 exceeded 5 million l. F. Bayard, "Le Secret du Roi: Etudes des comptants ès mains du Roi sous Henri IV," *Bulletin du Centre d'Histoire Economique et Sociale de la Région Lyonnaise* 3 (1974): 1–27. My thanks to Mlle. Bayard for a copy of the article and for having discussed her work with me.

Table 2. Revenans bons *of the French Monarchy, 1581 (in 000 l.)*

Source	Amount	Source	Amount
Paris	777	Montpellier	246
Châlons	320	Toulouse	178
Amiens	163	Burgundy	143
Rouen	1,221	Dauphiné	23
Caen	628	Provence	34
Bourges	370	Brittaɪ.y	291
Orléans	422	Subtotal of *généralités*	7,347
Tours	594	Blois (demesne)	8
Poitiers	603	Wood sales	677
Limoges	372	Clergy	69
Riom	454	*Parties casuelles*	10,638
Bordeaux	262	*Extraordinaires*	12,883
Lyon	246	Total	31,622

Source: BN, Ms. Dupuy 41, fols. 62 and ff.

Note: There are many copies of this document, apparently drawn up for the Assembly of Notables of 1583. See A. Chamberland, "Les recettes de l'Epargne en 1581 et une erreur de Forbonnais," *Revue Henri IV* 1(1905): 103–7. *Ecus* here converted to 1. at a ratio of 1:3.

together with the direct in a 1573 report.[101] Most of the demesnes and indirect taxes of the *généralité* of Lyon were alienated, which would explain their absence from the central estimate. The document from Bourges, however, makes reference only to the new 5 *sous/muid* of wine entering walled towns (mostly alienated) and to direct taxes. In part, the discrepancy is due to the different positions of the two *généralités:* Lyon had a separate *gabelle,* whereas Bourges was part of the large *gabelle* farm of the North. Nonetheless, the local discrepancies make it hard to know precisely what is in and what is not in the report of 1581.

    The more precise figures of Brittany give us some idea of the gap between real revenues and those listed on the 1581 estimate. Regular taxation was over 900,000 l., far more than the 290,000 l. in *revenans bons* (that is, the amount carried as the part of the Central

101. AD Cher, C 718 (*état* of 1579 for Bourges, done 6 March 1579); the king appears to have alienated half of the *taille* receipts of Bourges by 1579, and he took an advance on a special *crue* of 500,000 *écus* levied in the kingdom (Bourges paid 10,583.33 *écus* per quarter for this *crue*). AD Rhône, 8 C 312, 1573 account for Lyon. Some of the local assignations included 90,000 l. to the "duke of Florence," 41,200 l. for the Swiss (to the war treasurer), 70,000 to the Swiss Leagues.

Treasury). In addition, the Estates of 1588 claimed the king had levied over 800,000 l. in other money between 1583 and 1588: 110,000 l. for revocation of the *francs fiefs;* 57,000 l. in *crues;* 240,000 l. as a "forced loan" on the rich; 43,000 l. to abolish an edict selling the right to operate a tavern; 55,000 l. to dismantle two fortresses; and 120,000 l. as a special grant from Estates meeting in March 1588. The Estates had already voted 70,000 l. a year from 1583 to 1587.

Henry III's desperation is revealed in a series of royal letters from early 1589. Here he orders the treasurers of France to seize the receipts from the taxes and ship them directly to him. In a letter of 7 February 1589, he orders them to "faire conduyre seurement avec bonne escorte" an advance of 30,000 *écus* from the *fouages* by 25 February. The king further instructs the treasurers to make up the shortfall from nonpayment of *rentes, gages,* and other charges.[102] When we deduct such charges from the disposable income of the king, we are forgetting that, in emergencies, he could get his hands on some of it.

One can say that the king's total revenues from taxation rose from 10 to 30 million l. from the 1520s to 1580s. This amount did not, however, keep pace with inflation of 350–400 percent.[103] We also have little idea of the amount levied for (often by) troops. The one thing of which we can be certain is that, however much money the system produced, it was never enough to cover expenses.

Government Borrowing in Sixteenth-Century France

Henry III's letters to the Bretons remind us that there were two revenue problems in late sixteenth-century France: insufficient overall income and cash shortage. The king borrowed vast sums of money to cover short-term cash flow needs and to bridge the long-term gap between tax revenues and ongoing expenses. As one might expect, most of the long-term loans were related to military expenses; the tax system could not suddenly increase its levies to a

102. AD Loire-Atlantique, B 713.
103. Inflation at Paris was roughly 400 percent; at Toulouse some 350 percent. Meuvret and Baulant, *Les prix,* and G. and G. Frêche, *Les prix des grains . . . à Toulouse* (Paris, 1967). At Nantes, prices roughly tripled during the second half of the sixteenth century.

point sufficient to cover wartime military costs. Because the regular taxes were relatively custom bound (in terms of size), and because the extra resources needed for war expenses were raised by special taxes, the king could not easily continue the wartime tax level after the war was over. (And few respites from war existed in the second half of the century.) The king was therefore stuck with long-term debt and insufficient resources to pay it.

Let us begin with an evaluation of the king's position in 1596–98 and then move back to examine the manner in which he constituted this debt. Sully estimated this debt as 296 million l., of which 150 million l. was in alienated revenues and demesnes and the rest in unpaid loans and obligations.[104] While this estimate dominates the historiography on this question, it is not very helpful in understanding the real situation.

Sully's figures for the loans and obligations included some relatively fanciful listings, such as arrears (on *rentes*, on debts owed to the Swiss, and so on), and the debts of Henry III. These debts were certainly legitimate, but probably no one (save those with extremely good connections at Court) expected to be paid for them. In the event, they were not. In many cases, however, what was paid back, who got the money, and how much regulating the debts actually cost are very difficult to determine.

We can see this more easily if we take a specific case—that of the Swiss. Henry IV owed them 35.8 million l., of which 20 million l. were arrears. The French financial historian Albert Chamberland found that Henry owed 5 million l. to various Swiss colonels, but that he and Sully settled these (and other Swiss debts) for much less. Chamberland claimed that Sully settled 9.2 million l. of Swiss debts for 1.7 million l., and that he reduced the Swiss debt to 16.7 million l. by 1607 (in other words, to the original capital).[105]

Yet matters were not so simple, as the case of a certain Colonel Galatty shows. The king owed thirty-six companies of Swiss some 29,400 l. each in November 1593: 1,058,000 l. Unable to pay the debt during the League wars, Henry alienated the *impôts et billots* (wine taxes) of five Breton bishoprics and certain other local taxes.

---

104. M. de Béthune, duke of Sully, *Economies Royales* (Paris, 1837), 2 vols. These figures are discussed in R. Bonney, *The King's Debts* (Oxford, 1981) and, more usefully, by B. Barbiche, *Sully* (Paris, 1981).

105. A. Chamberland, "La comptabilité imaginaire des deniers des coffres du roi et les dettes suisses," *Revue Henri IV*, 2: 50–60. See also Barbiche's comments on this matter.

He also added a debt of 21,600 l. owed to a thirty-seventh company, that of Jean-Jacques Vallier.[106]

The king was supposed to pay 90,000 l. a year to René Trimault, *commis* for the Swiss in this matter. There was no question of getting this money at the time of the original letters (given that Henry did not control much of Brittany). The king had great difficulty both with the Breton Parlement (which registered the alienations, after *lettres de jussion,* only in 1600) and the Chamber of Accounts (which received the *lettres de jussion* in September 1599 and which registered the edict in the form requested by the king only in October 1601, "sur le très exprès commandement de Sa Majesté"). The Swiss were supposed to receive their 90,000 l. a year beginning in 1598: in fact, they got 14,500 l. in 1598 and another 60,000 l. in 1599.[107]

Anxious to settle, the Swiss sold their remaining claim to Sebastien Zamet and Florent Dargonges. They, in turn, sold it to Gilles Ruellan, farmer of these same *impôts et billots* and, after 1608, farmer of the special duties levied to repurchase them.[108] The taxes were alienated at a time of extremely low return, so that the actual annual cost of the alienation was far more than 90,000 l. per year.

The Estates of Brittany paid Ruellan 1.1 million l. to free these taxes between 1608 and 1611, and Ruellan certainly collected over 1 million l. more from the proceeds of the taxes from 1601 to 1611, to say nothing of his profits as farmer and of any possible fraud. The cost of regulating this debt of 1.08 million l. was, therefore, at least 2.2 million l., yet the Swiss saw nothing like this amount.[109]

We face this problem of supposed cost and actual cost whenever we treat the debts of this period. Many of the Leaguers, for example, claimed very large past due sums from the king because of his treaties with them, while simultaneously collecting large royal pensions.[110] The king could amortize such debts in various ways, perhaps the most unusual of which was marrying his bastard César

---

106. AD Loire-Atlantique, B 66, fols. 153v–54, 160v–62v, 184v–86v, 165v–66, B 71, fols. 108–9v, auditing of Ruellan's accounts in 1618.

107. AD Loire-Atlantique, B 71, fol. 109v.

108. Collins, "Taxation in Bretagne," chaps. 6 and 8.

109. Ibid., chap. 7, on true value of taxes. By 1605, they were undervalued by at least 50 percent, at the alienation price.

110. The duke de Mayenne was listed for a pension of 100,000 l. in 1609, of which he got 50,000 l. from the Central Treasury budget (BN, 500 Colbert 106, Central Treasury account of 1609), yet his heirs claimed and got a settlement of 160,000 l. in 1611 to cover his past debts (BN, Ms. Dupuy 824, fols. 3 and ff.).

of Vendôme to the daughter of the duke of Mercoeur, and then paying Mercoeur's debts to Henry's own son.[111]

Sully's figures for the short-term debt are, therefore, of little value. The figures for long-term debt, however, are a different matter. He took the figure, 150 million l., from the material presented to the Assembly of Notables of 1596. The manner in which this long-term debt was contracted changed dramatically in the course of the sixteenth century, and these changes had very profound consequences for the direct tax system of the late sixteenth and seventeenth centuries. Before turning to the figures themselves, therefore, we will briefly consider how this long-term debt came into being.

At the beginning of the sixteenth-century the king borrowed money from German and Italian bankers through the offices of the *généraux*. The *généraux* got liens on tax revenues to repay the loans. As part of the reform of 1523, the king turned to two new sources of loans: the *rentes sur l'Hôtel de Ville de Paris* (annuities guaranteed by the income of the city of Paris, later augmented by liens on various tax revenues) and direct borrowing from the same German and Italian bankers.[112]

By the late 1540s, the king borrowed regularly at the fairs of Lyon, paying the going rate of interest (10–16 percent) from fair to fair. The foreign bankers of Lyon worked out syndicates and then a general shareholder system called the *Grand Parti de Lyon*. Payments to the *Grand Parti* were secured by tax revenues from nearby *généralités*.

In 1547, Francis I owed about 6.8 million (about one year's regular disposable income).[113] By 1558, when the *Grand Parti* went into default, the king owed it over 16 million l. He also owed substantial sums to other banking syndicates. The failure of the *Grand Parti* led to significant changes in the structure of royal debt. Foreign bankers now insisted on collecting the tax revenues directly, by means of tax farms, in return for their loans. For example, the great financier André Ruiz was a creditor both of the king and of Catherine de Medicis, and was the tax farmer of several wine duties

111. In 1607, for example, one finds a listing of 150,000 l. for Vendôme and his mother-in-law (BN, Ms. Fr. 16626, fols. 73–82).

112. R. Doucet, "Le Grand Parti de Lyon," *Revue Historique* 171 (1933): 470–509 and 172 (1934): 1–41. R. Doucet, *Finances municipales et crédit publique à Lyon au XVIe siècle* (Paris, 1935).

113. BN, Ms. Fr. 3127, fols. 91 and ff.

and of the export-import duties of Brittany (at what the Estates argued were bargain basement prices).[114] The efforts of Henry III to centralize the indirect taxes in the 1570s and 1580s must be seen as part of this restructuring of the royal debt because one of his primary motivations was to provide sureties for the syndicates of foreign bankers who would farm these taxes (such as the *Cinq Grosses Fermes,* created in 1581 for a syndicate of Italian bankers).

The other half of the new royal debt policy was the extensive use of the *rentes,* issued both on Paris and on the clergy. One estimate of the early 1580s provides documentation for *rentes* worth some 45 million l. issued between 1557 (that is, the collapse of the *Grand Parti*) and 1584. The document does not seem to be a complete listing, but it shows *rentes* of 30 million l. on general revenues (mostly *rentes sur l'Hôtel de Ville de Paris* but some on Rouen and Lyon as well) and of 15 million l. on the clergy (see Table 3).[115] The annual interest payment on these annuities was some 3.75 million l., although contemporary comments on the *rentes* make it clear that the *rentes* were irregularly paid and that, when rentiers did receive something from the government, it was seldom the full due amount.

These annual interest payments were deducted from total payments on the *aides, gabelles, décimes,* and direct taxes. The king issued a *rente* of 25,000 l. against the *taille* receipts in Paris (1570) and another of 30,000 l. against those of Châlons (1573). The direct tax receipts of the *généralité* of Rouen carried *rentes* worth 215,237 l. (half-paid). In other words the king financed 5.17 million l. of the royal debt with the regional charges of Rouen.[116] To a considerable extent the revenue missing from indirect tax receipts and (to a lesser degree) direct tax receipts went to cover the debt service on royal borrowing from the late sixteenth century. This debt service is yet another example of the problem created by the use of the term *net revenue* to describe the share of the Central Treasury.

Two chief groups were buying these *rentes:* those to whom the king owed money and that somewhat elusive group George Huppert has called the "bourgeois gentilshommes," a group that had a

---

114. AD Loire-Atlantique, B 60, for leases to Ruiz. On Ruiz. H. Lapeyre, *Une famille de marchands: Les Ruiz* (Paris, 1955).

115. BN, 500 Colbert 41, fols. 51–62.

116. BN, Ms. Fr. 16624, fols. 249–317v.

Table 3. Rentes *Created, 1557–84, Partial List (in 000 l.)*

Year	Type[a]	Amount	Cash Paid In	Assigned to Revenues Of
1557	HV	15	—	*Gabelle*, Ile-de-France; Paris local taxes
1562	HV	100	610.8	*Gabelle*, Champagne
1562	HV	20	58.7	—
1563	HV	200	1,172.0	Paris local taxes (fish and wine)
1564	HV	60	—	Paris local taxes
1564	HV	76	—	Paris local taxes; *gabelle*, Normandy
1566	—	25	—	*Traite foraine* of Normandy and Champagne
1566	C[b]	50.5	—	Clergy
1566	HV	25	—	*Gabelle*, Picardy
1567	C	20	—	Clergy
1567	C	35.2	—	Clergy
1567	HV	83	456.0	Paris local taxes; *tailles* and *équivalents* of Paris, Meaux, Etampes, and Montfort
1568	HV	100	594.0	*Gabelle*, Loire valley
1568	C	75.8	—	Clergy
1568	HV	100	990.0	*Aides* and *équivalents* of 12 northeastern *élections; tailles* of Paris and Châlons
1569	—	125	670.0	5 *sous/muid* of wine entering walled towns in Picardy, Normandy, Champagne; salt tax in Burgundy; *tailles* in Berry, Touraine
1569	*Aides*	50	308.0	*Aides*
1569	*Aides*	100	619.0	*Aides* of Picardy, Normandy, Nivernais, Orleanais, Touraine; *gabelle*, Normandy, Tours; *équivalent*, Tours
1569	HV[c]	50	336.0	*Tailles*, Paris; *plus-valeurs*
1570	HV	50	—	*Impôts et billots* (wine tax) of Brittany; 55 *sous/muid* of wine passing Ingrande-s-Loire
1570	C	101	—	Clergy
1571	HV	50	—	Breton revenues
1571	C	30	—	Clergy

Table 3. (*continued*)

Year	Type[a]	Amount	Cash Paid In	Assigned to Revenues Of
1571	—	10.5	—	*Plus-valeurs* of 12d./1. on *draps*
1571	Marseille	25	—	*Epiceries* entering Marseille
1571	QM's dowry	67.5	—	General receipts of Poitiers, Bordeaux, Auvergne
1572	C	100	—	Clergy
1572	HV	50	511.0	*Sceaux des draps*
1572	—	100	971.0	Demesnes Toulouse, Picardy, Poitiers; *plus-valeurs*
1572	Alum	28	91.0	Entry duty on alum
1572	—	29.4	—	—
1572	HV	50	—	*Généralités* of Paris, Rouen
1572	—	3	—	—
1573	C	150	1,800.0	Clergy
1573	—	100	1,092.0	*Généralités* of Paris, Tours, Châlons
1574	C	12	144.0	Clergy
1574	—	50	441.0	*Généralité* of Tours
1575	HV	150[d]	—	Paris local taxes
1576	—	50	—	—
1577	—	12	—	—
1579	—	20	74.0	—
1582	—	25	—	—
1584	—	90	—	—

Sources: BN, 500 Colbert, 41, fols. 51–62, 67, and ff. BN, Ms. Fr. 16622, 16623, 16624. AD Loire-Atlantique, B 12871. R. Doucet, "Le Grand Parti de Lyon," *Revue Historique* (1933).

[a]HV—Hotel de Ville de Paris; C—clergy; QM—Queen Mother.

[b]*Rentes* on the clergy created before 1566 equalled 627,260 1.

[c]*plus-valeurs* are excess revenues on previously alienated taxes.

[d]Receipts to cover these *rentes* were 156,000 1.; this figure is an estimate of the amount, since none is given. All amounts are for the value of the *rentes*; the capital would be (in theory) twelve times this amount.

very substantial portion of royal officers. The first group was most
√ prominent in the 1560s. They would put up a given amount in old
royal debts (often obligations from the *Grand Parti de Lyon*) and
an equal amount in cash; their *rente* would be for the combined
amount. In other cases the financier had to put up two-thirds
cash.[117]

In the 1570s, the sale of *rentes* shifted to the bourgeois gentils-
√ hommes, especially to the officers. The detailed examination of Breton finances done for the Assembly of Notables of 1583 enables us
to know the rentiers for Brittany, for the period 1558 to 1583. It
√ shows a virtual monopoly of officers and merchants. Even the widows and orphans, to whom the Estates of Brittany so often referred
in their complaints about nonpayment or underpayment of the
rentes, were widows and orphans of officers and merchants.[118]

We can see in Table 4 the list of the rentiers of the bishopric of
Nantes. The first sale set the pattern for the later ones: one of the
√ chief purchasers of 1558 was Jehan Lelou, scion of a great officer
and merchant family. His son, Michel, later controller general of
Brittany, would buy *rentes* in 1569 and 1573. In both 1573 and
1575, the sales were likely forced loans on the officers: in 1573,
Michel Lelou, Jullien Rocaz (receiver general), Pierre Cornulier
(treasurer of France), and many other officers; in 1575, five *fouage* receivers, the receiver general, and various other tax officers.
Elsewhere in Brittany, the same social group bought the *rentes.*
In Vannes, virtually all of the rentiers styled themselves "sieur
de . . ." and were either merchants or officers. Many of the rentiers,
such as the receiver of the *fouages* of Léon, Pierre Morin, or Gilles
Lemoyne (later master of accounts), were also tax farmers. In
short, the rentiers were members of that element of the bourgeoisie
√ with capital to spend and an inclination to spend some of it in ways
that would benefit the government: offices and *rentes.*

There are indications that this pattern was true elsewhere. For
√ example, a list of the rentiers of the *généralité* of Poitiers in 1603
includes the demesne receiver, an *avocat du roi,* the receiver of the

117. Doucet, "Le Grand Parti." AD Loire-Atlantique, B 12871, *rente* of Pierre
Gasche, receiver of *fouages* of Rennes, created 1 May 1557, for 1,200 l., cash and
arrears of his *gages.*

118. AD Loire-Atlantique, B 12871. List of officers from series B, registers of
the Chamber of Accounts and F. Saulnier, *Le Parlement de Bretagne* (Rennes, 1909).
On intermarriage, registers of parish of St-Laurent of Nantes, AM de Nantes, GG
138, GG 141.

Table 4. *Rentiers of Nantes, 1583*

Name	Office; Ties to Officers
Jehan Lelou	Creditor of Estates; father of Michel Lelou
Michel Lelou	Controller general of Brittany, later master of accounts, mayor of Nantes; father of a *conseiller* at the Parlement
Pierre de Francheville	Master of accounts
Nicolas Fyot	Receiver of *fouages* of Tréguier, later receiver general
Jullien Rocaz	Receiver general
Georges Bernard	Controller general; large officer family
Guillaume Poullain	Alderman and mayor of Nantes
Robert Poullain	Receiver of the *fouages* of Vannes; Poullain family were treasurers of the Estates, 1608–46
Pierre Cornulier	Treasurer of France; founder of great robe dynasty (included Parlementaires, bishops)
Jan Rocaz	Receiver of the *fouages* of Vannes
François Jallier	Receiver of the *fouages* of Nantes
Pierre Morin	Receiver of the *fouages* of Léon, later receiver general
Bernard Desmontz	Master of accounts
Michel Loriot	Mayor of Nantes, seneschal of the *régaires* of Nantes
Lucas Moreau	Receiver of the *fouages* of Vannes

Source: AD Loire-Atlantique, B 12871.
Note: This is a partial list. Many other robe families also held *rentes;* usually, they were from the financial robe.

tailles of Compiègne, and a *secrétaire du roi*. The private *rentes* included annuities for two treasurers of France and three widows of treasurers (likely indicating a forced sale before 1585), as well as the receiver general and the widow of Marshal Schomberg (a military debt of Henry III). In 1620, presidents Nicolay and d'Ormesson of the Paris courts held *rentes* of 1,125 l. on Châlons and 895 l. 19 s. on Soissons, respectively.[119]

These last two *rentes* may fall into the category of the personal *rentes* issued by "lettres particulières" to very powerful individuals. Private *rentes* issued to the duke of Montpensier (2,506 l. 11s. 1d.), the heirs of Jan Lorquivilliers, sieur du Bruch (4,000 l.), and Hugues d'Aragon (4,200 l.), with a capital value of over 128,000 l., constituted 46 percent of the total *rentes* issued at Nantes from 1558 to 1583.[120]

119. BN, Ms. Fr.16623, fols. 98–148v (Soissons) and 190–230 (Châlons).
120. AD Loire-Atlantique, B 12871.

Henry IV made particularly extensive use of this device to satisfy his creditors. The duke of Nevers (79,000 l.), the heirs of the duke of Montpensier (43,000 l.), the count of Soissons (18,000 l.), and the prince of Condé (11,000 l.) had liens worth about 1.8 million l. in capital on the direct taxes.[121] Henry also used this technique on indirect taxes: 180,000 l. a year to Christian of Anhalt on the *aides;* 90,000 l. a year to Zamet, Gondi, and Le Grand on the *Cinq Grosses Fermes;* 60,000 l. a year to the heirs of Cardinal Joyeuse on the *gabelles* of Languedoc. He created other new taxes to meet obligations to Leaguers, such as the 24 l./*muid* of salt passing Ingrande for the duke of Mercoeur. (In fact, Henry simply kept the proceeds.)

These *rentes,* assignations, and new taxes, however, were quite different from the long-term *rentes* inherited by Henry IV. The latter were paid at half value and they were part of general sales in the 1560s (largely to financiers) and 1570s and 1580s (largely to royal officers and their relations). They were held almost exclusively by such officers and merchants, who often had an interest in tax farms. The special *rentes* and assignations were new creations, usually fully paid, and held primarily by the great nobility (Nevers, Joyeuse, Montpensier) and the king's largest creditors.

One of the most important legacies of the sixteenth-century tax system was this close interrelationship between royal borrowing and royal political contacts with French elites. On the one hand, there was a very close correlation between borrowing from the officers (and some merchants) and taxation of the bourgeoisie. On the other hand, the king's debts to the upper nobility colored his political relations with them. It is a measure of the political clout of the two groups that the debts to the nobility were often paid in full, while those held by the officers and merchants were paid at half value. The reliance on these officers to fund the debt, to collect the taxes, and to pay the bourgeoisie's share of the taxes was to have catastrophic consequences in the 1630s. We turn now to the immediate background of the first of the three great bankruptcies of the first half of the seventeenth century: the restructuring of the *rentes.*

---

121. BN, Ms. Fr. 16622, 16623, 16624. On the Nevers family, see also the appendix to Harding, *Anatomy of a Power Elite.*

2. Reform and Collapse: The Administration of Direct Taxes, 1596–1648

Overview

The period 1596–1648 has a certain symmetry about it, beginning with the end of one civil war and ending with the beginning of another. In the interim between the League wars and the Fronde, the king made major strides in centralizing and standardizing the administration of the kingdom. The crisis conditions of the 1620s through 1640s enabled him to do this, just as war crises in the twentieth century have greatly accelerated the centralization of modern governments.

During the first half of the seventeenth century, the most important element in this drive to greater centralization and standardization was reform of the tax system. The period began and ended with an attack on the financial officers, yet the relationship between the king and the officers in the intervening years was not entirely adversarial. Henry IV tried to restructure the tax system between 1596 and 1604. By 1604 Henry and the officers had reached a compromise that substantially reduced the royal government's obligations to the officers but, at the same time, preserved the latter's offices (and thereby investments) and authority. The king and the officers existed within the parameters of this agreement for about thirty years, although there was a significant change in their relationship after 1616.

The government sought to extend the existing royal direct tax system as late as 1632, with rather limited success. It did get *élections* into Guyenne-Gascony and Dauphiné but failed in its efforts to do so in Provence, Languedoc, and Burgundy.[1] The extension of

1. On the revolt of Aix, S. Kettering, *Judicial Politics and Urban Revolt: The Parlement of Aix, 1629–1659* (Princeton, 1978).

the *élection* system led to revolts in all five provinces. These revolts were often led by members of the local elite, such as the Parlementaires of Aix and Dijon or the Estates of Languedoc, and they helped provide a release mechanism for long-standing popular discontent with taxation.[2]

The failure of this effort to introduce the *élections* into almost all of the kingdom, and the king's concomitant expansion of his debts to the officers, led to a decisive step in 1634. The king changed the *droits aliénés* (rights to surtaxes, sold to the officers after 1616) into *rentes*, thus effecting a partial bankruptcy that would save him 15 million l. a year in interest. At virtually the same instant the king expanded the system of intendants throughout most of the kingdom, thus creating an administrative framework for bypassing the existing officer network.

The result of these steps was a gradual descent into administrative and, eventually, political chaos. The taxes were not paid in full. There were widespread and massive popular revolts. The rebels were often abetted by members of the local elites, notably by royal officers who either did not carry out their duties with sufficient ardor or who actively aided the rebels.[3] By the time the king jettisoned the old system entirely, in 1642–43, the kingdom's finances had fallen into shambles. The local financial records for the 1640s indicate that many areas paid no direct taxes at all (see Chapter 3).

The government backed off a bit after 1645, but when it resumed the offensive by abolishing the *paulette* in 1648, it touched off the first Fronde. At virtually the same time the government conducted its third partial bankruptcy in fifty years, again aimed primarily at the officer class (although, in this case, at only that part of it that was integrated into the new network of intendants and *traitants*).

This chapter has three elements. First, we will describe the reforms of 1596–1604, looking at both the problems to which they were addressed and the solutions themselves. Second, we will examine the system thus established by Henry IV. Third, we will analyze the change in that system entailed by the *droits aliénés*, and the

---

2. On Languedoc, W. Beik, *Absolutism and Society in Seventeenth-century France: State Power and Provincial Aristocracy in Languedoc* (Cambridge, England, 1985), 199–202. On Dauphiné, D. Hickey, *The Coming of French Absolutism: The Struggle for Tax Reform in Dauphiné, 1540–1640* (Montreal, 1986).

3. M. Foisil, *La révolte des Nu-Pieds* (Paris, 1970).

subsequent conversion of the *droits* (and abandonment of the system) in 1634. The actions of 1634 were a repudiation of over 250 years of administrative practice and evolution. We must begin with the reforms of 1596–1604 to see how this revolution came about.

Henry IV and the Assembly of Notables of 1596: The Tax Question

Henry IV's treaty with the duke of Mayenne (September 1595) made it possible for him to turn his attention to reorganizing the administration of the kingdom. Following the example of Henry III, he convened an Assembly of Notables, at Rouen in 1596. Its chief task was to reform the kingdom's financial system.

Henry IV owed a very great deal of money and he was in no position to pay it all back. One of his main concerns between 1596 and 1604 was to decide which debts to pay. His solution was to pay current debts by a mixture of immediate reimbursement, alienation, and issuance of private *rentes,* to write off past due interest, and to restructure the long-term debt, owed primarily to the royal officers. Henry was evenhanded in his approach to the past: he also forgave all tax arrears through 1597.

The League War of 1589–98 had had a less disruptive effect on the French direct tax system than one might think. The local tax bureaucracy continued to function throughout the war without the sanction of a strong central government. The tax system provided both sides with substantial revenues during the war, helping to prolong the hostilities. Henry IV and his opponents often made special truces to allow for tax collections and for harvesting; the contracting parties would keep the proceeds in areas they clearly controlled and split the money in disputed areas.[4]

The lack of strong central authority did allow local officials to engage in abuses of their authority; in their *cahier* of 1599, the Estates of Brittany, accurately reflecting the general sentiment of the times, called these officers "bloodsuckers."[5] The relationship between the officers and the population in the 1590s also reflected two other factors. The financial straits of the king and his oppo-

---

4. BN, Ms. Fr. 22342, fol. 204, truce with the duke of Mercoeur to split the proceeds of Breton taxation; an even split of direct taxes in the bishoprics of Tréguier, Léon, and Cornouaille, and of wine transit taxes levied at Ingrande-s-Loire.

5. AD Loire-Atlantique, C 2645, p. 456.

nents led to much heavier tax assessments, dissatisfaction with those assessments, and the sale of many new offices (such as those at the new *généralité* of Soissons, created in 1595). This problem was further complicated after 1594 by the agreements between Henry and League leaders. These agreements stopped troop depredations in the countryside and peace sharply reduced tax levels. But the agreements forced Henry to recognize the officers with whom the Leaguers had filled vacancies, thus increasing the cost of government. Henry also had to create new taxes to pay for his large settlements with League leaders.[6]

While the tax system continued to function, and even to grow, during the Civil War, nonetheless, the kingdom (and its administration) was in bad shape. Tax assessment levels were extremely high and, in a pattern that would repeat itself in the 1630s and 1640s, so were *non-valeurs*—unpaid taxes. As we shall see in Chapter 3, the most effective means of limiting royal tax demands was simple nonpayment. Such nonpayment reached very high levels during wartime, although the areas in which the army (or armies) was present could be ruined by forced collection of overdue taxes.[7] Despite the high assessment levels, Henry was desperately short of cash and borrowed heavily from foreign bankers and states and, by means of new offices and *droits,* from the bourgeoisie. Henry also sharply increased salt taxes.

The high tax assessments and the depredations of the troops led to another phenomenon that would be common from the 1620s through the 1640s: peasant revolts. The great Croquants rising of 1593–95 was one of Henry's chief spurs in seeking reform and peace at any price (in terms of settlements with Leaguers).[8] Yet Henry must also have seen the Assembly of Notables as a means of establishing broad-based support for his rule, and of legitimizing the steps he would take to reform the kingdom once he was completely in control. Henry's main proposals to the Assembly were all

---

6. G. Boussinesq, "Sommes promises aux chefs de la Ligue," *Revue Henri IV,* 1(1905): 164. AD Cher, C 974, fols. 1 and ff., showing salt surtaxes for Mercoeur, marshal Boisdauphin, and the duke of Elbeuf. AN, 120 AP 11 has further information on this issue.

7. BN, Ms. Fr. 22342, fols. 258–65, on depredations in Cornouaille. J. Collins, "Taxation in Bretagne, 1598–1648" (Ph.D. diss., Columbia University, 1978), chap. 5.

8. AD Haute-Vienne, C 551, on nonpayment and revolt in the Limousin (1594). Y.-M. Bercé, *Histoire des Croquants* (Geneva, 1974).

financial ones, but such proposals had important political ramifications. In reforming the tax system, Henry had to obtain a consensus from the elites whose support enabled that system to work. He achieved this consensus in a series of steps taken from 1596 to 1604.

The immediate financial situation of Henry IV when he called the Assembly of Notables in 1596 was not good, but the underlying situation held out some promise. Henry had a well-established and quite large tax bureaucracy and a substantial revenue base. The direct tax system would change little in the next quarter century; the nature of the levies would also remain about the same. Henry was certainly aware of the shortcomings of the existing system, and he acted quickly to eliminate abuses.

Henry seems to have coordinated troop levies into one *grande crue*. No specific document mentions the creation of a special tax of this name, yet we have a separate *brevet* for it in 1597, and records from Brittany, Champagne, and Languedoc list a garrison tax between 1594 and 1598.[9] In 1593, Henry proposed to levy 657,465 l. in the *généralité* of Châlons for "gens de guerre"; in 1594, he proposed a levy of 810,000 l. for "garnisons" as a special *crue*.[10] By 1598 or 1599, the *crue* was about 40 percent of direct taxation in the *pays d'élection*.[11] Its military portion declined sharply in 1600, but Henry added some 850–900,000 l. to it in 1602 as a replacement for the *pancarte*.

Henry's revenue base, while quite unsteady in 1596, was potentially very large. When peace returned, Henry was able to obtain some 16–16.5 million l. per year in direct taxation, from which he could expect to net about 13.5 million l. (total revenue minus the costs of collection). The *pays d'Etats* produced additional sums from direct taxation, but they often accounted for this revenue on budgets that included indirect tax revenues as well. Nonetheless, the five *pays d'Etats* produced close to 2.5 million l. each year in additional revenue from direct taxation.[12]

9. Collins, "Taxation in Bretagne," chap. 5.
10. AD Marne, C 2489, fols. 65v–66 for 1593, 105v for 1594, 234v for 1595.
11. A. Chamberland, "La répartition de la taille en 1597," *Revue Henri IV* 2 (1905–06): 82–85 and "Le budget de 1597," *Revue Henri IV* 1 (1905): 15–20.
12. L. S. Van Doren, "The Royal *Taille* in Dauphiné, 1560–1610," *Proceedings of the Third Annual Western Conference for French History* 3 (1975): 35–53, gives figures for Dauphiné of 986,000 l. in 1597 and 600,000 l. in 1598. In Burgundy garrisons cost 318,000 l. in 1592, the last year for which we have an accurate

Henry also had substantial resources from indirect taxation, perhaps 15–20 million l. of potential revenue. In 1596, however, much of this revenue was alienated, and a large portion of it went to cover debt service. The shadow of the enormous royal debt hung over all possible actions in 1596. The Amiens crisis of 1597 served only to exacerbate the situation. Before we turn to the steps taken by Henry IV to reform the basic system between 1598 and 1604, we must clarify this problem of the royal debt, because it was central to the actions taken by Henry after 1596.

Sully's figure for the debt, 296 million l., was based on the documents presented to the Assembly of Notables of 1596. He divided the debt into two parts: long-term debt (*rentes* and alienations) and short-term debt (essentially, Henry's own obligations). In the latter category he included certain obligations that were clearly not going to be paid, such as arrears on the *rentes* and some of the debts of Henry III. In fact Henry so ruled on the arrears of the *rentes* in 1604 and he repudiated the debts of Henry III in 1608.[13] These two actions alone cut 40 million l. from Sully's figures.

The king also owed substantial amounts to foreigners, notably German princes and towns, Italian bankers, the king of England, and the Estates of Holland. We have already seen that the king gave short shrift to the arrears owed to the Swiss (20 million l.), yet his actual cost of regulating the Swiss debt was far more than the simple 1.7 million l. suggested by Chamberland and the Central Treasury records. In both 1610 and 1611, the *états au vrai* carried 1.2 million l. in payments to the Swiss, yet those amounts were undoubtedly for current military matters. Henry paid the city of Geneva a pension of 72,000 l. a year from 1603 to 1610 (one that was also paid in 1611): 648,000 l. from 1603 to 1611.[14]

The king paid the United Provinces 13.2 million l. from 1594 to 1610 (10.35 million l. of it from 1603 to 1610) and another

---

figure. In Languedoc the regular direct taxes were 620,000 l., and the Estates voted substantial other sums, perhaps 1.13 million l. in all for both 1598 and 1599. In Brittany most of the taxes were on wine, but the direct levies in 1599 were on the order of 550,000 l. (they had been projected as more than twice that amount in 1597). For Provence we have no accurate figures because indirect and direct taxes were lumped together on the community budgets.

13. B. Barbiche, *Sully* (Paris, 1981).

14. F. Bayard, "Le Secret du Roi: Etudes des comptants ès mains du Roi sous Henry IV," *Bulletin du Centre d'Histoire Economique et Sociale de la Région Lyonnaise* 3 (1974): 17. BN, Ms. Fr. 18510, for 1610.

500,000 l. in 1611. By virtue of a 1603 treaty with England, one-third of the amount paid from 1603 to 1610 to the Dutch, was credited to the king's English debt, and the king of England received 300,000 l. more in 1611.[15] The original estimate of debts to the Dutch and English was 16.7 million l.; these payments add up to 14 million l. The French considered these debts fully paid in 1611.

If we exclude the amounts such as arrears and the debts of Henry III, the short-term debt in 1596 was still some 90 million l. Henry IV did not intend to pay all of this at once, but as the Dutch-English and Swiss examples show, he made significant progress at eliminating much of it. Henry could not pay past due interest on this debt and the principal as well, so we must be wary of the Sully figures on that score.

On the other side of the ledger, Sully's figures exclude Henry's borrowings from bankers such as Sebastien Zamet, Cenamy, and the Gondis, and from tax farmers (often the same bankers). Henry issued very large private *rentes:* those on the *tailles* alone were 150,000 l. (1.8 million l. in capital). He alienated various revenues—for example, over 125,000 l. in Brittany (another 1.5 million l. in capital). Zamet collected 769,000 l. from the Estates of Brittany from 1599 to 1605, another 330,000 l. from the receipts of the *généralité* of Rouen in 1598, an annual lien of 30,000 l. on the *Cinq Grosses Fermes* until 1606 (shifted to other revenue but fully paid, in 1607, reduced to half payment in 1610), nearly 80,000 l. from the *comptants ès mains du Roi* in 1602–3, and a final payment of 20,000 l. (as the *reste* of a loan of 180,000 l., made in 1600) in 1609.[16] Thus Zamet received known payments of 1.5–1.6 million l. during Henry's reign. Henry paid the Gondis 45,000 l. each year in a lien on the *Cinq Grosses Fermes*. In 1609 he paid them 100,000 l. as the rest of one loan and 26,490 l. as the remainder of another.[17]

The accounts of 1607 and 1609 show Henry repaying other foreign lenders. In 1609, the duke of Wittenberg got 4,256 l. (the rest of a loan of 204,256 l.) and 7,500 l. (as the rest of another). In that

15. BN, Ms. Dupuy 824, fols. 3 and ff. (1611). BN, 500 Colbert 445, list of sums paid to the Dutch, 1603–10. The Dutch may have received another 300,000 l. in cash from the Bastille treasure in 1611.

16. Bayard, "Le Secret du Roi"; AN, 120 AP 11; Collins, "Taxation in Bretagne," chap. 6; BN, Ms. Fr. 10839, fols. 223–26, 239–42; BN, Ms. Fr. 16626 (1607); BN, 500 Colbert 106 (1609).

17. BN, Ms. Fr. 10839, fols. 223–26 and 239–42; BN, 500 Colbert 106.

same year, as final payments for larger loans, the "count Palatine" of the Rhine received 40,000 l.; the "margrave" of Brandenburg, 20,000 l.; the burgermaster and town of Nurnberg, 20,000 l. Henry also gave an annual pension of 36,000 l. to the landgrave of Hesse. In 1610, Sully's *état au vrai* listed payments of 229,000 l. to German princes (again, one suspects they were more closely related to events in 1610 than to past debts).[18]

The short-term debt also included Henry's obligations to his tax farmers. Etienne Ringues, farmer of the Traite d'Anjou, for example, had a lien on it of 42,000 l. a year (probably repayment, with interest, of an advance). Antoine Feydeau, farmer of the *Aides Générales*, gave the king an advance of 200,000 l. in 1607, as well as a loan of 1.5 million l. He received his reimbursement (and interest) from the subsequent receipts of the tax farm. The king also owed money and favors to local or regional farmers: Henry ennobled Gilles Ruellan, turned his seigneurie into a barony, and allowed his villages to have fairs and markets.[19]

The other half of the debt situation was the burden of past annuities and alienations. The documents for the Assembly of Notables mentioned the following *rentes* and alienations: demesne— 1.8 million l.; *aides*—3.0 million l.; *rentes* on *gabelles, tailles, décimes, impositions*—7.5 million l.; and debts on salt taxes—1.8 million l. These amounts are a total of 14.1 million l., or 169.2 million l. of capital (at the *denier 12*). Yet the figures seem to overlap, and they do not accurately present the situation because the different sorts of revenue had different sorts of liens.

Many demesne alienations, particularly the smaller ones concerning land, were made at twenty or thirty times the annual revenue, as was customary for land. Other demesne alienations, such as local taxes and fees and alienations of entire holdings to powerful nobles, were done at twelve times the annual revenue. Not all of the demesne was alienated; for example, Henry IV would soon assign the duke of Brissac various Breton demesnes (and a few local taxes) to cover 400,000 l. in debts. It seems likely that the value of the alienated demesnes was about 40 million l., yet no French king had gotten much income from this source in some time. Henry actually began to carry out sizeable repurchases of alienations in

18. BN, Ms. Fr. 18510 (1610).
19. Collins, "Taxation in Bretagne," chaps. 6 and 7.

1605. In Brittany, for example, the Estates eliminated over 6 million l. of royal alienations and debts between 1605 and 1618.[20]

The listing for *rentes,* 90 million l., probably included the *rentes* on the *aides.* Another document from this period indicates alienations on the *aides* and other indirect taxes of some 1.35 million l.; under Sully, the charges on the *aides* were 1.5 million l. Such charges included *gages,* administrative costs, and new liens added by Henry IV (the lease to Feydeau at the end of Henry's reign, for example, included a lien of 180,000 l. each year for Christian of Anhalt).[21] The estimate for *rentes* on the second document is 5.5 million l., or 66 million l. of capital.

We must augment this figure with *rentes* assigned in the *pays d'Etats:* 1.2 million l. of capital in Brittany, plus another 1.0 million l. of alienated demesne and an unknown amount for the *greffes* (here leaving aside Henry's 1.5 million l. of new alienations), and 1.0 million l. of *rentes,* guaranteed by the Estates of Languedoc.[22] There were also *rentes* on the salt taxes of Dauphiné and Burgundy.

Henry's long-term debt, excluding the demesne, was some 70–85 million l. The debt service on this amount was at least 2.75 million l. and probably closer to 3.0 million l. (even allowing for Henry's policy of partial payment of *rentes*). This substantial amount was a barrier to workable financial reform, yet Henry was able to come up with a repayment schedule that worked fairly well.

We can get an approximate idea of the debts regulated from the Central Treasury budget (Table 5) in 1607: 3.44 million l. In addition, the document lists charges on the indirect taxes of 6.2 million l., and we know the *rentes* on the direct taxes were about 1.2 million l. more. The king also spent 3.3 million l. through the *comptants ès mains du Roi.* Of this amount, 1.95 million l. went to the Dutch, but little of the rest was for regular debts. From this total of 12.8 million l., we must deduct the *gages* (even though they were, in some senses, part of the debt service) and the administrative costs on the indirect taxes, and some 100,000 l. belonging to the Estates of Brittany. In all, debt service, excluding the *gages,* likely consumed 11–11.5 million l. in 1607, roughly 35–40 percent

20. Ibid., chap. 6.
21. See the lease of the *Aides* in 1611, AD Cher, C 985, fols. 161 and ff. On this lease, the *rentes* were paid at three-fourths value.
22. On Brittany, Collins, "Taxation in Bretagne," chap. 6. On *rentes* at Montpellier, BN, Ms. Fr. 16623, fols. 280–99v.

Table 5. *Debts Paid from the Central Treasury Budget, 1607*

Creditor	Amount (in 000 l.)
England and Holland	1,950
Swiss	120
Grand Duke of Tuscany	100
Duke of Lorraine	100
Duke of Guise	100
Cardinal Joyeuse (heirs) and others	100
Duke of Nevers	30
Duke of Vendôme and Duchess of Mercoeur	150
Duke of Mantua	45
Zamet, Gondi and Le Grand	90
Damages to *aides* farmer	209
Debts in Languedoc	75
Rentes at Rouen	72
Interest on advances	300
Total	3,441

Sources: BN, Ms. Fr. 16626, fols. 73–82; Ms. Dupuy 89, fols. 243–50.

of the king's net income. A significant portion of this expenditure, however, was for retirement of principal. The amount paid to carry the debt (as interest or annuity) was perhaps as low as 4–5 million l. (about 15 percent of net income).

To these sums, we must add the very substantial amounts thrust onto others, notably the towns. At the end of the League war, Breton towns often had debts running into six figures: Nantes, Rennes (120,000 l.), and Quimper (166,000 l.). Small Breton towns such as Vitré (70,000 l. +) and Dinan (60,000 l. +) had very large debts. Provençal towns were also deeply in debt.[23] The king recognized this problem in certain cases: he granted Bordeaux 82,885 l. for its

23. Breton figures from registration of town duties at Chamber of Accounts of Nantes, AD Loire-Atlantique, series B 66–78. R. Pillorget, *Les mouvements insur-rectionnels en Provence de 1595 à 1715* (Paris, 1975), 207, gives debts of 1.55 million l. for Marseille in 1598, as well as 360,000 l. for Aix and 700,000 l. for Arles (no date in the latter two cases, 60 n. 183). P. Deyon, *Amiens, capitale provinciale au XVIIe siècle* (Paris, 1967), 433 n. 1, gives that city's debts as 149,209 l. in 1608. E. Giraudet, *Histoire de la Ville de Tours* (Tours, 1873), vol. 2, 129, gives debts of 439,690 l. to the king in 1600. Dijon owed at least 240,000 l. in 1596; Autun borrowed 143,000 l. from 1589 to 1591; Chalon-s-Saône issued 75,000 l. in *rentes* during the war. As always, these debts are, from the perspective of the central doc-uments, unrelated to royal taxation.

debts between 1601 and 1604 and Orléans 43,200 l. in 1602.[24] The rural communities also had very high debts; many Burgundian villages were still paying these debts in the 1660s.[25] In all cases such debts were contracted to pay soldiers, often the royal army.[26] It seems a bit disingenuous not to count such debts as the king's own.

The king and his advisers must certainly have been aware of the problem of municipal debt: those who would have to fund such debt were the same people who held much of the royal debt. Nonetheless, the core of the royal debt problem was the combination of the long-term debt, in *rentes* and alienations, and the short-term debt, in farm leases (of taxes), straight loans, and special *rentes*. If we can fairly estimate Henry IV's debt service payments as some 9.5 million l. in 1607, it seems likely that his debts were on the order of 160 million l. that he would try to pay back. The overall problem appeared much worse than it would prove in 1596, because war expenses were still quite high and tax collections were relatively low (*non-valeurs* on direct taxes, interference with commerce on indirect sales taxes). Henry believed he had to attack the problem from both ends—expenses and income—and it was with the former that he opened his proposals to the Assembly of 1596.

He proposed to reduce household expenses by 300,000 l. and to cut the pensions list by 600,000 l.[27] *Rentes* were to be paid at the *denier* 12 (8.33 percent) of the capital actually invested in them; all offices created since 1574 were to be abolished when their current

24. AN, 120 AP 11.

25. L. Ligueron, "Les dettes des Communautés du bailliage de Dijon au XVIIe siècle," *Annales de Bourgogne* 53 (1981): 65–79. Ligueron found that of 138,000 l. of debts whose origin in time he could trace, 110,000 l. were contracted before 1636. The village of Lantenay, for example, sold 2,100 *journaux* of land to meet its debts in 1596 and 1618. The total debt of Burgundian communities, eliminated by the action of the intendant Bouchu in the 1660s (using local indirect taxes and a special salt tax), was 2.73 million l. plus interest.

26. Deyon, *Amiens*, 433 n. 1, indicates that of the 315,975 l. owed by Amiens in 1660, some 176,700 l. was for war costs. The borrowings of the Burgundian communities, cited above in n. 23, were all for war costs; those of Breton towns, such as Vitré or Quimper, were for the same purpose.

27. BN, 500 Colbert 41, fols. 92–102. A Chamberland published a copy in *Un plan de restauration financière en 1596* (Paris, 1904). J. R. Major, "Bellièvre, Sully and the Assembly of Notables of 1596," *Transactions of the American Philosophical Society* new ser. 64 (1974): 3–31, credits the chancellor, Pomponne de Bellièvre, with authorship of the plan, while Chamberland believed it was one of the *secrétaires d'Etat*, Forget de Fresnes. See also Chamberland, "Le conseil des finances en 1596 et 1597 et les 'Economies Royales,'" *Revue Henri IV,* 1–2(1905–6): 21–32, 152–63, 250–60, 275–84. The specific proposals are on pp. 9–12 of *Un plan.*

occupant died. The officers holding these places would annually receive 10 percent of the capital they had invested as their *gages*. The king expected to save 7.32 million l. each year by these two measures.

These measures were aimed at all groups. The nobility would suffer through the reduction of the household expenses and pensions; the officers would find their offices abolished and their income from *rentes* greatly reduced in theory. As we have seen in Chapter 1, many of the *rentes* had been purchased with a mixture of cash and obligations from previously unpaid royal debts, including unpaid officers' *gages*. By repudiating *rentes* based on noncash payments, the king would cut the total annuity burden by nearly one-half. The greatest burden in these original proposals fell precisely on the officers, who would, in the event, bear the brunt of the coming partial bankruptcy.

The revenues were to be increased by removing the liens granted to various financiers against the indirect taxes, such as the *aides* and the *gabelles*. In addition, the king proposed two new taxes on the towns: a *subvention* of 3 million l. to replace a similar reduction of the *tailles* on the countryside and the *sou pour livre* (*pancarte*), a sales tax of 5 percent. This second tax was expected to produce 4.5 million l.

The Assembly, however, had other ideas. After noting that the disorder in the administration of the kingdom's finances was the "desolation . . . of this state," and admonishing the king that he had a paternal responsibility to his people (children), they asked him to restore justice and order in the kingdom. They claimed that the people were crushed by "extortions, pillagings and extraordinary levies 'si inhumaines et impitoyables.'" To aid the king in this process of reconstruction, the Assembly offered 15 million l. in taxes: 5.5 million l. for the *taille* and *taillon;* 750,000 l. for the *subvention des villes;* 1.5 million l. for a two-year tax of 3 l./*muid* of wine; and the rest from the *gabelles,* demesne, *parties casuelles,* and other sources.

The Assembly asked the king for letters to be sent to each bailiwick, specifying that no other monies were to be levied during the year and that the troops stationed in the bailiwick were to be paid in full from the taxes being levied there. The troops, in turn, were to pay cash for all supplies taken from the population. The Assembly also recommended that the peasants be given the right to sound the tocsin and pursue soldiers who had taken goods without paying for them as if the soldiers were ordinary thieves.[28]

The Notables proposed a tax of 25 *sous/minot* of salt to pay the *rentes* on the *gabelles* and wanted to suppress all gifts, alienations, and engagements of "aides, décimes, gabelles, subsides et imposi-tions." They requested that the king make new leases for the *ga-belles* and that such leases be done by local area, not as a general farm. No rebates were to be granted to any farmer.

The Assembly further requested that the *taillon* be used for its avowed purpose (payment of the men-at-arms), and they wanted all nonfrontier garrisons to be abolished. Governors of provinces were to lose their guards, unnecessary forts and chateaux were to be dismantled or razed, and the unpaid taxes of 1588–94 were to be discharged. They also asked the king to abolish the new *gabelle* officers at the *denier* 12 and to reduce his own household to the level of 1558.

The picture drawn by the two sides was thus remarkably similar: taxes on the countryside were too heavy; the abuses of the soldiers had to be stopped; and the power of the *grands,* particularly the provincial governors, had to be curbed. The Assembly also sought to eliminate the powerful general farmers/financiers who had come to control the indirect taxes through their farms and their loans to the king.

All the Assembly's proposals, and even some of the king's sug-gestions, would seem to have been doomed to failure by the constellation of political forces running France at that time.[29] Henry IV needed the support of governors such as Montmorency and Lesdiguières, and he was in no position to challenge their au-thority. Similarly, it would seem that his finances would not have allowed him to alienate the great financiers such as the Gondis or Sebastien Zamet.

The immediate aftermath of the Assembly was the siege of Amiens and its attendant financial crisis. Henry responded with some traditional financial practices: he made *comptable* officers triennial; he created new *gabelle* officers; he raised the *gabelle*

---

28. BN, 500 Colbert 41, fols. 103–5v, response of the Assembly to the king, arts. 1–10, 16, 17, 21–23.

29. R. Harding, *Anatomy of a Power Elite: The Provincial Governors of Early Modern France* (New Haven, 1978); H. Drouot, *Mayenne et la Bourgogne* (Paris, 1935).

proper.[30] In short, Henry followed much the same policy he had used to deal with the Leaguers, mortgaging future revenues to solve a short-term financial problem. In 1597, with substantial *non-valeurs* still common in the direct tax system and with Henry already heavily in debt to bankers such as Zamet, Henry was unlikely to get immediate cash from creditors unless he specified a source of repayment over which the creditor would have some control. New offices were the time-honored solution to such a problem.

As soon as this crisis passed, however, Henry acted immediately to strengthen his control of the kingdom and to reform its administration. In the political realm he moved into Brittany, bringing Mercoeur and the Leaguers to terms (paid for by the Estates of Brittany, as was the expedition itself).[31] He also shifted the governors of many provinces, temporarily weakening their local power bases.

Henry's first target, indeed his main target, was the royal tax administration. He began with an investigating commission, a *Chambre de Justice,* in 1597. While the commission proved to be ephemeral (it led only to a general fine against the officers), it was a signal to the officers that they would soon be under more serious attack. In 1598, Henry abolished collegiality (the *bureau des finances*) in order to make easier attribution of individual responsibility. He recognized the futility of this action in 1608, when he rescinded the original edict.[32]

With the exception of the disasterous *pancarte*, which prompted riots in the Loire valley and had to be abolished in 1602 (in return for an addition to the *grande crue* of some 850,000 l. or more),[33] the rest of Henry's reforms took root. He began to free himself from Italian financiers in the period 1599–1604. He leased the *Cinq Grosses Fermes* to a French syndicate headed by Charles du

30. The new *gabelle* officers were eliminated by means of a *traité,* financed by a salt surtax.

31. Collins, "Taxation in Bretagne," chaps. 6 and 8. The Estates gave the king 600,000 l. for his trip to the province and 2.4 million l. to settle with the Leaguers.

32. J.-P. Charmeil, *Les trésoriers de France à l'époque de la Fronde* (Paris, 1963), 11.

33. On opposition, see F. Lebrun, "Les soulèvements populaires à Angers au XVIIe et XVIIIe siècles," *Actes du 90e Congrès National des Sociétés Savantes,* 119–40. The Estates of Normandie, in art. 8 of the *cahier* of 1602, claimed the *pancarte* was so onerous that the peasants could pay neither their *tailles* nor their rents. (De Beaurepaire, *Cahiers des Etats de Normandie, règne* Henri IV, 2: 4–5.) The king added 39,000 l. to the *crue* of Champagne, which would mean 850–900,000 l. for the kingdom.

Han in 1599 and the *Aides Générales* to a syndicate led by Jean de Moisset in 1604.[34] The *gabelles,* too, went to French farmers.[35] Henry shifted the financial center of the kingdom from Lyon, dominated by foreign (especially Italian) bankers, to Paris, where French bankers (from Paris, Rouen, and the Loire cities) held sway.[36] Henry continued to use Lyon as a payment center, but no longer would Italian and German bankers lease the great farms or provide vast amounts of credit to the king. The necessity of finding an alternative source of ready capital would have a profound effect on the direct tax system.

The shift from Italian to French bankers responded very positively to one of the reform proposals of the Notables. In the other half of the credit situation Henry and his finance minister, the duke of Sully, acted to reform the *rentes* between 1602 and 1604. They set the official rate of interest at 8.33 percent, although, as we shall see, they paid either 6.25 or 4.17 percent (depending on the *rente*).

Sully investigated all *rentes* with a view to repudiating those he felt were of dubious title, a convenient way of cutting out the *rentes* based on unpaid royal debts and obligations. Henry decreed that he would not pay the arrears on any of the *rentes*. It is unclear if any of the *rentes* were truly repudiated—powerful robe interests argued against such repudiation—but it is interesting that Sully agreed to pay the *rentes* for only half (on the *tailles*) or three-quarters (on the *Cinq Grosses Fermes*) of their face value. While the king claimed that he would try to pay the *rentes* fully in the future, nonetheless, this arrangement was a de facto repudiation of the *rentes* not bought with cash. The decision was an inspired compromise because it preserved the legal existence of these *rentes*, while, at the same time, it eliminated the need to pay them.[37]

The repudiation of the *rentes* and the fixing of the rate of interest may appear, at first glance, to have little to do with direct taxation,

34. BN, Ms. Fr. 16626. See also R. Bonney, *The King's Debts* (Oxford, 1981), chap. 1, for some useful comments on this action, as well as Barbiche, *Sully,* pp. 78 and ff. BN, Ms. Fr. 10839 has various lease prices under Sully.

35. The famous *bail* Josse, on which see: E. Le Roy Ladurie and J. Recurrat, "Sur les fluctuations de la consommation taxée du sel dans la France du nord aux XVIIe et XVIIIe siècles," *Revue du Nord* (1972): 385–98, table II n. 5.

36. Mlle. Françoise Bayard graciously shared a copy of another of her articles on this subject, "Fermes et traités en France dans la première moitié du XVIIe siècle," *Bulletin du Centre d'Histoire Economique et Sociale de la Région Lyonnaise* 4 (1975): 45–80.

37. It must be reemphasized that the *rentes* were rarely (if ever) paid at full value in the 1570s and 1580s, and that they were not paid at all from about 1585 to 1598.

because most of the *rentes* lay against indirect taxes. Yet the direct taxes in the *pays d'élection* carried *rentes* of about 770,000 l. (excluding private *rentes*). The savings from half payment were an increase of about 5 percent in the king's net return from direct taxation.

The savings on interest expenses were an important element in the *rentes* reform of 1602–4 and its impact on the direct tax system, but the partial repudiation of the debt had a far more important impact on the system than the simple savings alone suggest. Many of the *rentes* were held by royal officers, particularly by royal financial officers. The repudiation of the *rentes* must therefore be seen as being very closely connected to the simultaneous introduction of a new system of heredity of office, the *paulette*.

The Direct Tax System of Henry IV: The Reforms of 1598–1604 and the New System

In 1604 an important change took place in the status of financial (and nearly all) officers: the creation of the *paulette*. This change was part of the great reform movement of 1598–1604, but the reasons for the king's action have been debated since the time of the edict. Francis I had made offices legally hereditary in the early sixteenth century, but the mechanism of inheritance remained unclear until the *paulette*. There were several systems of inheritance in the sixteenth century; by 1600, however, the method of resignation was the *quart denier* with a forty-day survival clause. The officer could resign his position to whomever he wished by paying the king one-fourth of the office's assessed value, provided that the resigner survived by forty days the receipt of the resignation tax by the treasurer of the *parties casuelles*.[38]

The inconvenience of such a system for the officers was obvious, although families owning offices whose occupant died suddenly could often make a special deal with the king to keep the office (such deals, as one might expect, were quite expensive).[39] In 1604,

38. R. Mousnier, *La Vénalité des Offices* (Rouen and Paris, 1945, 1971).
39. One example among many is in AD Loire-Atlantique, B 67, fols. 142–43, Claude Lefevre getting the office of Jan Verdier, master of accounts, paying a dispensation of 15,000 l. (the usual tax was 2,250 l.).

Henry IV acted to eliminate the forty-day clause. He instituted a yearly payment of one-sixtieth of the official value of the office (the *paulette*) and reduced the resignation tax to one-eighth. The government drew up a table of official values in 1604, but these values were well under the going rate for most offices and became an even smaller proportion of the actual value in the office price inflation of the early seventeenth century.[40]

The reason for the creation of the *paulette* is hotly debated by historians, with some taking the view that it was done to increase revenues and others that it was done for political reasons. Even seventeenth-century figures differed on the motivation. In his *Testament Politique*, Richelieu gave the opinion that it was politics that had counted.

> Nothing gave as many means to the Duke of Guise to make himself powerful in the League against the King and his State than the great number of offices, which his credit introduced in the principal charges of the Kingdom, and I learned from the Duke of Sully that this consideration was the most important motive of the late King in the Establishment of the *paulette* . . . and that, while financial matters counted for a great deal with him, *raison d'Etat* was more important than it on this occasion.[41]

Henry, and the Assembly of 1596, had sought to curb the power of the *grands,* especially the provincial governors. The ability to control access to royal offices was one of their key powers of patronage, but the *paulette* did not eliminate this ability. In fact, the process became more complicated in this period, as the royal officer corps, notably the Sovereign Courts, developed their own standards for admission. Offices were *not* available to all who could pay for them.

For example, in the Chamber of Accounts of Brittany, the Chamber refused to accept the resignation of the office of René du Verger to Joachim Le Coq, forcing Le Coq to sell it to René Pinard in 1633. In 1618–19, the Chamber refused to accept Joachim Descartes, *conseiller* in the Parlement (and father of René), as its first

---

40. BN, 500 Colbert 256, lists official prices of 1604.
41. A. Richelieu, *Testament Politique* (Paris, 1947), 233–34. He is supported by J. R. Major, "Henry IV and Guyenne: A Study Concerning the Origins of Royal Absolutism," *French Historical Studies* 4 (1966): 363–84. Mousnier, *Vénalité,* advances the fiscal argument.

president, forcing him to resign in favor of Jacques Barrin, a president of the Parlement.[42]

The most extraordinary case at Nantes was that of the office of auditor of accounts owned by Patrice Bizeul. He sold it to Pierre Lelou, who passed it along to Jan Trippart, who gave it to Sébastien de Bruc. De Bruc passed it along to Guillaume Marceau, who sold it to François de Bruc, brother of Sébastien. The Chamber refused to accept either of the de Brucs. The king sent three orders to the Chamber to receive François de Bruc and issued an *arrêt,* giving the Chamber fifteen days to accept him. The Chamber refused, so the king had de Bruc received by a group of Masters of Requests. The Chamber agreed it would examine de Bruc six months later. De Bruc finally gave up, passing the office to René de Bruc, who sold it to Louis Hernouet, who gave it to Nathan Huzeau. Six years after the original resignation, Huzeau was finally received by the Chamber.[43] At Nantes, as elsewhere, a combination of good connections among the upper provincial nobility and within the robe itself (especially the court in question) were what mattered to those seeking office.

There is some merit in the political explanation, but it does not provide a satisfactory answer, given how little the situation changed with respect to patronage. The key opponent of the *paulette* at the time of its introduction, the chancellor Pomponne de Bellièvre, however, believed the increase in revenue was the key factor in the promulgation of the edict. Bellièvre wrote to Villeroy, another member of the council, on 29 November 1602:

> The affair was strongly considered and disputed; at the end, it passed according to the opinion of M. de Rosny (Sully); God grant that good comes of it. As soon as one speaks of money, it is thereafter necessary that all reasons cease . . . If such an edict is allowed, first, the king will no longer have the choice of any officer. . . . The officers will no longer be officers of the king; they will be officers of their purses. . . . There are an infinite number of other inconveniences, but money talks and reason and honor are silent.[44]

42. AD Loire-Atlantique, B 71, fols. 104–6. Biographical information on Descartes and Barrin in F. Saulnier, *Le Parlement de Bretagne, 1554–1790* (Rennes, 1909).

43. AD Loire-Atlantique, B 68, fols. 270–76.

44. P. de Bellièvre, "Contre la paulette," *Revue Henri IV* 1 (1905): 182–85. Quotation from pp. 182–83, second quotation from p. 184.

Bellièvre did see some utility in the measure: the 400,000 l. increase in the revenues of the *parties casuelles*—"a thing worthy of very great consideration." For Bellièvre, however, "one must take care that the remedy is not more dangerous than the illness." Buttressing his point, he argued that "half of the *tailles* are employed in the payment of officers' wages."

The exact reasons for the promulgation of the *paulette* are diffi- cult to determine; the political perspective fits in well with the re- forming efforts of this period, but Sully was struggling to balance the budget as well. Each of these explanations has fundamental weaknesses. Offices continued to be filled by favoritism. For ex- ✓ ample, the officers in the engaged parts of the king's demesne paid their entry fees to the *engagiste,* and the king often granted casual revenues to third parties, such as the Queen Mother. She would receive the revenue from office transfers in the given area and would play the key role in filling offices. Most provinces had an adminis- tration dominated by clients of powerful nobles, such as the Condés in Burgundy, the Longuevilles in Normandy, or the Mont- morencys in Languedoc. As for revenues, Roland Mousnier has shown that the *paulette* may actually have decreased overall income for the *parties casuelles* because the resignation tax dropped from one-fourth to one-eighth and the king no longer "inherited" any offices. The first three *traitants* of the *paulette* lost money. On the financial side the strongest point was perhaps the advance Charles Paulet made to Henry IV; Henry would have had to reimburse him had he rescinded the edict.[45]

Three major reasons account for the introduction of the *pau- lette:* its role in the reform and rationalization of the administration of the kingdom; its attractiveness to the officers; and its importance to the king in his efforts to restructure his debts. First, Sully and Henry sought to standardize the administration of the kingdom between 1597 and 1604; the *paulette* should be seen as part of this effort because it produced a regular income flow and ended the constant dickering between the king and the families of officers who had died without resigning far enough in advance.[46]

The *paulette* followed by only a few years Henry's attempted

45. Mousnier, *Vénalité,* 259–66.
46. On the other hand, it would not be the first (or last) time the king ignored such a problem. He could easily have levied the money on the officers themselves. There are many examples of the dickering in AD Loire-Atlantique, B 66–78.

abolition of the *bureaux des finances* and his simultaneous attack on the number and function of the treasurers of France. The *paulette* must be seen as part of this effort, because it responded to the strongest wish of the officers—the elimination of the forty-day clause.[47] While the sixteenth-century system allowed virtually all offices to be passed on hereditarily, the *paulette* eliminated the necessity of bribes to various people and a large indemnity to the king for dispensation of the clause.

As part of the standardization process the *paulette* belongs with such actions as the creation of *élections* in Guyenne. The *paulette*, producing a stable rather than an erratic annual revenue, would have fit in quite well with the general stability of taxation under Sully (see Chapter 3). Sully believed in having specific expenses assigned to specific revenues in order to obtain a more accurate budget, and one consideration involved in the creation of the *paulette* was that it provided a specific amount of revenue each year, against which given expenses could be assigned.[48]

The second major reason for the promulgation of the *paulette* was that it was the price paid by Henry IV and Sully for the officers' acquiescence in the reduction of the *rentes*. It was the carrot in the carrot-and-stick policy pursued by Henry IV and Sully with respect to the royal officers. The officers had to accept the permanent reduction in the rate of return on their investments in *rentes*. In return they got a regular payment of their lower interest, and most important, they got absolute heredity of office. This compromise was essential to the effective relationship of the king and his officers.

In the long run, by providing greater stability, the *paulette* made offices much more lucrative investments. In this sense the *paulette* greatly increased royal revenue from the sale of offices: the assured heritability of offices made them much more valuable, and the king could now sell offices for much more than their "official" value. It was a measure of the popularity of the *paulette* with the officers that they were willing to pay 5 percent of the official value of their offices in 1621 to continue the privilege, a further 20 percent for the same privilege in 1630, and 12.5 percent in 1639 for a third

47. C. Loyseau, *Cinq Livres du Droit des Offices* (Paris, 1613, 1644). P. de l'Estoile, *Journal . . . pour le règne de Henri IV* (Paris, 1948–60), tells a famous anecdote of the officers lined up in the mud to get their payments in on time.

48. Buisseret, *Sully* and Barbiche, *Sully*.

renewal.[49] In 1648, the proposed abolition of the *paulette* precipi-
tated the first Fronde.

While the officers had accepted their loss of power in the early
1640s, rather grudgingly it must be admitted, the threatened loss
of their investment capital finally prompted them to revolt in 1648.
This behavior demonstrated the extent to which the offices were
regarded by the bourgeoisie as investments as well as a means by
which to share the king's power.[50] The king was able to take advantage of this attitude after the Fronde when he maintained the integrity of the officers' investments while simultaneously eroding their
authority with the intendants. The frequent lack of active officer
resistance to this erosion of power merely reflected their concern
with investment values over political power. Their most effective
resistance came through inaction rather than action: the failure
to carry out the wishes of the central government (see Chapters 3
and 4).

The government saw a darker side to the officers' financial stake
in their offices: corruption and malfeasance. The government as-
sumed, not without cause, that all levels of the tax bureaucracy
were rife with corruption and collusion. The *Chambre de Justice,*
or reforming commission, charged with punishing wrongdoers,
was a regular part of the system. There were *Chambres* in 1597,
1601, 1607, 1624, 1635, and 1648.[51] For example, the *Chambre* of
1607 imprisoned the receiver general of Riom, A. Girard, and
seized the goods of his clerk, Le Gendre.[52] It investigated other officers and assessed large fines against several of them.

These *Chambres* were essentially fiscal devices, since most officers simply paid a nominal fine to escape prosecution. Each office,
such as receiver general, had a fixed fine to pay, regardless of the
wrongdoing of the officers in question; one can see this arrangement either as an admission that all were guilty, or as proof that
the *Chambre* was merely a revenue-raising device, not a serious

49. Collins, "Taxation in Bretagne," 391–92.

50. The nobility granted by such offices was also important, both for economic
(tax exemption) and social reasons. We shall see in Chapter 4 that officers could
provide very valuable service to patrons, clients, and family.

51. J. F. Bosher, "*Chambres de Justice* in the French Monarchy," in *French Government and Society, Essays in Memory of Alfred Cobban,* ed. J. F. Bosher (London,
1973), 19–40.

52. BN, Ms. Fr. 16626, fols. 266v–73.

reforming tool. Even Colbert, in the great *Chambre* of 1661, finally had to levy fines. He did assess fines according to guilt, but he eventually had to reduce their amounts. One of the reasons he had to give up was that so many important personages, including members of the royal family, were involved in the tax farms (and their frauds). Despite all these limitations, however, the *Chambres* of the period up to 1667 were of some value in curbing excesses because some officers were imprisoned and their goods actually seized during the early stages of the investigation.[53]

The third element in the creation of the *paulette* involved its value to the government, rather than to the officers. As we have already seen, the government altered the way in which it paid the *rentes* in the period 1602–4. It also altered, by means of the *paulette*, that portion of the royal debt represented by offices. One aspect of the creation of the *paulette* was the promulgation of an official table of value for offices: for example, a treasurer of France was valued at 25,000 l.[54] As the government paid these people *gages* (a sort of annuity in the guise of a salary) at the *denier 10* (10 percent), it now had fixed *gages* (or interest) to pay on all offices. The heredity of office helped fuel a substantial increase in the cost of offices in the early seventeenth century, and the government sold its new offices at the going prices. The *gages* for these new offices, however, were fixed at the *denier 10* of the *official* price. For the 258 new offices of treasurer of France sold between 1621 and 1637, this rate would represent an annual savings of some 650,000 l. or more in *gages* by 1638.[55] The rate of interest on officers' capital, therefore, dropped from 10 percent to closer to 4 or 5 percent (in other words, about what the government was paying on the *rentes*). By the late 1630s and early 1640s, the government was

53. D. Dessert, "Finances et société au XVIIe siècle: à propos de la Chambre de Justice de 1661," *Annales E.S.C.* 29 (1974): 847–81. See also, D. Buisseret, "A Stage in the Development of the Intendants: The Reign of Henri IV," *Historical Journal* (1966): 27–38. On the punishments meted out under Sully, BN, Ms. Fr. 16626, fols. 260, 268, 349v.

54. Values for all offices in BN, 500 Colbert 256. In Paris an office of treasurer was worth 25,000 l., one of receiver general 62,000 l. or 55,000 l.; in Brittany an office of treasurer was worth 40,000 l., one of receiver general 24,000 l. The offices of treasurer ranged in value from 18,000 l. in Provence and Burgundy, to 40,000 in Brittany. In seventeen of twenty-one *généralités,* they were worth 21–24,000 l.

55. Charmeil, *Les trésoriers de France,* on real office prices.

officially paying only part of the officers' *gages,* so the rate of interest was even lower.[56]

If we turn away from the officers and the question of debt service, we find that Henry IV and Sully followed up on many of the Notables' other suggestions. They sent *commissaires* out to the provinces in 1598–99 to reform the direct tax collection process. The *commissaires* conferred with the treasurers of France and *élus* about the rolls of the *tailles* for each parish. They checked possible favoritism by the *élus,* investigated the competence of the parish assessors, and checked to see if there had been any outside interference in the drawing up of the parish rolls. They also checked the accounts of the receivers. In Normandy they ordered the *élus* of the *élections* that included the towns of Harfleur, Lisieux, Pont-Audemer, Quillebeuf, Pont de l'Arche, and Louviers to follow the *commissaires'* own repartition of the *tailles,* not that of the Estates of Normandy.[57]

The *commissaires* found that the most frequent abuses were those involving privilege and exemption. In an effort to reform these abuses, they repartitioned the *tailles* of Poitou in conjunction with the *élus* (for 1599) and did the full job themselves in Normandy. They also recommended a remission of a third or a quarter of the *tailles* and reforms of the *gabelle* system. Lastly, they recommended severe punishments against royal sergeants; the *commissaires* in Champagne noted the sergeants, "like vermin, gnaw at the people by the great exactions they make."[58]

These commissioners did reform the system in some ways. The great *règlements* on the *tailles* of 1599 and 1600 were clearly a reflection of the abuses catalogued by the *commissaires.* The king acted immediately on a number of issues. He made the parish assessors responsible for the collection, and thus for its unpaid arrears, rather than allowing the jobs of assessor and collector to be held by separate individuals, as had previously been the case. Henry believed that the assessors would act more fairly if they had

56. BN, Ms. Fr. 18510, fols. 354–56v, one-quarter cut in 1640, three-eighths in 1642.

57. B. Barbiche, "Les commissaires députés pour le régalement des tailles en 1598–99," *Bibliothèque de l'Ecole des Chartes* 118 (1960): 58–96.

58. Ibid., 72. Barbiche notes, p. 85, that the appearance of these *commissaires* in the countryside coincided very closely with the edict forbidding meetings of the *bureau des finances.*

to collect and be responsible for the money.[59] He ended all surtaxes to the *tailles*, such as the 73,000 *écus* levied in Berry for troops in 1597, and regularized the levies for troops by creating the *crue des garnisons*.[60] This *crue* was not the one usually referred to in tax ordinances. (The previous *crues* had been created by Francis I and Charles IX). Rather it was an effort to standardize the amount required for garrison troops. It was known as the *grande crue*. Henry soon added other, nonmilitary elements to it, such as a replacement tax for the *pancarte* (abolished in 1602).[61] At the urgent insistence of the *commissaires,* local officials, and the remaining provincial Estates (and the Assembly of 1596–97), Henry remitted all back taxes due for the years prior to 1596; he later extended this to 1598.[62] As we shall see in Chapter 3, he also reduced the taxes themselves.

Henry IV's reforms of 1596–1604 significantly altered the French direct tax system, indeed the governmental system as a whole. In terms of revenues, he sharply increased the proportion of money coming from indirect taxes. He did this in three ways: (1) he cut the direct taxes, basically by reducing the *crue*; (2) he increased the *gabelle* from 1589 to 1597, raising it from about 300 l./*muid* to about 400 l./*muid;* and (3) he greatly increased revenue from sales and transit taxes by better supervision and, more importantly, by restoring the peace necessary for commercial expansion. Contrary to what is often asserted, Sully did not raise indirect taxes (other than the *gabelle*); he did increase indirect tax revenue.[63]

With respect to the direct tax system, Henry and Sully made several far-reaching changes. First, let us consider the manner in which Henry levied the direct taxes and then we can turn to the specific changes he made in the relationship between the Crown and the officers of the tax system. These latter changes had pro-

59. "Edit de mars 1600," in *Règlements rendus sur le fait des tailles* (Rouen, 1710).

60. AD Cher, C 974, fol. 5.

61. AD Marne, C 2490, fols. 138–51.

62. AD Cher, C 974, fol. 12v, fols. 19v–20.

63. Bonney, *King's Debts,* is somewhat contradictory on this point, as he states, p. 59, that "Sully greatly increased the burden of indirect taxes, although part of the increase was the result of improved collection." In fact, nearly all the increase was due to improved collection. Sully did raise the *gabelle,* although the increase well antedates the increase in *gabelle* revenues, and added a few minor indirect taxes, such as the ones on salt levied on the Loire and Seine. Virtually all the increase in indirect tax revenues, however, came from better management.

Table 6. *Direct Taxation in the* Elections *of Rouen, Tours, and Châlons, 1620 (in* livres)

Tax	Rouen	Tours	Châlons
Equivalent	0	352	500
Taille	34,950	54,987	12,650
3d./l. to receivers	(340)	403	187
Levees	0	1,470	0
Postal service	107	264	300
Gages	6,214	7,700	5,400
Taillon	3,863	8,393	12,510
Constabulary	1,462	5,134	
Garrison tax	(54,250)	30,425	8,825
City repairs	546	0	6,600
Governor's *état*	672	0	0
Estates' commission	800	0	0
Roads and bridges	0	0	800
4d./l. bridge at Châlons	0	0	600
Taxe of *élus*	0	0	601
Pont Neuf	0	0	600
Total	103,204	109,128	49,573

Sources: BN, Ms. Fr. 16622, fols. 203–47 (Tours); 16623, fols. 190–230 (Châlons); 16624, fols. 249–317v (Rouen).

Notes: This document does not list a 3d./l. for the receivers as a revenue in Rouen, but it carries 340 l. as an expense. The document also excludes the *crue* in Rouen, estimated from other sources (AD Seine-Maritime, C 1438). For Châlons, *taillon* and constabulary tax were listed as one combined levy.

found effects on the local workings of the tax system, and it is only by understanding them that we can understand how the system worked at the level of the *élection* and the parish.

The king levied the direct taxes in about 60 percent of France.[64] As we can see in Table 6, the commission for the *tailles* included a vast array of other taxes, such as the *taillon* or the levy for postal services. There were many local taxes, such as the levy for the Pont

64. There is remarkably little on this subject. M. Marion, *Dictionnaire des institutions de la France aux XVIIe et XVIIIe siècles* (Paris, 1923), is the standard work, but concentrates on the eighteenth century. R. Mousnier, *Les institutions de la France sous la monarchie absolue* (Paris, 1974, 1980) is a modern synthesis. The best work on the *taille* remains E. Esmonin's remarkable, *La taille en Normandie au temps de Colbert* (Paris, 1913). On the administrative side, see also, L. Batiffol, "Essai de synthèse de l'organisation de la France vers 1600," *Revue Henri IV* 2(1905–6): 257–94.

Neuf of Paris, or for the dikes and levees of Touraine. In addition, there were substitute taxes, such as the *équivalent,* levied in the *généralités* that were subject to the *aides,* in return for the abolition of certain of those *aides,* or the *équivalent du sel* levied in lieu of the *gabelle* in Auvergne. Most additions to the direct tax burden of the early seventeenth century, were made to the *grande crue,* which was quite flexible. The *taille* and associated levies changed very little from year to year. The separation between the two went down to the village level: most villages had a separate roll, or at least separate listings on the roll, for the *taille* and its associated levies and for the *crue* (see Chapter 4).

The five *pays d'Etats*—Brittany, Burgundy, Dauphiné, Langue-doc, and Provence—did not pay the royal *taille,* nor did certain enclaves, such as the viscounty of Turenne, the *pays* of the Pyrenees (Béarn, and so on), or the Ile de Ré. Many towns did not pay the *taille;* indeed, many bourgeois of privileged towns (Lyon, Paris, many others) did not pay the *tailles* on their rural property. Because of the widespread urban exemption and the special exemptions of the clergy and nobility, the *tailles* were essentially a tax on peasants. They were levied on the basis of parishes and of *feux* (hearths) within the parishes.

The system of repartition at four levels had very important local consequences. While the king sometimes granted special, short-term exemptions for cause (fire, hail, flooding), he often readjusted the taxes of the entire district so that the global amount did not change. More important, because the *tailles* were a fixed sum for each area, divided among its inhabitants, a loss of inhabitants or eligibles, either due to population decline or exemption, did not lead to a reduction in the total levied. The amount was now divided among fewer taxpayers, thus raising their individual contributions. Such was not the case in all areas. In Brittany the *feu* exemptions bought in the 1630s reduced the share of the village by a given number of *feux* (or fraction of a *feu*) and therefore reduced its con-tribution (which was set at *x livres/feu*). This Breton procedure, however, had the effect of exempting the richest taxpayers at pre-cisely the moment when the king would double the direct tax bur-den; it reinforced the already overwhelming preponderance of the peasantry on the tax rolls.[65]

65. Collins, "Taxation in Bretagne," chap. 5.

The local division of the tax burden also meant that the local elite could control the manner in which the taxes were raised; in the most privileged areas, such as Brittany or Provence, they could also control, to some extent, the amount levied. The systems of assessment varied from one province to the next: the two most common, as we have seen, were the *taille personnelle,* levied in the North, and the *taille réelle* of the South. Yet in Brittany both nobles and noble land were exempt from the hearth tax. In Provence the *fouage* was not necessarily a direct tax. The amount levied was determined by a vote of the Estates of Provence; it was divided among the communities (*communes*) on the basis of an *affouagement* (estimation of property values) of 1471, periodically adjusted (very minor adjustments). Each *feu* was the equivalent of 35,000 l. of taxable goods (*biens*). The assessment of each community was then levied by the community in the manner chosen by it; most used a combination of direct and indirect taxes, but there was no requirement to have direct taxes and some communities did not have them.[66]

The definition of *feu* or hearth varied sharply from province to province. In Brittany the number of *feux* was set in the 1420s and then revised for population losses and purchased exemptions from the 1420s until 1501. The number of *feux* then remained fixed from 1501 to 1789, except for purchased exemptions (forced sales in the 1570s and 1630s and 1640s). Each *feu* represented three real hearths in the original division, but one can imagine how inaccurate such counts were by the seventeenth century. Other areas used different systems: in the Southwest some districts defined a *feu* as a specific amount of land. In Normandy the tax assessment was based on the *octroi,* a sort of register of taxpayers of each village. The Estates of Normandy and the local officials periodically reformed the list, in the "changement de l'octroi." In the interim between reformations, taxpayers were assessed in the village to which they owed a contribution in the year in which the *octroi* had been drawn up.[67] In the 1620s and 1630s, this caused tremendous hard-

66. R. Pillorget, *Les mouvements insurrectionnels en Provence entre 1595 et 1715* (Paris, 1975), 58–65 on Provençal taxation. Bercé, *Histoire des Croquants,* 79–80 on southwestern exemptions. *Ordonnances,* 6: 36–37, on viscounty of Turenne.

67. J.-B. Voysin de la Noiraye, *Mémoire sur la généralité de Rouen en 1665,* ed. E. Esmonin (Paris, 1913), on Norman system. The possibilities for exemption were endless: Bordeaux, for example, paid the *taillon* but not the *taille.*

ship in the western part of the Cotentin because many peasants, seeking to escape the exorbitant Norman tax levels, fled to Brittany. Those who left were still assessed within the villages, but it was virtually impossible to get money from them because the complainants had to seek justice through the Breton court system. The Bretons, eager to protect local privilege, refused to allow summons of any Breton to a court outside the province. The Parlement of Brittany further refused to allow assignment of any immigrants who had lived more than one year in the province.[68]

Certain areas, such as Burgundy, kept serious records of hearths and based their contributions on them. The assessment of the village was based on its number of hearths; apportionment within the village was not so based but was done by the villagers themselves.[69] In the area in which the *taille* was *réelle,* the local officials kept a *compoix:* a register of the land and its value within the village. Each village had a cadaster of its *allivrement* (poundage value of the land). Each plot was assessed according to its cadastral value.[70]

As we have seen, the direct taxes varied in content from one region to the next and even from one *élection* to the next. As we can see in Table 6, there was great variation even within the so-called homogenous mass of the *pays d'élection.* The *équivalent* of the *aides* existed in the nine *généralités* of Paris, Soissons, Châlons, Tours, Poitiers, Riom, Moulin, Bourges, and Lyon: it came to 125,000 l. per year. Eight of these *généralités* (Paris was the lone

68. M. Le Pésant, "Un centre d'émigration en Normandie sous l'Ancien Régime: Le cas de Percy," *Bibliothèque de l'Ecole des Chartes* 130 (1972): 163–225. The heaviest period of emigration was 1650–79, during which nearly half the 588 emigrants of the period 1630–1749 departed. Le Pésant cites a *cahier* of the deputies of Avranches to the Estates of Normandy in 1617 to the effect that "several parishes of the *élection* of Avranches, as many as 25 or 30, which border on the sea, are being completely depeopled of inhabitants, who, because of their poverty, are leaving for the province of Brittany, as much to be discharged from their *tailles* and *crues*" (p. 181).

69. The "Règlement des finances de 19 janvier 1599," *Revue Henri IV* 1 (1905): 189–90, spells this out (a practice that dated from the fourteenth century, as we have seen). The "Edit de mars 1600," art. 12, states that parishes with a contribution of more than 900 l. should have four men to collect and assess the taxes; those with a lesser total, should have two. In fact, the evidence from the many rolls I have examined (see Chapter 4) indicates that the peasants did as they pleased.

70. E. Le Roy Ladurie, *Les paysans de Languedoc* (Paris, 1966), criticized by G. Frêche, "Compoix, propriété foncière, fiscalité et démographie," *Revue d'Histoire Moderne et Contemporaine* 18 (1971): 321–53.

exception) also paid the *subvention des villes,* a tax of another
125,000 l. levied on the towns.[71]

The *équivalent* of the *aides* was not levied in former Burgundian
lands, such as Burgundy proper or Picardy, or in other areas that
had composed with the king in the fourteenth century. The *élection*
of Rethel, for example, lay in the *généralité* of Châlons, which paid
the *équivalent.* But Rethel did not, because it had had a separate
composition in the fourteenth century, and was thus exempt from
the *aides.* There were also other special exemptions, such as that of
the entire *généralité* of Amiens from the garrison tax, because so
many troops were always quartered there.[72]

The process of dividing the contributions for this array of direct
taxes will be fully covered in Chapter 4. The process was usually
done on the bases of the previous year's assessments (the most important consideration) and the information gathered by the treasurers during their (obligatory) inspection tours of each *élection.*
Reductions in assessment could be granted for local disasters, both
natural and man-made (that is, military). The king then had the
choice of reducing the amount due from the district as a whole or
of redividing the same amount among the other parishes or *élections:* he used both procedures.[73]

The administrative personnel of this direct tax system was quite
extensive. At the regional level (*généralité*) there were ten treasurers
at each of eighteen *généralités,* seven treasurers at Grenoble, five at
Aix and, two at Nantes. The number of treasurers jumped sharply
after 1620: the total reached twenty-three per *généralité* for nineteen districts, nineteen for each of the three Norman *généralités,*
but still only two in Brittany.[74] Each district had three offices of
receiver general and controller general, exercised every third year.
In fact the same man often held two or even all three offices; alter-
natively, the two pre-1597 officers bought out the third office and
shared it. The regional office also had a requisite number of sub-
ordinate personnel, such as clerks and bailiffs.

71. BN, Ms. Fr. 16622, 16623, 16624, gives the figures for 1620 for most *généralités* (Paris, 1622). Only Limoges is missing from the *pays d'élection.*

72. BN, Ms. Fr. 16623, fols. 150–88.

73. AD Cher, C 974–75, for examples. AD Gironde, C 4832, shows temporary
relief of 7,267 *écus* in Figéac due to a late harvest.

74. Charmeil, *Trésoriers,* 33.

At the local level there were the *élus*, numbering five to fourteen in any given *élection*. The *élection* personnel included three receivers and three controllers (again, three offices but not three officers, in most cases) and the subsidiary personnel. The *élection* officers made extensive use of royal sergeants to carry out their orders in the villages. The Breton courts alone had close to 700 such sergeants, which gives some indication of the number in the kingdom as a whole.[75] As with the *généralités*, the number of *élections* rose from 1620 to 1640, and the number of officers jumped even more sharply. The king created over twenty new *élections* between 1620 and 1640, as well as the new *généralités* of Alençon and Montauban.[76] While these creations of offices raised substantial amounts of money, most of the money obtained from the officers came not through sales of offices but through the sale of the *droits aliénés* (which will be described fully in a moment).

Until 1634 Henry IV and Louis XIII sought to expand this overall system of *élections*, *généralités*, judicial bodies, and occasional *commissaires*. They tried to convert France to this system and to centralize government action through the mechanism afforded by the existing bureaucracy. For example, Henry and Louis established *élections* in Guyenne-Gascony in the period 1602–26. It was indicative of the difficulties of overcoming localism that each king created and abolished the *élections* before Louis' definitive action of 1621. Even this action prompted a revolt in Quercy in 1624; the *élus* did not assume full authority until 1627.[77]

In the 1620s, Louis expanded the authority of all the treasurers to include judicial competence over transportation.[78] Louis also introduced *élections* into all the *pays d'Etats*, except Brittany, between 1628 and 1633. His efforts to establish *élections* in Languedoc prompted an uprising that coincided with the revolt of Gaston

75. AD Loire-Atlantique, C 3276, payments for continuation in office, 1611. This would imply at least 7,000 in France.

76. Appendix A gives a list of *élections* in 1583, 1620, and 1640.

77. Bercé, *Histoire des Croquants*, 98 and ff. J. R. Major, "Henry IV and Guyenne," and "French Representative Assemblies: Research Opportunities and Research Published," *Studies in Medieval and Renaissance History* 1 (1964): 181–219. Buisseret, *Sully*, 58 and 97. L. de Cardenal, "Les dernières réunions des trois ordres de Périgord avant la Révolution," and "Les Etats de Périgord sous Henri IV," in *Etudes présentées à la commission internationale pour l'Histoire des Assemblées d'Etats* 2 (1978): 111–27 and 3 (1979): 163–81.

78. Charmeil, *Trésoriers*. See also the articles by Georges Pagès cited in the bibliography on the meaning of this action.

d'Orléans and the duke of Montmorency, governor of the province. Montmorency's family had ruled the province for over 100 years. His execution, which is so puzzling to many historians, may have been an object lesson in the dangers of provincial governors using local Estates to oppose the king. The province itself paid a huge indemnity and the king abolished the *élections*.[79] One may see this action as a recognition that the great nobles were the greatest threat to the king's power, and thus had to be dealt with firmly, while the particularist Estates, dangerous in conjunction with such nobles, were themselves obstructionist rather than threats to the king's very power.

The simultaneous introduction of *élections* into Provence, Dauphiné, and Burgundy led to popular riots in all three areas. In Provence the Coriolis faction of the Parlement led the revolt. Each of these provinces tried to "compose" with the king; Provence and Burgundy were successful, Dauphiné was not.[80]

This failure in Languedoc, Provence, and Burgundy may have convinced Louis XIII and Richelieu that a new method was necessary to break the particularism best represented by the *pays d'Etats*. They may also have realized that the massive sales of offices in the 1620s had compromised the authority of the king's officials and reduced many positions to a mere form of investment. The investment aspect of the offices had always been important, but after 1620 or so, it started to become the sole purpose of officeholders. The investment was both economic (office prices rose sharply during the first half of the seventeenth century and the return on investment was sometimes quite respectable) and social (most offices ennobled the holder and, under varying conditions, his descendants).[81]

For example, Louis added two new treasurers in each *généralité* in 1621, four more in 1623, and seven more by 1637.[82] The prestige and power of each individual office obviously declined as the number of such offices rose. The multiple attractions of officeholding—tax exemption, social status, an annual income, high resale

79. BN, 500 Colbert, fols. 53–63 on the apportionment of the 1632 levy to abolish the *élections*.

80. Kettering, *Judicial Politics*, and Pillorget, *Les Mouvements*, 320–48.

81. This complex matter is best discussed in Mousnier, *Vénalité* and Mousnier, *Institutions*.

82. Charmeil, *Trésoriers*, 11–16.

value—kept office prices high during the reign of Louis XIII, but, by the reign of Louis XIV, the value of the offices declined sharply due to their proliferation. By way of contrast, in Brittany, where concerted opposition by the local elite kept the number of treasurers at two, the offices remained extremely powerful and very expensive—on average, 150 percent more than their French counterparts.[83]

To understand the relationship among the tax administrators, the Crown, and the people, we must remember that there were two aspects to the royal administration. It was the national bureaucracy and had all the aspects of a national administration for the central government. But the bureaucracy was also a major source of tax income; that is, it both *collected* and *produced* tax income. This tax income came from the sale of offices and the sale of rights attached to these offices, the *droits aliénés*. (The *droits* were a perpetual surtax sold to tax officers in return for an advance payment equal to ten times the annual surtax. As we shall see, they were essentially forced loans on the officers.)

The sale of offices and *droits* was a major source of income for the seventeenth-century French monarchy. More important, such sales were a major source of immediately disposable income. These sales were a form of taxation. The monarchy had great difficulty taxing the wealth of the middle classes, just as it could not reach the income of the clergy and nobility in a direct manner. The sale of offices and *droits* allowed the king to tap the wealth of the middle classes on a regular basis.

The king's efforts to tax the privileged classes deserve some mention here, because these classes did not seem to contribute to direct taxation: they were all exempt from the *tailles*.[84] In fact they did pay some direct taxes. The clergy paid a special annual grant, the *don gratuit*, whose value was 1.2 million l. under Henry IV and rose under Louis XIII. The lay landlords, commoner or noble, seem

---

83. Ibid., 33, cites a typical value of an office of treasurer of 50–70,000 l. after 1610 or 1620. In Brittany, where there were only two treasurers, the office rose in value from some 30–40,000 l. in 1600 to 150,000 l. by 1636.

84. This blanket statement cannot be applied everywhere. In the area of *taille réelle*, noble land was exempt, nobles (as individuals) were not. In Brittany both noble persons and noble land were exempt. In Provence the situation was even more complicated because there were no provincewide taxes of this nature. In the regular *taille* area, as we shall see, nobles often paid half the share of their *métayers*, and all noble tenants paid taxes on their share of the output.

to have been paying some of the taxes of their tenants (on which, see Chapter 4). Nonetheless, such groups were substantially under-assessed.

The royal tax administration was the central element in the king's extraction of tax money from the middle classes. In the six-teenth century he had sold the middle classes various offices and *rentes*. The number of offices rose sharply. For example, the trea-surers of France grew from one per district in the 1550s to ten per district in the 1580s; the *élus* jumped from one or two per district to an average of nine by 1600; the number of districts, at both levels, also increased sharply. These officers had to buy *rentes* in the period 1561–88: such *rentes* were both a form of taxation, a way of getting the officers to contribute to the king's needs, and the prin-cipal mechanism of floating the royal debt. Because so many of the *rentes* sales were obligatory, and because the *rentes* were so badly paid, it is hard to argue that they were exclusively a manner of floating the debt: a loan implies a certain willingness on the part of the lender. In the sense that the officers had no choice in the matter, the *rentes* were a form of direct taxation.

In the seventeenth century this system changed. There was a hia-tus between 1600 and 1620 or so, with very few sales of offices or *droits*. After 1616, and, more heavily, after 1620, the king sold many new offices and a bewildering variety of *droits*. The *droits* allowed the king to anticipate future direct tax revenues and to tap the capital of the urban dwellers. One of the most intriguing as-pects of this process was that in the eighteenth century, when the *vingtièmes* and capitations allowed the king to get to the capital of the privileged classes, especially the middle classes, the sale of of-fices declined sharply and that of *droits* virtually disappeared.[85] While there is no direct proof of causality, one is tempted by the strong coincidence to connect the two phenomena.

The variety of offices created in the seventeenth century boggles the mind. In Brittany, where the number of officers was much lower than in any other province (save perhaps Provence and Languedoc), the king sought to create a guard for the charters in the chateau of

85. There are, in fact, two questions to answer here: (1) Did these taxes replace the earlier sales in their function of tax? Louis XIV certainly continued to sell offices during the War of the Spanish Succession, but creations and sales dropped sharply after 1715. (2) Did the availability of other credit make the loan function of offices/ *droits* unnecessary in the eighteenth century?

Nantes (price: 500 l.), a controller of fortifications (1,320 l.), and hereditary owners of the free taverns of Rennes, to cite only a few examples.[86] In provinces in which there were no provincial Estates to pay for the suppression of such ridiculous positions, the offices came into existence.

Big money could also be made from the sale of superfluous additions to the regular bureaucracy: the value of the 258 treasurers of France created between 1621 and 1637 would have been about 15 million l.[87] Louis XIII also sold offices in the financial courts, the law courts, and the indirect tax administration. If he did not wish to create new offices, he could raise the *gages* of the existing ones: at the Chamber of Accounts of Brittany, in 1626, Louis added 27,000 l. in new *gages,* for an advance of 263,500 l.[88]

The creation and sale of a bewildering variety of lesser offices, particularly at the *élections* and in the administrations of the sale and wine taxes, however, dwarfed these sales of legitimate (albeit superfluous) high-level offices. The king added new *élus,* clerks, *greffiers,* guards of the seal, measurers of salt, *jaugeurs* of wine, receivers, and controllers of various indirect taxes. He also created many lower-echelon judicial offices, to say nothing of offices created to collect newly created taxes. (In the latter case the officer would receive the right to a surtax; thus the king would pay him no wages. For example, an inspector of hides would get x pennies per hide, paid by the manufacturer.)[89]

The *Droits Aliénés* and the Collapse of the Direct Tax System

Within the enormous literature on the sale of offices one finds little mention of the financially quite substantial sale of rights to these officers. The sale of these rights, the *droits aliénés,* constituted one of Louis XIII's major contributions to the relationship of the officers and the Crown. In the long run the *droits* played the key role in undermining that relationship and in forcing Louis to change the nature of his government. They were also a major factor

86. Collins, "Taxation in Bretagne," chaps. 7 and 8.
87. Charmeil, *Trésoriers,* 33.
88. AD Loire-Atlantique, B 73, fols. 94v–109, on wage increase; B 74, fols. 282v–83 on new offices.
89. The tax on hides led to a revolt at Caen. See Foisil, *Nu-Pieds.*

in the widespread popular uprisings of the period 1624–48. Let us first define these *droits* and then move on to an examination of their influence on French society.

The *droits aliénés* were the rights purchased by the officers to surtaxes on various taxes. They were sold on both direct and indirect taxes; the largest shares went to the officers of the direct tax system and to the *gabelle* officers. We are concerned here with the officers of the direct tax system, who bought the largest share of the *droits*.

The sale of the given *droit* was handled by a *traitant*. The king received a fixed sum of money, and the *traitant* then sold the specific *droit* to anyone he chose. The obvious choice was the officer involved in collecting the tax, but the royal letters creating these *droits* made it absolutely clear that they could be sold to a third party if the officer concerned did not wish to buy. In one case in Brittany the receiver general, Guillaume Martin, bought a *droit* of 3d./l. for both offices of receiver general of Brittany. He did not have enough money to pay for both of the *droits* himself (at some 23,160 l. each), so he borrowed the money from a third party. The third party sued and received a royal ruling that the *droit* was to be paid on the same basis as the respective shares in its cost (in this case, 13 to 10 rather than the equal split demanded by Martin).[90]

In most cases, however, the given officer bought the *droit*. The price was fixed at ten times the annual value of the *droit* itself, plus a 5 percent surcharge for "costs." The *droits* were, in fact, another form of *rente* and, as such, a continuation of the dual role of the *rentes* as a mechanism for floating the royal debt and as a tax on bourgeois capital stocks. Let us take the example of the 10d./l. sold to the *greffiers* and master clerks of the *élections* in 1623. In 1623, in the *généralité* of Châlons, the king levied 26,715 l. 16s. 1d. for the 10d./l. of these officers. In 1624, however, the *brevet de la taille*, using the assessment base of 10d./l., listed only 25,362 l. 2s. 7d. because the principal of the direct taxes was less in 1624 than in 1623. The officers protested to the king that they were being cheated of a fair return on their investment; they felt they should be paid interest on the basis of their original investment, which was

90. Martin borrowed 13,160 l. from his father to help pay for the *droit* of the office of the *ancien* receiver and 13,160 l. from Nicolas Vauguin, *écuyer,* for the office of *alternatif* receiver's *droit.* Vauguin won the case (AD Loire-Atlantique, B 74, fol. 187).

calculated on the higher 1623 levies. The king ruled in their favor, perhaps because he wished to keep the goodwill of the officers in order to sell them more *droits*. Some *droits* rose when the direct taxes went up, however, which was a major difference between them and the *rentes*.

The evolution of an individual *droit* depended on its origin: those *droits* taken from the 2s./l. collection costs (originally paid to the parish collectors) went up whenever the direct taxes went up. Some *droits* were sold with limitations as to which levies they were based upon, while others were sold with the provision that they be levied on all assessed direct taxes. They reached 125d./l. (52 percent) in 1634, with additional *droits* on the *taille* (5 percent) and the *taillon* (3.75 percent).

In 1634, the king converted the *droits* into *rentes*, turning the analogy to his own ends. The *rentes* were to be paid by a special surtax of 8 million l., which would take the place of the *droits*. There were two catches here: first, the *droits* had been listed for 14 million l. on the *commission des tailles* of 1634 and, second, the *rentes*, like all *rentes*, were paid at only half their face value. In fact, only 3.5 million l. were levied for these *rentes* in the late 1630s, and part of even this sum went to pay cavalry.[91] It was, in short, a bankruptcy of some 10.5 million l. per year.

The difficulties in enforcing this edict were such that the man in charge of collecting it, Nicolas Drouin, could not find his assistants in Guyenne in 1635.[92] The conflict between the old officers and the intendants and the *traitants*, including Drouin, was extremely intense from 1634 to 1654. The local officers took whatever steps they felt were necessary to protect their investments and their power. To that end, the *élus* in some areas of the Southwest eliminated the *droits* of their own authority. The king, meanwhile, continued to sell new *droits*, this time assessed in set amounts per parish rather than in *deniers/livre*, as early as 1635–36.[93]

The officers became discontented with their increasing financial outlays and their decreasing political power. The treasurers of France claimed to have paid more than 30 million l. from 1624 to 1648, only to find their offices had declined two-thirds in value

91. BN, Nouvelle Acquisitions Françaises 200, fols. 1 and ff.

92. Bercé, *Histoire des Croquants*, 361.

93. AD Marne, C 2498, fol. 174v for 1636; C 2499, fol. 46 for 1637. AD Calvados, 4 C 394 for Caen in 1636.

during the period. Their *gages* were often not paid, especially after 1640. Indeed the treasurers of Bourges, writing in the mid-1640s, claimed that they had not received any money since 1640.[94] This nonpayment was made possible by the presence of the intendants and, later, by that of the army.

As we shall see in Chapters 3 and 4, the nonpayment of wages and *droits* to the officers was a major part of the "fiscal screw turning" of 1634–36. The increase in taxation from 1634 to 1636 was not only an increase in the amount being levied but also a much more drastic increase in the portion being levied for the king. The reduction in payments for the *droits,* some 10.5 million l. per year, represented a 60 percent increase in the amount of direct tax revenue available to the king.

One important reason for the collusion of many officers with the various peasant revolts was that the officers themselves footed most of the tax increase after 1633. In the 1630s, there were two levels of opposition in areas such as the Southwest. On the one hand, the *élus* represented the old system; yet, in the eyes of the locals, they represented an innovation. On the other hand, the tax resisters and peasant revolters of the 1630s demanded an abolition of the *élections,* along with tax reduction, and a return to the Estates system.[95] The king used both approaches, buttressing the old system by adding a *généralité* at Montauban in 1634, and undermining that system and the loyalty of its officers by cutting their *droits* in the same year.

In the late 1630s and 1640s, the process was completely out of hand. The intendants well understood the problem of using violence to collect taxes. In May 1644, for example, the intendant of Bordeaux, Lauson, wrote to chancellor Séguier: "Quant à la levée des tailles j'ay tasché d'éviter la procédure violente et de conserver les peuples pour la payer plus d'une année."[96] Using troops to collect the money, a common procedure throughout the Southwest in the 1640s, often paid short-term dividends. But, by using force to collect the money, the intendants risked ruining the villages visited by the troops and rendering them incapable of paying future taxes.

The new role of the army was a major shift in administrative

94. BN, Ms. Fr. 18510, fol. 388.
95. Bercé, *Histoire des Croquants*, vol. 2, documents.
96. B. Porshnev, *Les Soulèvements Populaires en France avant la Fronde* (Paris, 1963), piece 46. BN, Ms. Fr. 18510, fol. 391, reports a battle between peasants of

policy. The correspondence of the intendants with chancellor Séguier is filled with references to the use of the regular army to collect the taxes and, in certain areas, to the creation of a special army for tax collection. These troops were expensive—one report tells of soldiers demanding 3 l. a day—so that the net gain for the king's coffers was often quite small. The pillaging of troops was a cause of persistent complaint in sixteenth- and seventeenth-century France; its effect is easily seen in reduced hearth counts in combat areas.[97]

The troops left a trail of destruction behind them wherever they went. The receiver general of Champagne tendered his resignation in August 1639 because he had not received any money from the *élection* receivers for that year's taxes. He noted the "ruin and desolation of the said province, occasioned as much by the raids of the enemies of the State as by the armies and men of war that His Majesty has been constrained to maintain here for the past four years." [98]

Bercé, who calls the housing of troops the heaviest burden on the communities, makes the following comment on the role of the troops in the tax-collection process.

> Starting with the entry into the war, the receivers, for the most part, could no longer fulfill their task. They were caught between the ruin or revolt of the taxpayers, on the one hand, and the legal pursuits of the holders of *quittances* of the Central Treasury, on the other. . . . Starting with the entry into war, in 1635, the superintendants [of finance] were engaged in a vicious circle. The recovery of the *tailles* and the other direct taxes could not be assured without a systematic recourse to force. From fiscal terrorism, there resulted an epidemic of revolts, which required the minister to maintain permanently, throughout the kingdom, a sort of tax army.[99]

The process was all the more vicious because it was virtually impossible to get the money back from the troops once they col-

---

St-Hilaire de Soisey and cavalry. The villagers had refused to make the *assiette*— that is, they had refused to apportion their taxes.

97. AD Côte d'Or, series C, hearth investigations of 1551, 1578, and 1588, parish tax rolls for same years. The population went up between 1551 and 1578 but dropped about 20 percent from 1578 to 1588.

98. AD Marne, C 2499, fol. 176. Cited by M. Pelicier, *Inventaire Sommaire des Archives Départementales de la Marne*, series C (Châlons, 1892), 2: 77–78.

99. Bercé, *Histoire des Croquants*, 117–18 and 170.

lected it. The recourse to force, however, did not come first in the process. The direct taxes could not be collected because the local officers had been alienated by the central government, through the *droits* repudiation of 1634. Having once alienated the officers, the king found he could not rely on them. He anticipated this problem by sending out the intendants; however, they could not carry out their mandate without local support. When they could not get it from local elites, closely tied to the officers, they had to use the army.

Recourse to the army became necessary in 1634 because the local officials began to be systematically stripped of their financial stake in the levies. It was this disenchantment of the local and regional officers with the central government, more than the tax increases after 1634 (which were less than has been imagined, as we will see in Chapter 3), which led to the necessity of using the army to keep the peasantry under control and to collect the taxes. It was not the increase in taxes alone that caused the revolts, although that was a major factor. The combination of the increase and the disenchantment of the officials assigned to collect it led to the trouble.

The old officers could no longer be trusted by the government because the king had reduced the payments on their invested capital and was forcing them to make further (very risky) investments. By squeezing the officers, the government alienated its major governing tool in the countryside and had to employ another one—the intendants and the army. The hostility of the officers also increased the percentage of the proposed taxes that was not actually collected (the *non-valeurs*) because the officers lost interest in the levies. After all, they were no longer getting their share.

The proliferation of *non-valeurs* will be discussed at length in the next two chapters, but a few examples here will demonstrate the extent of the problem. In the *généralité* of Caen, in 1635, *non-valeurs* were 64.1 percent.[100] The intendant of the Limousin, Vautorte, wrote to Séguier in September 1643 that "arrivant en ce pays j'ay trouvé qu'on n'avoit payé guères plus du quart des impositions de 1642 et rien de 1643, la moitié des rolles n'estans faict dans les paroisses." De Heere, intendant of Tours, used troops to force several parishes to draw up their rolls in October 1643.[101]

100. Caillard, "Soulèvements populaires," 132.
101. Mousnier, *Lettres et mémoires*, I, 544 (quotation), 553.

The government had destroyed the workings of the old system by robbing the officers of their incentive, thus putting the officers in an ambiguous position within French society after 1634. They had become the third party in a tripartite conflict among the government, the mass of the population, and the officers themselves. Some of the officers were coopted into the new system; for example, some *élection* receivers became subfarmers for the collection in their district after 1643. Others supported, both openly and tacitly, various local revolts.[102]

Georges Pagès emphasized the sociopolitical importance of these venal offices for the sixteenth- and seventeenth-century French monarchy: "the multiplication of the . . . offices, the ease of access to them given by their venality, associated . . . large social classes with the administration . . . and gave the absolute monarchy solid foundations in the nation."[103] The *droits aliénés* strengthened the ties of these groups to the monarchy, and the abolition of the *droits* in 1634 quite naturally deprived the government of its most important allies. The monarchy made substantial financial gains from the original bankruptcy, but its loss of officer cooperation led to long-term financial problems. The monarchy needed local assistance to collect its taxes; when the king alienated the officers, he simultaneously cut himself off from his taxpayers.

The intendants were a new start and could therefore be used everywhere. They obviated recourse to local privilege, eliminating, for example, the argument that one could not introduce the institutions of Maine into Brittany. They were a recognition of the failure of the *élection-généralité* system. The system failed for three basic reasons: (1) the venality of offices, as Bellièvre had warned, made their occupants "officers of their purse not officers of the king"; (2) the massive increase in the number of officers weakened their individual authority and reduced their collective credibility; and, most important, (3) the particularism of the system meant that it could not be an effective tool for centralization. The system *represented* the very particularism the king was trying so hard to overcome; not surprisingly, therefore, it had to be jettisoned when particularism was attacked with renewed vigor under Richelieu.

The king's attack on the officers was not an assault on an iso-

102. Bercé, *Histoire des Croquants;* Foisil, *Nu-Pieds;* and, especially, Kettering, *Judicial Politics,* have many examples.
103. Pagès, "Essai sur l'évolution des institutions," 26.

lated group. The officers had strong ties to their noble patrons, powerful mutual interests with other landlords, and close familial ties to municipal oligarchies (both political and mercantile). The situation was something of a stalemate, because the officers had both a common cause with the king—expansion of the power of the royal bureaucracy—and common cause with other local elites—maintenance of their supremacy in the area.

The attack on the officers must also be seen as part of a general policy of overcoming particularism. The king needed greater financial resources, and he had to restructure his contracts with those groups in society that did not carry a fair share of the burden. The landlords were certainly affected by the higher direct taxes on their tenants (who paid the bulk of such taxes, as we shall see in Chapter 4), yet it was the bourgeoisie who bore the brunt of the early assault. The officers and the bourgeoisie itself were under tremendous financial pressure after the bankruptcy of 1634 and the forced loan of 20 million l., first levied in 1637.[104] Yet they were not the only privileged group from whom the king sought more money. After 1620, the king increased pressure on the *pays d'Etats* to pay more in taxes.

In the *pays d'Etats* the king tried to eliminate the old administrative arrangements, first, through the *élections* and then, when that failed, through the intendants. The pressure had a notable effect: in Brittany the wine duty of the Estates quadrupled from 1621 to 1640, and when wine could support no more taxes, the direct tax (the *fouage*) was doubled in 1643.[105] The other *pays d'Etats* had to pay far more, particularly after 1630. Much of this contribution went directly to troops in the field.

The increased financial needs of the monarchy could no longer allow anachronisms such as the Breton *fouage,* which was the same in absolute terms in 1642 as it had been in 1484, to retard the flow of money to the center. The failure to expand the existing institutions, such as *élections,* was a strong incentive to introduce an entirely new package of administrative personnel and taxes. One can see the old standardization drive of Sully in much of this—for example, in the effort to raise the costs of winter quarters for the

104. Ibid., 52 n. 2. Bullion wrote to Richelieu that the loan "was important not only for the present year but also for the future" (O. Ranum, *Richelieu and the Councillors of Louis XIII* [Oxford, 1963]).

105. Collins, "Taxation in Bretagne," chaps. 6 and 8.

troops through specific taxes rather than through irregular levies of *étapes*. All these changes were an attack on the existing bureaucracy, and that bureaucracy's resistance took many forms: recalcitrant Parlements, officer inaction on royal edicts, officer support of peasant revolts, and officer failure to collect the taxes.

The conflict between central authority and local autonomy or, in legal terms, between "pleine puissance" and "privilèges, droits, libertés et franchises" was the central motor in the administrative developments of the seventeenth century. The king's conflict with the local elites who possessed these privileges was most acute when he wanted more money. They were the only ones who had the money he needed.

The old tax system could not reach this money effectively. It could tap the wealth of the nobility indirectly, through its tenants, yet the limits of this approach, as we will see in Chapter 4, were reached in the early 1630s. The old system could tap the wealth of the Church only by means of special agreement, and it was noticeably unable to do so in this period. Moreover, much of the wealth of these two groups lay in the land itself, and it was quite difficult to capitalize such wealth.

The third wealthy group, the one with substantial amounts of liquid capital, was the bourgeoisie. The king tapped this capital largely by borrowing, since the bourgeoisie was substantially underassessed by the tax system. This borrowing took three forms: tax farms and *traités*, sales of offices, and sales of *droits aliénés*. As we have seen, one of the ways in which the king met his financial needs in the 1620s and early 1630s was to anticipate his future revenues by borrowing against them from the officers. He also reduced his interest payments, which went largely to these same officers, on the existing debt (both pre-1600 and for office *gages*). In 1634, he tapped the resources of this group once again by seizing a substantial portion of the interest due to them. He continued this process in the late 1630s and 1640s, when he reduced payment of *gages* and *droits* by one-quarter, then by three-eighths, then by one-half. In effect the sale of offices and *droits* (*rentes* in the sixteenth century) was, in addition to a form of borrowing, the king's method of taxing the bourgeoisie.

The king's constant probing of privileges was most effective against the bourgeois gentilshommes, perhaps partly because of their anomalous position in society—that is, they lacked well-defined rights and privileges. One suspects, however, that the principal reason for the king's efforts to get their money was that they had such substantial amounts of liquid capital.

The king's assaults on the privileged groups in French society led to coalitions of opposition that focused on the defense of specific interests (thus the financial and judicial officers, so often at loggerheads, acted together in defense of the *paulette* in 1648). One of the long-term problems of opposition to royal centralization in the seventeenth century was precisely the instability of such coalitions. Yet the other aspect of such instability was that it made full centralization more difficult to achieve. There was no constant group of allies within local elites to whom the king could reach out. The king could obtain a measure of centralization, as under Colbert, but the underlying currents of regionalism and localism could not be defeated. The cooperation of local elites was essential for success and, in the eighteenth century, the preexisting elite continued the same process of cooptation of the officer/*commissaires* of the new system—the intendants and their subdelegates.

It took a full generation, from 1634 to 1661, for the new system based on the intendants to come to a working compromise with the old. Because this new system was a compromise with the old, it, too, would prove inadequate as an agent for modernization of government. The new system never fully rejected the old differentiations and thus could never overcome them. This problem, so closely related to the way in which the king raised money, was a fatal flaw in the administrative structure of the Ancien Régime.

3. A French Peru: Revenues from Direct Taxation, 1598–1648

Jean-Roland Mallet and the Central Treasury Figures

The greatest difficulty facing historians of early seventeenth-century French fiscal problems is the lack of accurate figures on which to base their analyses. Historians have normally used the figures supplied by Jean-Roland Mallet and François Forbonnet.[1] Mallet, the most frequently used source, was the chief clerk of controller general Desmarets between 1708 and 1715. His book is based on the "budgets de l'Epargne," or the "bordereaux de l'Epargne," for the period 1600–1715. It provides the only continuous series of figures for the early seventeenth century, which explains its attractions for historians of French taxation. Moreover, Mallet is scrupulously accurate in presenting his material.[2]

The problem lies with his source, the *bordereau de l'Epargne*. The *bordereau* was the receipt and expense book of the Central Treasury. The nature of the receipts and expenses on these documents has clearly been misunderstood by most historians, who see these receipts as net revenue. Mallet himself points out that the local and regional charges were not included on the *bordereau*, but he does not detail as fully as he might either how important those charges were or what they represented.[3]

We must, therefore, treat this problem of revenues from two angles: first, we must examine what the revenues and expenses

1. J. R. Roland Mallet, *Comptes rendus de l'administration financière de la France* . . . (London, Paris, 1789); F. Forbonnais, *Recherches et considérations sur les finances de la France* (Liège, 1758).
2. BN, Ms. Fr. 16627, for 1605–15, as a check on Mallet's accuracy.
3. A point made by Roger Chartier in his comment to J. Collins, "Sur l'histoire fiscale du XVIIe siècle: Les impôts directs en Champagne entre 1595 et 1635," *Annales E.S.C.* 34 (1979): 325–47.

really were, and, second, we can then turn to an examination of
the figures themselves. The theoretical procedures of the system are
well described by Martin Wolfe, in his section on "control and disbursement of funds":

> The Renaissance monarchy, so far as possible, spent its money within
> the *élection* . . . where the funds were raised. By keeping the "porte et
> voicture" of cash to a minimum, the king saved himself a considerable
> amount of money, since these shipments were expensive as well as dan-
> gerous. Examples of local expenditures were charitable contributions
> of all kinds, wages of garrison soldiers, all regular and special wages of
> the whole corps of local royal officials, the upkeep of royal chateaux
> . . . and the repair and maintenance of fortresses. All such items and, of
> course, the expenses of shipment would be "assigned" on the local rev-
> enues.
>   The system of localized expenditures explains why all edicts and
> Renaissance writings refer to the money that was actually shipped to
> the king as a residuum—*les restes*. It was "that net (amount) which
> remains or comes in," or money which comes in as cash (*au clair* or
> "free and clear"). This did not mean, of course, that the *restes* were
> unimportant—on the contrary. For the government, this was the func-
> tion of the revenue system that mattered most.[4]

While Martin Wolfe is entirely correct in his belief that the government preferred to spend money at the local level, largely because
of the expense and danger of shipping coinage, the cash that came
to Paris was not in any way "net" revenue. The amount of cash
shipped to Paris was very small, as we shall see.

The French monarchy spent its direct tax revenues in five ways.
The first expenditure was the local and regional charges. These
charges were those to which Wolfe refers: officers' *gages*, garrison
costs, and chateaux and fortress upkeep. Yet one must be careful
here, because the money spent for the *taillon* (tax for men-at-arms)
was carried as a regional charge even if the money was spent outside the area in which it was levied (and thus charged). The second
group of expenses was what might be called "regular" assignations. In order to minimize the shipment of money, the government
assigned expenses to certain revenues. Thus a major noble, such as

---

4. M. Wolfe, *The Fiscal System of Renaissance France* (New Haven, 1972), 279.
It should be emphasized that the focus of Wolfe's book is not the local practice of
the tax system but rather its *theoretical* underpinnings, as seen through royal ordinances and the writings of sixteenth-century fiscal authors (Bodin, et al.).

the prince of Condé, would be assigned 60,000 l. as his pension and would obtain the money from the receiver general of, say, Moulins. This expenditure was carried on the share of the Central Treasury (*partie de l'Epargne*) and was duly registered in the expenses listed on the *bordereau de l'Epargne*. Condé would give the receiver general a *mandement de l'Epargne* (an order to pay him such-and-such an amount from the share of the Central Treasury), and the receiver general would use this document to justify the expense when he had his accounts audited. (As one might expect, the prospect of actually going to a remote location to collect money was not a popular one. A frequent way to avoid this was to sell the *mandement* at a discount to a merchant/financier of Paris.)

The third group of expenses might be called the extralegal or "irregular" assignations. This group is particularly difficult to define because it did not technically exist, and there is no administrative or legal term for it. The king might assign a certain expense, usually a payment to a major noble or a war-related outlay, to an *élection* or *généralité*. This arrangement allowed the king to give exorbitant amounts of money to an individual but to disguise the action by spreading the payments among several different accounts. While the king had the legal right to do as he wished with the money, this method of assigning money was clearly outside the realm of standard administrative practice because these assignations were not listed on the *bordereaux de l'Epargne*.

The fourth major expense was the costs of collection. In the period prior to 1616, these costs were always 10 percent, of which 8.33 percent went to the parish collectors and 1.67 percent to the king (he took it from the collectors in the 1590s to pay for demesne repairs). The original 2s./l. had been divided into the collector's fees—1 *sou*—and the costs of collection (1 *sou*)—for paper, candles, wood, writing fees and costs, signature fees, and so on. The 4d./l. taken by the king in 1595 continued to be levied as a surtax. Thus it was not listed on the official accounts at any level, but it was paid to the king. After 1616, the costs of collection included the *droits aliénés*, a series of surtaxes that equalled 88 percent of the principal of the *tailles* by 1634.

The fifth category, by far the smallest, was the cash shipped to Paris. As the seventeenth century wore on, bills of exchange and letters of credit were sometimes used in place of cash for the trans-

ferral of funds from the provinces to Paris.[5] Considerable amounts
of cash were also shipped from various provinces to Lyon, which
continued to function as a major payment center for the French
monarchy during the first half of the seventeenth century.

Mallet's figures include only the cash shipped to Paris (and Lyon)
and the "regular" assignations. The *bordereaux* did not list expenses for local and regional charges, the "irregular" assignations,
or the costs of collection. These last three categories, as we shall
see, made up an ever-increasing portion of the money spent.

These distinctions might seem to be enough to enable us to divide French revenues into categories such as net and gross, but in
fact, they are not. The great difficulty is that the various sorts of
expenditure, notably military outlays and debt service, were spread
out among the different categories. By excluding all charges paid at
the local and regional levels, we introduce wide regional disparities
and gloss over the idiosyncrasies of the French budgetary system of
the seventeenth century.

If we start with the figures of Mallet, we would get the French
monarchy having a "net" revenue from direct taxation of some 10
million l. under Henry IV (on gross revenues of some 16.5 million
l.), a rate of about 60 percent. By the late 1620s and early 1630s,
net revenue, so defined, would have been about 7 million l. (sometimes less) on levies of 28–35 million l.; that is, a return of 20 to
25 percent at the most (in the *pays d'élection*). As Mallet explains,
some missing money came into the Central Treasury in the form of
extraordinary revenues. In fact this extraordinary revenue was little
more than disguised direct taxation, levied on groups who were
theoretically exempt from such taxation. Most of the missing 75
percent went to the royal officers, largely in the form of the *droits
aliénés;* that is, the money was spent on debt service.

This brings us to the issue of net versus gross revenues and central versus regional and local expenses. The king borrowed vast
sums of money (well over 100 million l. from 1616 to 1633) by
means of the *droits aliénés* on the direct taxes. Should the money
spent on the interest to pay these *droits,* this financing of the national debt, not count toward the full central budget? Can we de-

5. AD Loire-Atlantique (ADLA), E 1188, private papers of Bernadin Poullain,
treasurer of the Estates of Brittany, covering payments to the Central Treasury in
1636–37. See pp. 130–31 for details.

duct this expense from gross income in our determination of net income? In his recent article on the subject, Alain Guéry does not do so when he discusses the eighteenth century. He stresses the importance of debt service as a portion of the central budget (over 50 percent of it in 1788). Indeed Guéry argues that debt service was the most important strain on *net* revenue in 1788.[6]

If we are to accept such principles for the eighteenth century, we must accept them for the seventeenth as well. The fact that the seventeenth-century monarchy borrowed in a different fashion from the eighteenth-century monarchy is no excuse for excluding debt service as a critical cost of the central government in the early seventeenth century.

The second major drain on the finances of the state in the seventeenth century was, of course, the military. All historians agree that military expenses should be counted against net revenue and that they should be considered a central government expense. The records reproduced by Mallet, and used by all subsequent historians, up to Guéry and Richard Bonney, carry specific listings for the various war treasurers: the *trésorier de l'extraordinaire de guerre*, the *trésorier de l'ordinaire de guerre*, the treasurers of the *marines* (navies) of the Levant and of Ponant, and the special *comptables* for artillery and fortifications. One of the most mistaken assumptions that one can make about the figures listed for these individuals on the *bordereau de l'Epargne* is that they represented all, or even almost all, of the money spent by the given individuals. A very significant part of the war budget was paid at the regional and local levels.

If we consider the *pays d'élection*, we find that the *taillon*, a tax levied for the payment of permanent men-at-arms, was paid as a regional charge. The same was true of the *crue des prévôts des maréchaussées* (constabulary tax). The king levied 1.8 million l. a year for these two taxes between 1600 and 1620; this amount represented 11 percent of total direct taxation. Can we really omit both this revenue and this expense from our consideration of the actions of the central government? Given that other men-at-arms costs were included in the budget carried on the *bordereau de l'Epargne*, can we really consider one set of men-at-arms a central

6. A. Guéry, "Les finances de la monarchie française sous l'ancien régime," *Annales E.S.C.* 33 (1978): 216–39.

expense and another set a regional expense? This point is particularly true given that the *taillon* was often spent for expenses incurred outside the area in which it was levied.

The *taillon* and the constabulary tax are easy enough for us to figure back into the budget because we know their size for each year. The real difficulty comes with on-the-spot military levies, such as *étapes*. In a province such as Provence or Dauphiné, most of the direct taxes would have been collected and spent in this fashion; none of this money would have appeared on the *bordereau de l'Epargne*. The problem of *étapes* was common both in *pays d'Etats* such as Dauphiné and in *pays d'élection* such as Champagne; other military expenses, however, were also paid for locally in the *pays d'Etats*. In Brittany the treasurer of the marine of Ponant alone received more money in some years than the Central Treasury was supposed to get as "net" revenue from Brittany. The king's half-brother, César of Vendôme, received a grant of 198,000 l. in 1626 to pay for the costs of outfitting ships for the king. We will say nothing here of the costs of defending cities and towns, which were covered by direct taxes on the towns' inhabitants and often on those people living in the surrounding countryside. The Central Treasury figures simply ignore all of this.

The situation is just as confusing with respect to other government services. Local royal courts were paid from seigneurial revenues; presidial courts were often paid from three sources—demesnes, salt taxes, and direct taxes. The Parlements were paid by salt tax revenues (Paris and Rouen), by general revenues (Aix, Grenoble, and Rennes), and even by wine taxes (Rennes). The one fact that all courts had in common was that their costs were not carried on the *bordereau de l'Epargne*. How can we say that the *gages* of the Parlement of Paris were not a genuine expense against net revenue?

In short, "net" revenue as defined by the *bordereau* (and Mallet and others) excludes the money used to pay the entire judiciary, the financial apparatus, most of the standing army, the mounted constabulary, some of the army and navy expenses (especially fortifications and *étapes*), and various ill-defined outlays, such as the *rentes* on the direct taxes held by the duke of Nevers (over 78,000 l. in 1620) and others on local and regional revenues. In addition, virtually all of the debt service of the state was paid in the form of *rentes* and *droits* that were not listed on the *bordereau*.

There can be no question that the government knew very well what was happening to this money. Colbert had access to the figures a half-century later: "From 1620 until 1633, they [direct taxes] were from 12 to 18 million, even 20; but the *droits aliénés* grew from 10 to 18 millions, which led to the conversion of these *droits* into *rentes.*"[7] Colbert was certainly right. In 1627 and 1628, for example, the *bordereau* listed 4.85 and 4.9 million l. in direct taxes in the *pays d'élection.*[8] The actual levies, excluding military surtaxes for *étapes*, were some 20 million l. in 1627 and 21 million l. in 1628. These figures represented 4.2 million l. in debt service through the *droits* and 13–14 million l. per year in spendable income from direct taxation. The levies for *étapes* in the time of the La Rochelle siege would, of course, have added considerably to these totals.

Spending the Tax Money

Local and regional charges.

A brief comparison between the figures given by local archival records for the *généralité* of Lyon between 1600 and 1634 and those given by Mallet for the same period will demonstrate the diminution in the receipts caused by local and regional charges. Of the total levied in the *généralité* from 1600 to 1610, *excluding* the 10 percent costs of collection, 24 percent was spent at the local and regional levels. If one includes the collectors' fees, the provincial costs were 30.85 percent (see Table 7).[9]

These figures, which show a median reduction of 29.8 percent at the provincial level, while alarming in themselves, are actually extremely low. Lyon had a higher percentage of its taxes listed on the *partie de l'Epargne* than most of the other *généralités* because there were only three *élections* in Lyon and the expense for officers was therefore quite low (Lyon ranked third among fifteen in portion carried on the *partie de l'Epargne* in 1620, see Table 8). It

7. G. P. Depping, ed., *Correspondance administrative . . .* , vol. 2 (Paris, 1850–54), 125.

8. Central figures from Mallet, *Comptes rendus*, 200–201.

9. J. Permézel, *La politique financière de Sully dans la généralité de Lyon* (Paris, 1935), app. I and AD Rhône, 8 C 32 to 8 C 41. Compare with Mallet, *Comptes rendus*, 186–87.

Table 7. *Share of the Central Treasury in Lyon, 1600–1634*

Year	Total Levied (in 000 l.)	Share of the Central Treasury as % of Total Levy
1600	652.3	69.5
1601	705.1	72.6
1602	699.6	73.0
1603	765.6	60.7
1604	662.2	70.3
1605	662.1	70.2
1606	662.1	71.7
1607	662.1	69.3
1608	649.0	73.0
1609	649.0	65.3
1610	649.0	65.8
—		
1617	755.5	61.5
1618	683.7	63.7
1619	695.1	58.3
1620	702.0	58.7
1621	1,030.1[a]	66.7
1622	767.6	65.6
1623	788.4	43.9
1624	716.4	66.3
—		
1626	762.5	70.5[b]
1627	817.2	23.2[c]
—		
1634	1,572.0	28.0

Sources: J. Permézel, *La politique financière de Sully dans la généralité de Lyon* (Paris, 1935), app. I. I have added the collection costs (10 percent). Figures for 1607 (BN, Ms. Fr. 16626, fols. 73–82); 1608 (AN, 120 AP 17); 1610 (AN, 120 AP 13, showing 654,400 l.) checked on archival sources. Figures for 1617–19 and 1621–27 from AD Rhône, 8 C 32 to 8 C 41. Figure for 1620 from BN, Ms. Fr. 16623, fols. 234–75v. Figure for 1634 from BN, NAF 200, fols. 1 and ff. Share of the Central Treasury from J. R. Mallet, *Comptes rendus de l'administration financière de la France* (London, 1789), checked, for 1605–10, on BN, Ms. Fr. 16627.

[a]The figure cited in local documents, 596,000 l. plus 2 s./l. (AD Rhône, 8 C 35, fols. 125v and 130v) is clearly wrong because the Central Treasury share was 678,380 l., the local and regional charges at least 221,000 l. more, and the *droits* roughly 15 percent.

[b]The total levied likely excludes unknown military levies, which makes this percentage too high.

[c]The sharp drop is probably due to the shifting of resources from the Central Treasury's share to direct payments to the war treasurer.

Table 8. *Share of the Central Treasury in Fifteen* Généralités, *1620*

Généralité	Share of the Central Treasury as % of Total Levy[a]
Caen	70.2
Bordeaux	70.2
Lyon	63.0
Poitiers	60.4
Riom	57.1
Rouen	55.1
Orléans	52.3
Bourges	52.0
Tours	49.7
Moulins	48.5
Soissons	38.6
Paris (1622)	37.4
Montpellier	34.6
Châlons	27.8
Amiens	23.9

Sources: BN, Ms. Fr. 16622, 16623, 16624.
Note: [a]These figures *exclude* the 10 percent collection costs at the parish level.

should also be pointed out that the period 1600–10 was one of relatively honest and efficient fiscal administration and one in which the *droits aliénés* did not exist. As for "irregular" assignations, under Sully the three years of highest local and regional expenses—1603, 1609, and 1610—were years in which military expenses in Lyon were highest. The military surtax (*crue*) of 1603 was the highest of this period, while 1609–10 saw the buildup of forces for the Cleves-Julich crisis. Lyon was the major payment center for both the Piedmont army and the Swiss mercenaries. Lyon's percentage of return to the Central Treasury remained high until the late 1620s.

The *brevets de la taille* for fifteen of the twenty-one *généralités* for 1620 (1622 for Paris) provide a bleaker, and much more accurate, representation of the normal rate of return, measured in the percentage listed as returning to the Central Treasury (*partie de l'Epargne*). Table 8 presents these percentages, excluding the collections costs, which would reduce them even further.

How can one explain the wide variations? First, the North and

Northeast had many more officers than the other areas; thus their local costs were higher. For example, the *élection* of Provins had a net revenue of only 48.9 percent; the rest of the money levied there went to officers' wages and local costs. Again, this excluded the 10 percent cost of collection. The areas such as Riom, which had only two full-scale *élections* and two subbureaus (*tabliers*), or Lyon, which had three large *élections,* paid far less for local costs. The *élections* in the *généralité* of Bordeaux were reestablished in 1621; only Périgord and the Agenais had *élus* in 1620, which partially explains the high rate of return there. The two Norman districts (Rouen and Caen), which rank first and sixth, had fewer *élus* per *élection* than the other areas: Amiens had 9.33/*élection,* Châlons, 8.67, Paris 9, while Caen had only 6.88 and Rouen 6.33.

One of the major differences between the northeastern provinces and the other provinces was that the costs of the *prévôt des maréchaussées* (mounted constabulary) and the *taillon* were far greater in the former area. The *taillon,* which was levied to pay the men-at-arms (garrisons), was only 3.7 percent of the money levied in Caen, while it was 14.7 percent in Châlons and 15.2 percent in Amiens. The mounted constabulary received only 1.1 percent in Caen, while getting 8.1 percent in Châlons and 7.4 percent in Amiens. Table 9 shows the figures for all the *généralités* and indicates the comparatively high level of the Northeast (Châlons, Amiens, Soissons, and Paris).

The cost of garrisons was higher in Châlons and Amiens because they were frontier provinces, but the reason for the higher mounted constabulary costs is perhaps less obvious. As a general rule, one of the major tasks of the provost and his archers was to keep order between the peasants and the soldiers. The larger garrisons of the Northeast would have required larger concentrations of the provost's men. Both the provost's levy and the *taillon* were listed on the regional charges and neither appears on the *bordereaux de l'Epargne.*[10]

To understand the complications of this system of payments, we can turn to specific provinces, in which there are records detailing the process. Before studying these provinces, however, we must first describe in more detail the charges paid at the local and regional

10. Compare the *états de la valeur des finances* for 1620, which list regional and local costs (BN, Ms. Fr. 16622, 16623, and 16624), with the *bordereaux* for various years found in Ms. Fr. 16627.

Table 9. Taillon *and Constabulary Tax as a Percentage of Total Levy in
          Thirteen* Généralités, *1620*

Généralité	Taillon	Constabulary Tax	*Taillon* and Constabulary Tax
Amiens	16.6	7.1	23.7%[a]
Châlons	15.3	8.2	23.5
Soissons	13.1	7.0	20.1
Paris (1622)	10.9	4.3	15.2
Moulins	9.0	5.1	14.1
Bourges	10.6	3.2	13.8
Bordeaux	10.9	2.5	13.4
Tours	7.7	4.4	12.1
Lyon	8.7	3.2	11.9
Orléans	7.8	3.6	11.4
Poitiers	7.1	2.7	9.8
Rouen	3.8	1.4	5.2
Caen	3.8	1.2	5.0
In *pays d'élection*	8.5	3.5	12.0

Sources: BN, Ms. Fr. 16622, 16623, 16624.
[a]The garrison tax was not levied in Amiens, which warps its figure somewhat.

level. It will then be possible to move to a consideration of specific provinces, and then back again to the general system.

The regional (*généralité*) and local (*élection*) charges included, not only the *taillon* and provost's wages, but postal costs (regional) and public works expenditure (local). In some districts the roads and bridges levy was a separate listing on the revenues and the expenses, while in others the revenue for it was simply lumped in with the *taille*. In all *élections* the revenue for postal service was a separate listing on the *brevet*, as were the *taillon* and provost's wages. The *taillon* went to a separate receiver; the other direct taxes went to the receiver of the *tailles*. In fact, the two offices were often held by the same man.

There were also *rentes* at both levels, *gages* of local and regional officers, and in some cases the *gages* of the Parlement.[11] All the judicial officers not paid by the salt tax revenues or demesne re-

11. The Parlements were often paid by salt taxes, although that was not always true. In Brittany the Parlement was paid by a mixture of regular revenues (that is, it was carried as a regional cost) and a special wine tax, the *petit devoir*.

ceipts were paid at the local or regional level. Local charges were almost exclusively *gages* and *rentes,* with some public works spending thrown in. Special expenses were sometimes added on, such as a surtax of 51,964 l. spent on dikes in the *généralité* of Châlons in 1620. At the lowest level, the parish, further special levies were often added by the peasants themselves. These additional levies could add as much as 2,000 l. to the parish's tax bill.[12]

The government spent considerable sums by assigning expenses to local and regional receipts and to their budgets. The best example is the *taillon,* carried as a separate listing on the *brevet* and paid to its own receiver. The listing for the *taillon* on the *bordereaux* was for the surplus revenue from the tax—that is, the money left over after the garrisons had been paid.[13]

Other taxes, particularly those levied for military purposes and those raised in the *pays d'Etats* were simply listed, not on the *bordereaux,* but on separate accounts by the official responsible for their expenditure—usually the war treasurer (*trésorier de l'extraordinaire de guerre*).[14] The most confusing aspect of these accounts is that the *bordereaux* listed payments made to the war treasurer among the regular expenses; these sums must not be taken as the total expenditure of that official, because he drew substantial sums from other sources.[15]

A third provincial expense not included in the *bordereaux* was the costs of collection. While some of these costs, such as the regular *gages* of the receivers or the *élus,* were included in the local and regional charges, other parts of the collections costs were not included in any accounts. The most important of these costs were the *droits aliénés.*[16] The *droits aliénés* were not listed on the *brevets*

12. AD Cher, C 985, fol. 64v, parish of Mougues levying 332 l. for church repair, fol. 66, parish of Estreches levying 350 l. for debts (both 1612).

13. BN, Ms. Fr. 16626 shows the *taillon* as 600,000 l. in 1607 (fols. 73v–82), noting expenses were only 153,000 l. BN, Ms. Fr. 16627 lists the *taillon* on the *bordereau de l'Epargne* for 1610 as 390,000 l.; for 1613 as 262,090 l.; and for 1614 as 430,000 l. The *taillon* did not vary; it was 1,528,000 l. in 1608 (AN, 120 AP 17), a figure that agrees with other citations throughout this period. The figure from the *bordereau* can only be for the amount remaining after the expenses officially paid by the *taillon* had been met for the given year.

14. There was also a *trésorier de l'ordinaire de guerre,* who met most of his expenses from the *taillon.* He seems to have been concerned primarily with certain garrisons.

15. J. Collins, "Taxation in Bretagne, 1598–1648" (Ph.D. diss., Columbia University, 1978), chap. 6 for examples.

16. AD Marne, C 2492, fol. 113v. For a similar office in Gisors AD Eure, C 196.

Table 10. *Local Charges as a Percentage of Total Expenses in Châlons,*
         1620

Election	Charges	Charges, Excluding Roads and Bridges Surtax
Châlons	41.0	32.4
Reims	26.1	17.4
Troyes	26.3	18.2
Langres	27.7	20.0
Chaumont	27.0	24.4
Sézanne	27.6	21.6
Rethel	50.4	42.4
Epernay	38.7	26.9
Vitry	42.3	32.3
Total	32.5	24.3

Sources: BN, Ms. Fr. 16623, fols. 190–230. For 1621, the figures are much the same:
AD Marne, C 2492 (Receipts only).

as a specific amount, but each *droit* was given in d./l. at the end of
the document. It was also listed separately on the parish roll.[17]

The problems raised by these three major omissions from the
bordereaux are considerable, and the use of Mallet can lead one to
believe that taxation went down after 1614, when, in fact, it rose
sharply. The increase was hidden in the three omissions from the
bordereaux, especially in the *droits aliénés.* Let us turn to these
three omissions, concentrating particularly on Champagne, to see
how this process worked.[18]

The main costs at the local level were *gages* and *rentes.* In Champagne, 55.1 percent of the local charges, excluding a special surtax
levied to repair local roads and bridges, went to the *gages* of the
local officers in 1620. The main regional charges were *gages,* police
costs, garrisons, *rentes,* and public works spending. We can see the
evolution of these various charges in the accounts of 1602 and
1620 for Champagne (Tables 10 and 11). The accounts of the two
years are remarkably similar and show how little local and regional
spending evolved during this period.

There was only a slight increase in the *élection* charges, but the

17. AD Haute-Vienne, C 145; AD Deux-Sèvres, C 511.
18. Much of this material was previously set out in Collins, "Sur l'histoire fiscale
du XVIIe siècle."

Table 11. *Accounts of Châlons in 1602 and 1620 (in 000 l.)*

	1602	1620
Receipts		
Taille	392	364
Taillon	98	98
Constabulary	52	52
Garrison tax[a]	40	117
Total receipts (includes others)	582	636
Droits	49	64
4d./l. for buildings, to king	10	
Expenses		
Regional charges	192	165
Local charges	151	155
Roads and bridges surtax[b]		52
Bureau des finances	41	51
Rentes	16	23
Share of the Central Treasury	152	184
Charges paid to Central Treasury	30	6
Total expenses	582	636

Sources: BN, Ms. Fr. 16623, fols. 190–230 (1620); AD Marne, C 2490, fols. 123–26 and 138–51 (1602). Published by A. Chamberland, "Le budget de la généralité de Châlons en 1602," *Revue Henri IV* 1(1905): 144–87. J. Collins, "Sur l'histoire fiscale du XVIIe siècle: Les impôts directs en Champagne entre 1595 et 1635," *Annales E.S.C.* (1979): 341–42 for a more detailed analysis.

[a]This amount is much lower than normal for the period. The range 90–100,000 l. was customary.

[b]This tax was levied only in 1620 (perhaps over two years).

costs of the *bureau des finances* went up 25 percent. The listing for *rentes* rose 6,000 l. at the regional level because of the creation of three payer-receivers and three controllers of *rentes*. The local and regional charges rose much more sharply after 1620. For example, the *bureau des finances* was augmented by two *trésoriers* in 1621, two more in 1626, four more in 1627, and five others by 1640: the ten *trésoriers* of 1620 became twenty-three by 1640.[19] By 1640, the *official* charges on the regional level were 264,000 l. and those at the local level 738,970 l. (including the new *droits*). The word *official* is stressed here because no one received anything like these amounts; the official levies were 2,064,004 l., yet, in 1639, as we

19. J.-P. Charmeil, *Les trésoriers de France à l'époque de la Fronde* (Paris, 1963), 11.

have seen in Chapter 2, the receiver general had not gotten a penny by mid-August.[20]

The regional charges were also increased in 1628 when the king raised the *taillon* and decreased the *taille*. The *taille* was the general-purpose direct tax, while the *taillon* was pegged to the wages of specific garrisons. The *taillon* was a regional charge, and since it covered a fixed expense, any increase in it was an increase in the surplus not covered by the Central Treasury accounts. The government did not have to account for the surplus because it was listed on the regional account as being paid to the *taillon* receiver.[21]

As one can see from Tables 8 through 13, one of the main problems of dealing with local and regional charges is that they varied greatly from one area to another. Table 12 shows the percentage of charges on each *élection* in the *généralité* of Châlons. The *rente* of the duke of Nevers on the *élection* of Rethel makes its charges more than 50 percent; his *rente* alone (22,307 l. 5s. 6d.) equals 32.65 percent of the money levied in the *élection*.

Tables 11 and 12 percent a slightly warped picture of the French system as a whole because Châlons had an unusually high level of local charges. The median level of local charges for sixteen *généralités* was about 15 percent. If one includes the special roads and bridges spending, only Montpellier had a higher level than Châlons; if one excludes that expense, Montpellier, Paris, and Moulins had a higher level. Table 13 shows the percentage of the total levied paid for local charges in the sixteen *généralités*.

Montpellier had the highest level because of the large number of *rentes* against the dioceses there; these *rentes*, worth 36,176 l. per year, were guaranteed by the Estates of Languedoc, whose credit was better than that of the king. The old *rentes* were even paid in full (27,123 l.).[22] Paris had the highest number of officers and the expenses included the costs of the two new *élus* added to each *élection* during 1622. Moulins had an enormous *rente*, equal to 17 percent of the total spent on local charges, paid to the duke of Nevers on the receipts of the *élection* of Nevers (26,667 l.) Similarly, the charges of Châlons were raised significantly by the *rente* the duke had on the receipts of Rethel (22,307 l.).

At the other end of the scale, Rouen and Caen, as we have seen,

20. AD Marne, C 2498.
21. AD Marne, C 2494, for examples.
22. BN, Ms. Fr. 16624, fols. 280–99v.

Table 12. *Local and Regional Charges as a Percentage of Total Expenses in Châlons, 1620*

Election	Officers	Local Charges Rentes	Duke of Nevers	Affranchissements
Châlons	19.6	10.4		
Reims	9.5	6.9		
Troyes	9.0	8.2		
Langres	15.4	3.7		
Chaumont	16.7	5.8		
Sézanne	14.1	3.5		
Rethel	6.6	1.6	32.7	
Epernay	18.2	6.8		
Vitry	9.3	12.9		8.1

Regional Charges Expense	% of Expenses
Bureau des finances	7.8
Taillon, constabulary, military	26.1
Other offices	3.4
Rentes	2.6
Pont Neuf	1.5
Total[a]	41.4
Local charges	31.3
Central Treasury	27.9

Source: BN, Ms. Fr. 16623, fols. 190–230.

[a]The additional 0.6 percent went to the Central Treasury, for unfilled offices (it was technically not part of the regular expenses of the *généralité*). The additional revenue came from the 24,000 l. of the *subvention des villes* (a special tax on towns, collected as a lump sum, raised as the town saw fit).

had fewer *élus/élection* than the other areas, while Nantes had no *élections* at all. There were only two receivers in each Breton diocese, thus the low charges (officers' *gages* were only 3.8 percent of direct taxation). Indeed if one includes all Breton direct taxation (some of it is left off the *brevet*), local charges there were only 6.8 percent. Bordeaux had only three *élections* at this time, only one of which had *élus*. (All of the districts, the *pays*, had receivers.) One need hardly point out that the reintroduction of the *élections* in 1621 raised the percentage of local charges in Bordeaux.

What happened to this money? As noted earlier, most of it went

Table 13. *Local Charges as a Percentage of Total Expenses in Sixteen*
           Généralités, 1620

Généralité	Local Charges
Montpellier	34.5
Paris (1622)	27.4
Moulins	25.7
Châlons[a]	24.3
Soissons	21.8
Amiens	18.7
Orléans	18.3
Tours	16.7
Bourges	13.9
Lyon	13.8
Riom	12.4
Poitiers	12.0
Rouen	11.8
Caen	11.6
Nantes	10.3
Bordeaux	9.4

Sources: BN, Ms. Fr. 16622, 16623, 16624.
[a]Excludes roads and bridges surtax, which would raise it to 32.5.

to the officers, *rentes,* and public works expenditure. The cost of
the 124 *élections,* 3 *tabliers,* and 13 *pays* in the 14 *généralités* of
Paris (20 *élections*), Soissons (7), Amiens (6), Châlons (9), Rouen
(21), Caen (9), Tours (14), Orléans (12), Poitiers (9), Riom (2, 2
tabliers), Moulins (8), Lyon (3), Bordeaux (1, 13 *pays*), and
Bourges (3, 1 *tablier*) was about 1.15 million l. in 1620. This figure
is about 7.7 percent of the total levied in those areas. The sum
includes two amounts, the spending for shipment (*port et voiture*)
and that for the costs of preparing the accounts (both the making
up of the account—*façon*—and the *épices* of the relevant Chamber
of Accounts) not necessarily spent within the *élection.* If one excludes these two amounts, 18,170 l. and 106,748 l., respectively,
the percentage of money spent for the running of the *élections* was
only 6.8 percent.[23]

The average cost of an *élection,* shipment and makeup included,

23. The *épices* paid to the Chamber of Accounts were fixed by custom. In most
cases they went to the Paris Chamber.

was about 8,000–8,500 l. (the higher figure if one excludes the *pays* of the Southwest), while the median figure was either 7,100 l. or 7,700 l., depending on whether one includes the *élections* of the *généralité* of Bordeaux. Because the cost of an *élection* was relatively fixed, there was a strong negative correlation between the amount of money levied and the percentage of local charges. The less money raised in an *élection*, the higher the percentage of local costs because the main component of those costs, *gages* and *droits,* was relatively limited in range. In the *généralité* of Amiens, for example, the correlation between the amount levied and the percentage of local charges in 1620 was $r = -0.93$, while in the *généralité* of Paris, in 1622, excluding the *élection* of Paris itself, it was $r = -0.69$. Most of the other districts lay within this range. If one takes the median as 7,700 l., and the standard deviation as 2,400 l., then some 60 percent of the *élections* lay within this range.[24]

Yet such statistics are virtually meaningless when applied to individual cases. The *généralité* of Rouen, for example, with its relatively streamlined staff and its high tax contribution, had a much lower cost per *élection* than the kingdom as a whole, and its size (roughly one of every seven *élections*) warps the figures for the system. Nineteen of its twenty-one *élections* paid less than the median cost; the median cost of its *élections* was only 5,948 l. At the other end of the scale, the areas of the Midi, with their enormous *élections* (there were only two *élections* and two subbureaus in Riom, for example), had tremendous nominal local charges because the *droits* paid to the officers were based on such large amounts of money. In the *élection* of Lower Auvergne, the total levied was 397,500 l., while in Forez it was 307,200 l. By way of contrast, in the tiny *élection* of Lyons in Normandy (60 parishes), the total levied was only 13,400 l. Officers' costs were three times higher in Forez (16,526 l.) than in Lyons (4,574 l.), but the proportion of local charges was obviously much higher in the latter (41 percent as against 13.7 percent in Forez).[25]

One can also see this relationship in the comparison of the fifteen largest *élections*, in terms of costs, as opposed to the fifteen smallest. The fifteen largest paid 22.2 percent of the total costs for

24. BN, Ms. Fr. 16622, 16623, 16624. The *élection* of Paris is excluded because it, alone among the *élections,* had substantial charges for the upkeep of the royal court and for royal officials located in Paris.

25. Number of parishes per *élection* from AN, 120 AP 17.

all of France (they represent 11.8 percent of the 127 *élections* dealt with here), while the fifteen smallest paid only 6.1 percent. In terms of the money levied, these fifteen largest contributed 25.9 percent of the money raised, while the other fifteen contributed only 5.0 percent. If we look at the figures in terms of parishes, however, the larger districts paid only 57 l./parish in costs, while the smaller ones paid 66.7 l. As a percentage of money levied, the parishes of the larger districts paid 7.5 percent, while the smaller ones paid 10.6 percent, for cost of officers.

The second greatest local cost was public works, a total of 611,600 l. in the fourteen *généralités*. The contributions ranged from 15,100 l. in Bordeaux to 98,500 l. in Paris (total for all local districts). Much of this money was spent on dike and levee maintenance: 136,000 l. was levied for that purpose, primarily in the *généralités* of Tours, Moulins, Orléans, Riom, and Bourges. In Tours a number of parishes received exemptions from direct taxation in return for upkeep of dikes and levees; these exemptions reduced local receipts by 16,425 l. In addition, money was raised in four *généralités* to pay 40,000 l. for the bridge at Amboise, while four other *généralités* contributed a like amount to the cost of the Pont Neuf in Paris. In Poitiers local expenditure also covered some 7,530 l. for maintenance of sea dikes.

The third great expense was the *rentes*. The total for the fourteen *généralités* was 248,000 l., but the distribution among them was very uneven. In Poitiers, for example, there were no local *rentes*. Almost 20 percent of this total was made up by two *rentes* held by the duke of Nevers on the *élections* of Rethel and Nevers (two family duchies). The *rentes* (1.65 percent), officers' costs (7.6 percent), and public works spending (4.1 percent) made up about 85 percent of the local charges; the remainder consisted of officers' *gages* unrelated to the tax system (usually local judicial offices), and, on occasion, demesne costs.

Cash shipped to Paris.

Most of the money collected for the Central Treasury was not shipped in cash to Paris. We have the exact figures for 1609, based on the figures for *port et voiture* for each *généralité,* and they indicate that only a third of the Central Treasury's share went to Paris; this amount would be only 20 percent of the total collection in 1609. Table 14 indicates that only Caen (84 percent), Rouen (82.1

Table 14. *Cash Shipped to Paris in 1609, as a Portion of the Share of the Central Treasury*

Généralité	% of Cash
Caen	84.0
Rouen	82.1
Tours	54.9
Bourges[a]	53.6
Nantes	42.0
Orléans	39.2
Châlons	31.5
Poitiers	30.3
Limoges	24.0
Bordeaux	22.9
Amiens	22.0
Dijon	5.0
Toulouse	4.9
Moulins	4.7
Montpellier	4.5
Soissons	3.6
Lyon	1.3
Riom	0.7

Source: BN, Ms. Fr. 16627, fols. 76v–80.
[a]The listing for Bourges, 253,950 l., is likely an error. I have used a figure of 153,950 l., but even that may be too high.

percent), Tours (54.9 percent), and Nantes (42 percent) shipped more than 40 percent of their *partie de l'Epargne* to Paris in coins. Roughly half the money shipped to Paris (1.68 million l. of 3.4 million l.) came from Normandy.[26]

The large volume of money from Normandy represents the proximity of that area to Paris and the consequent lower shipping costs, as well as the easy access of Normandy to Spanish bullion. It is clear, as Jean Meuvret has pointed out, that cash moved from west to east in France. The Loire area shows a medium percentage of cash shipped to Paris, while the frontier provinces—Soissonais, Burgundy, Dauphiné, Provence—shipped virtually nothing to Paris (less than 20,000 l. for all four combined). Since 1609 was a year of military buildup, the document may represent a lower level of

26. BN, 500 Colbert 106.

cash return than peacetime years would, especially in the North-east.

The receipts of Riom, Moulins, Lyon, Montpellier, and Toulouse were spent locally and at Lyon. Throughout the sixteenth and early seventeenth centuries, Lyon was a major payment center of the monarchy. For example, the treasurer of the Swiss and Grisons was assigned 1.2 million l. for his expenses in 1602, and he received the money from the following districts: Moulins (225,000 l.); Riom (450,000 l.); Lyon (240,000 l.); Montpellier (120,000 l.); Bourges (50,000 l.). In addition, he received assignations on the *pancarte* receipts of Limoges, Bourges, Poitiers, and Riom for 65,000 l. and on those of Moulins for 27,000 l.[27] Richard Gascon has stressed the importance of the Limoges-Lyon route in the sixteenth-century international trade pattern; there is little reason to doubt that this axis, leading receipts from Bordeaux, Poitiers, and Limoges to Lyon, was a major method of funneling cash to Lyon in the seventeenth century.[28]

A listing of 1629 *quittances de l'Epargne,* representing cash payments of various *généralités,* also shows a low rate of cash return: 20.3 percent for the *partie de l'Epargne* of the kingdom as a whole (excluding Brittany). This list (Table 15) shows Caen and Rouen to be the big contributors once again, but both their percentage of the *partie de l'Epargne* delivered in cash and their share of the total cash shipments declined sharply. The document also lists *mandements,* orders to pay, and here we find Lyon (307,613 l.), Caen (225,701 l.), and Rouen (207,554 l.), among the leaders, with Brittany (389,000 l.) now figuring prominently on the list.[29] This list accounts for another 25 percent of the *partie de l'Epargne,* so the document covers slightly less than half of that total for 1629.

The types of coins used in the different parts of the kingdom also reflected the regional economic systems. In the East one finds primarily French coins: for example, in the *généralité* of Châlons some 60 percent of the coins shipped from the *élections* to Châlons itself were one-quarter *écu* pieces (15 s.), and most of the rest was in francs and half-francs.[30] From 1624 to 1628, such shipments of

27. BN, Ms. Fr. 10839, fols. 103–9.
28. R. Gascon, *Grand commerce et vie urbaine au XVIe siècle: Lyon et ses marchands* (Paris, 1971), fig. 1 and p. 163.
29. AN, P 3438.
30. AD Marne, C 2530.

Table 15. Quittances de l'Epargne *for Cash Delivered to Paris and Elsewhere*, 1629

| | | | | Cash to Paris as % of: | |
Généralité	Cash to Paris	Cash to . . .		Share of Central Treasury	All Taxes
Paris	265,783			49.4	14.0
Soissons	28,300			35.3	3.8
Châlons	38,500			38.5	4.0
Amiens	23,170			21.9	4.8
Bordeaux	4,883	Montauban	270,000[a]	0.4	0.02
		Bordeaux	7,811	23.2	17.1
Montpellier	0	Béziers	1,500	0.0	
Toulouse	0	Toulouse	16,795	0.0	
Dauphiné	6,000			8.9	
Provence	0	Aix	5,000	0.0	
Burgundy	18,000	Dijon	2,250	8.5	
Rouen	205,000			25.3	7.9
Caen	275,000			37.6	19.3
Orléans	162,500	Orléans	6,116	45.2	11.3
Tours	145,000			23.1	8.0
Bourges	0			0.0	0.0
Moulins	25,000	Moulins	2,637	13.8	3.2
Poitiers	153,545			19.0	8.4
Riom	107,610			25.1	9.3
Lyon	33,300			9.6	4.2
Limoges	145,000	Limoges	26,000	26.0	9.5
		Avignon	170,000[a]	61.1	22.3
Brittany	0			0.0	

Sources: AN, P 3438. On share of the Central Treasury, J. R. Mallet, *Comptes rendus de l'administration financière de la France* (London, 1789). The estimates of total direct taxation are based on extrapolations from the known figures of 1620 and 1634, and from the known figures for 1629 for Caen, Châlons, Lyon, and Bordeaux. The figures must therefore be treated as orders of magnitude, although they are probably fairly close to the actual ones because the extrapolations from both directions are usually quite close.

coins were 150–200,000 l. per year, of which only 30–45,000 l. went on from Châlons to Paris. In Brittany, though, two-thirds of the money collected in the parishes of the westernmost bishopric, Léon, came in as réals and other Spanish coins.[31] Indeed Pierre Jakez Héliaz notes in his memoirs of life in a western Breton village in the early twentieth century that old Breton peasants still figured sums in réals and Spanish coins at that time.[32]

The relatively small portion of the *partie de l'Epargne* shipped to Paris in the form of cash must make us wonder about specie drainage from the countryside. The Champenois example indicates that specie tended to stay in its region of origin, although one must admit that Champagne was an area in which the monarchy spent a great deal of cash (for military purposes). If we take another example, that of one of the chief specie suppliers, Brittany, we see a similar phenomenon. Let us examine two examples: in 1606 and 1635–36.

In 1606, the receiver general of Brittany, René Sain, noted on his *état au vrai* that he had shipped 86,678 l. to Paris of a total budget of 568,624 l. (15.2 percent). Even this larger amount fell far short of the actual level of taxation because certain taxes were alienated and the document does not include the special taxes voted by the Estates. The cost of shipping the 86,678 l. to Paris was 1,936 l.: eighteen horses, carrying 5,000 l. each, taking twenty-four days to reach Paris—1,296 l. (3 l./day) and 640 l. for four trips by *commis*, at 5 l./day and thirty-two days per trip.

The matter was, however, more complicated than these simple figures suggest. Sain's *commis*, Jehan Jonneaux, was taking 19,226 l. to Paris when he stopped at Ancenis on 15 November 1606. He submitted evidence that he did not see the thief, since it was 5:30 at night, and that the thief made off with 3,000 l. The king refused to accept this excuse because "les deniers du Roy doibvent estre voicturer entre deux soleils." The costs of the investigation and trial were 600 l.[33]

The second case, from 1635–36, is still more informative. It concerns the account rendered by Jean Guilbaud, *commis* of Bernadin

31. ADLA, B 3011.
32. P.-J. Hélias, *The Horse of Pride: Life in a Breton Village* (New Haven, 1979).
33. BN, Ms. Fr. 10839, fols. 248–68, "état au vrai" for 1606, by René Sain, receiver general of Brittany, approved 6 March 1608.

Poullain, treasurer of the Estates of Brittany. Guilbaud was Poullain's representative in Paris. The total receipts were 1.81 million l., of which 64,455 l. (3.6 percent) were shipped in cash: *pistoles, écus, quart d'écus,* with an emphasis on the *pistoles* (28,572 l. of 29,572 l. described).[34] Most of the money came in the form of paper: letters of exchange and blanks of the Central Treasurer. The blanks of the Central Treasury accounted for some 925,278 l. (51 percent) in *quittances* and *mandements.* The letters of exchange were usually drawn on Rouen, by means of merchants of Morlaix—354,323 l. (19.5 percent)—or by letters directly from those involved in the office of treasurer of the Estate—406,400 l. (22.4 percent).[35]

These two examples make it seem quite likely that paper money, either in Central Treasury documents (*mandements* or *quittances* of the Central Treasurer) or, somewhat later, letters of exchange, took pride of place over cash in the regulation of French tax payments going from the regional centers to the Central Treasury. We must therefore question the old assumption that high tax levels meant a specie drainage in the direction of Paris. Very little cash seems to have been involved in regulation of payments to Paris, even in provinces such as Brittany, which had substantial mint output.

Assignations.

Because so little money was shipped to Paris, the rest of the king's share of the direct taxes had to be spent at the local level. By giving his creditors assignations, the king shifted the burden of obtaining payment of this money from himself to someone else. Sully carried this policy to an extreme, as he attempted to assign all ex-

34. ADLA, E 1188, papers of Bernadin Poullain.

35. The financial obligations of the post of treasurer of the Estates of Brittany had become so great by 1635 that the treasurer associated others in his office (including his subsequent successor, César de Renouard). The problem of specie drainage in general is best treated in two articles by Jean Meuvret: "Circulation monétaire et utilisation économique de la monnaie dans la France du XVIe et XVIIe siècles," *Etudes d'histoire moderne et contemporaine* 1 (1947): 15–28; and "Comment les Francais du XVIIe siècle voyaient l'impôt," *XVIIe Siècle* 25–26 (1955): 59–82. James Riley, in a paper, "Ideology at Odds with Evidence: The *Annales* School and Old Regime Material Life," given at the Indiana University Economic History Workshop (9 September 1982), has argued that there was not a constant cash drainage from the countryside (that, in fact, the very idea is logically impossible). My thanks to Professor Riley for a copy of this paper.

penses to specific revenues at the beginning of the year. This effort was partially successful during the stable years of Henry IV, but proved too inflexible in the more uncertain conditions prevailing after his death.[36]

The regular assignations were the manner in which money was paid to almost everyone. There was a certain logic to the manner in which this policy was handled. For example, in 1629, we find a *mandement* for 389,000 l. drawn on the receipts of Brittany; it is made out to the treasurer of the Navy for the cost of ships outfitted in Brittany. Similarly, the garrison at Rouen was paid from the receipts of Caen, as were the garrisons of Lower Normandy. Bread and grain for the armies fighting in Languedoc were paid for by *mandements* on nearby *généralités*—such as Poitiers and Riom. Nobles were paid their pensions in areas in which they had some ties: the prince of Condé, governor of Burgundy, received a *mandement* of 40,000 l. on the receipts there, and another 80,000 l. on the receipts of Moulins (for the Bourbonnais, a family stronghold). Similarly, the large landholdings of the princess of Condé (by birth a Montmorency) in Normandy led to her receipts of 20,000 l. there.[37] Sully, whose holdings were in the Midi, received assignations on Poitiers and Bourges.[38]

It is difficult to distinguish these regular assignations from the irregular ones. The *rentes* assigned to major nobles can be one example of the latter. For instance the duke of Nevers received *rentes* on the *généralités* of Orléans, Bourges, and Moulins and on the *élections* of Clamécy, Nevers, and Rethel. The total paid in these six locations was 79,390 l. 11s. 4d.[39]

Two major points may be made about these *rentes* held by Nevers: (1) as we noted earlier, the two largest *rentes,* on Nevers and Rethel, were assigned to *élections* within family duchies, and (2) these *rentes* have nothing to do with his regular pensions. The king preferred to give these *rentes,* and regular assignations as well, to the major nobles in areas in which they had some influence; this arrangement made it easier for them to collect the money, because

36. B. Barbiche, *Sully* (Paris, 1980) and D. Buisseret, *Sully and the Growth of Centralized Government in France* (London, 1968) both describe this process under Sully.

37. BN, Ms. Fr. 16624.

38. AD Cher, C 985, fol. 79.

39. BN, Ms. Fr. 16622, 16623, 16624, *brevets* of 1620.

the local officials would likely have some clientele ties to them. As for the pensions, Nevers received 6,000 l. as governor of Champagne, 7,000 l. for other offices, and 30,000 l. ("rest and perfect acquittal of 450,000 l.") for his marriage to the duchess of Longueville. These pensions were duly noted on the accounts of the Central Treasury.[40]

The major form of irregular assignations, however, was the effort to have money from a given *généralité* assigned to a creditor of the Crown or to another *comptable* (other than the Central Treasurer), usually the war treasurer. These assignations were easiest with special increases in the *crue* in the *pays d'élection* and with the free gifts (*dons gratuits*) in the *pays d'Etats*. The Central Treasurer himself seized the receipts of the *Convoi de Bordeaux* (an import-export tax) in 1628 to help finance the siege of La Rochelle.[41] The seizures of direct tax revenues were even larger.

The king also ordered many special surtaxes fo military or other needs. An army surtax of 81,200 l. was levied in the *généralité* of Châlons in 1621, and 28,700 l. was assessed there in 1626 for repayment of *étapes*.[42] *Etapes* of 87,141 l. were levied in 1627 and repaid in 1630; 63,500 l. was hurriedly raised in the *élections* of Langres, Chaumont, and Bar-s-Aube in 1630 to pay the Swiss; the cavalry surtax of 1634 was supposed to be 196,800 l. in Châlons, roughly 5 million l. in the kingdom as a whole. None of the money collected for such taxes was accounted for on the *bordereau;* they were assigned directly to the receiver in question, who then presented a separate account for them.[43]

While we have some indications about these massive military levies, particularly those raised on a national scale, we know much less about the more constant parish level surtaxes. Sometimes such levies involved outside obligations: the prince of Condé received 500 l. from the parish of Conti in 1620.[44] The *élection* of Figéac, in Quercy, levied surtaxes for all manner of needs: 24,297 l. in 1611 and 1612 for suppression of offices; 2,967 l. in 1613 for the entry

40. BN, 500 Colbert 106.
41. Y.-M. Bercé, "La bourgeoisie bordelaise et le fisc sous Louis XIII," *Revue Historique de Bordeaux* 13 (1964): 55.
42. AD Marne, C 2492–2499 has many examples. C 2492, fol. 111 (1621); C 2494, fol. 39v (1626).
43. AD Marne, C 2495, fol. 141; BN, Nouvelles Acquisitions Françaises (NAF), 200.
44. AD Somme, C 1702.

of the prince of Condé into Cahors and Montauban; 12,603 l. for the debts of the *pays* of Quercy in 1628 (and a lesser sum for that purpose virtually every year); 21,568 l. 8s. 10d. for damages done to the property of three of the newly instituted *élus* of Figéac in 1625; 10,803 l. for Figéac's share of the munitions costs of the army that had besieged Montauban in 1622 (levied in 1625).[45]

The records of the *généralités* of Bourges, Lyon, and Châlons show that similar patterns prevailed in those districts. In Bourges, sixty-five parishes obtained grants for special levies in 1612–13: twenty-one for 300–350 l.; thirteen for over 200 l.; and two more for over 400 l.[46] The amounts in these sixty-five parishes ranged from under 100 l. to one levy of 2,127 l. In the *généralité* of Lyon, one finds many similar cases. The syndics of the *pays* of the Lyonnais, of Forez and of the Beaujolais usually raised an annual sum for their needs: in 1618, 3,150 l. in the Beaujolais; in 1619, 6,476 l. for the Lyonnais.[47] Bourg-Argental levied 3,996 l. in 1616 to pay men-at-arms stationed there; two years later, it raised 584 l. for the same purpose.[48] In 1618, parish levies ranged from 46 l. 4 s. in St-Martin-en-Haut, to 3,563 l. 10 s. for the demolition of the chateau of Thisy.[49] In 1616, sixty-four parishes received permission for extra levies ranging from 30 l. to 2,000 l.: under 100 l.—eight parishes; 100–199 l.—twenty-six; 200–299 l.—five; 300–399 l.—nineteen; 400–499 l.—three; over 500 l.—three (1,200 l., 1,403 l., and 2,000 l., respectively). Three years later, St-Cire-au-Mont-d'Or levied 2,045 l. for two new church bells.[50] The king himself introduced a new local levy into the Lyonnais in 1620: he replaced mandatory service on the repairs of the walls of Lyon with a levy of 15,000 l. (30,000 man-days of labor at 10 s. per day) on the Lyonnais.[51]

In the *généralité* of Châlons, one finds taxes to repair local levees

45. AD Gironde, C 4832.

46. AD Cher, C 985, contains listings for each parish.

47. AD Rhône, 8 C 33, fol. 1 on the Beaujolais; 8 C 35, fol. 28 on Lyonnais; 8 C 35, fol. 22v, shows 4,324 l. levied for the syndics of Forez in 1619.

48. AD Rhône, 8 C 32, fol. 2 (1616); 8 C 33, fols. 3v–4 (1618).

49. AD Rhône, 8 C, fol. 7 (St-Martin); fols. 117–17v (Thisy).

50. AD Rhône, 8 C 32 on 1616; 8 C 35, fol. 12 on St-Cire.

51. AD Rhône, 8 C 33, fol. 41v on *corvée* for Lyon walls in 1618, 8 C 35, fols. 36–37, letters of 1620 converting labor to direct tax. In 1619, the king also created, at the request of the syndics of the Lyonnais, a company of twenty mounted arquebusiers to ensure the safe passage of men-at-arms in the *pays*. The cost was 10,000 l. a year for ten years.

(11,666 2/3 l. in both 1630 and 1631); to repair the king's demesne at Mouzon (8,783 l. plus interest in 1630); to pay the town debts of Langres, Mouzon, and Chaumont (33,363 l. from 1628 to 1631); to repair the town bell of Bar-s-Aube (3,000 l. in 1630 and 1631); and to repair local bridges. The list is virtually endless. None of this money was listed on the *bordereau*.[52]

There were other special levies in Champagne in 1630–31: an indemnity of 10,100 l. in the new *élection* of Bar-s-Aube to compensate the officers of Vitry, Troyes, Langres, and Chaumont for loss of jurisdiction; a surtax of 70,000 l. for the destruction of the forts at La Rochelle and St-Martin-de-Ré (of 1.5 million l. nationwide); the surtax for levees, itself part of a nationwide total of 560,000 l. As with the parish surtaxes, these amounts were not listed on the *bordereau*, even when, as in the case of the levy for the destruction of the forts, they were levied nationwide for a central government expense.[53]

The droits aliénés.

The local and regional charges, the assignations of revenues to third parties, the decrease in the *taille* to increase the *taillon*, and the extra levies were all important reasons for the "hidden" increase in French taxation, but the rapid increase after 1620 cannot be fully explained by these devices. The most important new charge put on the taxpayers of France after 1616 was the *droits aliénés*. From a surcharge of 10 percent in 1616, the *droits* rose to equal more than 85 percent of the principal of the *tailles* in 1634 (proposed levy).[54] A comparison of the *brevets de la taille* for Châlons in 1620, 1625, and 1634 will demonstrate the extensive use of this means to raise money between 1616 and 1634.

The *tailles* of 1620 were encumbered by a surtax of 10 percent: 1s./l. for the *commissaires des tailles* created in 1616, 4d./l. for the master clerks and guards of the petty seals created in 1618, and 8d./l. for the parish collectors. This surtax did not represent any increase over the earlier levels, however, because the *sou* of the *commissaires* was the original one of the collectors for the costs of

52. AD Marne, C 2492 to 2499.
53. AD Marne, C 2494, fols. 141 and ff. on levee repair (560,000 l. over two years), C 2493, fol. 211 on fort destruction.
54. BN, NAF 200. This is corroborated by provincial documents, such as AD Calvados, 4 C 392; AD Marne, C 2495, fol. 122v; AD Gironde, C 4832.

collection (writing costs, paper, and so on). The 4d./l. of the master clerks and guards of the petty seals was the 4d./l. the king had taken for building repairs in 1595; it was sold to these officers in 1618.

In 1621, 8d./l. was added to the *droits* for the *greffiers* of the *élections* (6d./l.) and the *greffiers des affirmations* (4d./l.—of which 2d./l. was taken from the 8d./l. of the collectors). This 8d./l. was included in the regional charges on the *tailles* in both 1622 and 1623 (indeed in those areas where the officers had not yet paid for it, the king collected it for himself), but it was declared part of the *droits aliénés* in 1624.[55] By 1625, the *droits* were a surtax of 58d./l. (24.2 percent). The major additions were s./l. for a second *commissaire des tailles* (this office was sold by parish) in 1624 (6d./l. from the hereditary sergeants created in 1621 and suppressed in 1624 and 6d./l. from the collectors) and 10d./l. for the *greffiers* (3d./l. each) and master clerks (2d./l. each) of each *élection*.

The *droits* continued to grow from 1625 to 1634, reaching 125d./l. on the *tailles* in 1634 (52 percent). The *droits* were also levied on each other, but precisely in what manner it is impossible to say. The *commissaire des tailles* got their s./l. on everything right from the start, but it is unclear if others did.[56] A *traité* of 31 October 1633 sold Martin Violette the right to sell to the *greffiers* and master clerks the *droits* of their offices on the *tailles* for the other *droits* as well. He also got an earlier (1631) *traité* to do the same to the *commissaires des tailles* for their 12d./l. (can one guess here that they were being sold the 12d./l. on all *droits* created after their offices—that is, after 1616 and 1621, respectively?). In return for this privilege, Violette gave the king 400,000 l. in cash and promised to pay him 6 million l. in 1634 in six bimonthly payments.[57]

This practice had obviously been an ongoing process, since the Estates of Normandy complained in 1629 that:

> If we complain, with reason, of the great and excessive *tailles* demanded of us, we have even more subject to redouble our complaints, in that they are levied and collected with surcharges (*frais*) as excessive and

55. AD Marne, C 2492, fol. 200v; C 2493, fols. 58–60 and 152–54v.
56. AD Somme C 1702; AD Haute-Vienne, C 400. The *commissaires des tailles* got their *sou/livre* on everything because it had originally belonged to the parish collectors (to pay for the cost of drawing up the rolls—paper, candles, and so on), who always received their percentage on the total levy.
57. BN, Ms. Fr. 18205, fols. 178–80.

onerous, or more, than the *taille* itself, and this, in the name of a worthless group of officers ("un tas d'officiers de néant"), such as *commissaires des tailles et des vivres, greffiers des affirmations,* guards of the petty seals, and other similar ones, the which, like caterpillars, born to no other effect than for gnawing on and ruining your people, carry off, by their hereditary *taxations,* the best revenue ["le plus beau et meilleur" part—thus best in the sense of from the surest part, from the best part—perhaps profit—and in the sense of the better part of the taxes] of the province, and this, under the pretext of having financed a few pennies to the Central Treasury, from which they take back excessive usuries, the greater part [of the officers] only possessing these rights at the *denier huict ou neuf* [i.e., they paid only eight or nine times the value of their right, not the official rate of ten], *et le plus hault à dix,* now it seems by the letters patent sent by Your Majesty to open this assembly, it is mandated that these *droits* will be levied the one on the other, which is properly to levy the *droit* of a *droit.*[58]

Yet it is unclear how this was done. For the *brevets* of 1634, the process seems to have been to make a doubling on the principal of the *taille* alone. In Champagne, for example, the *droits* are determined on the basis of 125d./l. of 850,000 l.; the *tailles,* 525,000 l., plus the *taille* alone, 325,000 l., added a second time. A similar base of calculation was used in the other *généralités.* There is no evidence that such a basis was used, and one may perhaps speculate that it was done simply to ease the mathematical intricacies of determining how much each *droit* would have to be.[59]

There were also *droits* levied on parts of the whole, such as the 12d./l. of the receivers of the *taille,* assessed only on the *taille* and the *crue des ponts et chaussées,* of the 9d./l. of the receiver of the *taillon,* levied only on that tax.

The 125d./l. did not include the 6d./l. given back to the collectors in 1626, presumably because they proved somewhat reticent to perform their odious task without being paid for it. Indeed the Estates of Normandy had complained of the situation there in 1626:

Today, Sire, one has entirely taken from the collectors the said 20 pence, which is properly each year to ruin two of your subjects in each parish

58. C. de Robillard de Beaurepaire, *Cahiers des Etats de Normandie, règnes Louis XIII et Louis XIV,* vol. 2 (Rouen, 1888), 150–51.
59. BN, NAF 200. This issue is a very vexing one, but there seems to be no other explanation for the totals given in the documents.

Table 16. Droits Aliénés *in Champagne, 1620–34*

Year	*Droits* (in d./l.)	%	Total Paid (in 000 l.)	Total as % of Taxes Levied
1620	24	10.0	63.1	9.1
1621	38	15.8	110.5	13.7
1622	48	20.0	132.4	16.7
1623	58	24.2	161.2	19.5
1624	58	24.2	147.1	19.5
1625	58	24.2	147.1	19.5
1626	58	24.2	154.0	19.5
1627	64[a]	26.7	191.3	23.0
1628	64	26.7	200.5	23.0
1629	78	32.5	251.5	26.4
1630	78	32.5	397.2	34.1
1631	83	34.6	363.3	36.9
1632	117	48.8	510.3	44.4
1633	119	49.6	558.3	45.6
1634	125	52.1	557.0[b]	42.7

Sources: AD Marne, C 2490–2499, for 1621–1633; BN, Ms. Fr. 16623, fols. 190–230 for 1620; BN, NAF 200 for 1634. This table is adapted from a more detailed table in J. Collins, "Sur l'histoire fiscale du XVIIe siècle: Les impôts directs en Champagne entre 1595 et 1635," *Annales E.S.C.* (1979).
[a]From this point, there was also 6d./l. for the parish collectors.
[b]Plus an unknown share of the cavalry tax of 196,200 l.

and render them all miserable, and, by the revolving of a certain number of years, to put them, one after the other, all in a sack, to deprive you of both *tailles* and collectors.[60]

The monetary importance of the *droits* (listed below, Table 17) can be seen from the evolution in Champagne between 1620 and 1634 (Table 16). They were 63,000 l. in 1620, up to 150,000 l. in 1625, and more than 557,000 l. projected for 1634. The *droits* of 1634 were 463,000 l. on *tailles* of 525,600 l., 93,900 l. on the *grande crue* of 222,100 l., and an unspecified amount on a cavalry surtax of 196,200 l. The collectors would have gotten 6d./l. on all of this, a further 37,600 l.: the total levied would thus have been

60. De Beaurepaire, *Cahiers,* 102.

Table 17. *Droits Aliénés, 1634*

Droit	Owner
10d./l.	Petty seal holder (1618, 1622, 1632)
6d./l.	*Greffier* (1620)
4d./l.	*Greffier des affirmations* (1621)
10d./l.	*Greffiers* (2), master clerks (2) (1623); *greffiers* get 3d./l. each, clerks 2d./l. each
12d./l.	Three *commissaires des vivres* (1622, 1634)
24d./l.	*Commissaires des tailles* (1616, 1624)
6d./l.	Three *commissaires des droits aliénés* (1629, 1631, 1632)
ob./l.	Clerks of the *bureau des finances*
ob./l.	Controllers of the *greffes* (1632)
d./l.	Controllers of the *élections* (1632)
6d./l.	*Elus* (1627, 1632)
12d./l.	Three *greffiers* of the *élections* (1629)
12d./l.	Officers of the *élections* (1632)
12d./l.	Controllers of the apportionment and collection of *tailles* (1632)
4d./l.	Controllers of the *commissaires des tailles* (1633)
3d./l.	Three controllers of *élections* (1632)
2d./l.	Receivers of the *tailles* (1633)
12d./l.	Receivers of the *tailles*, on the *taille* and roads and bridges levy only: 4d./l. "ancien"; 4d./l. (1629, 1633)
9d./l.	Receivers of the *taillon*, on *taillon* only: 6d./l. "ancien"; 3d./l. (1629)
3d./l.	Controllers of the receivers of the *droits aliénés* (on the *droits* only) (1633)

Sources: BN, NAF 200. For individual *généralités*, there are many illustrations, such as AD Gironde, C 3990, for Bordeaux in 1629.

1,537,700 l. (by way of comparison, Mallet gives a return from Châlons in 1634 of 93,000 l.).[61]

The pattern we have followed in Champagne was also true in Normandy, where the *droits* were s./l. in 1618 (for the *commissaires*), and 3s. 6d./l. in 1622, including the 6d./l. of the collectors.[62] This latter amount represents a number of adjustments in the period prior to 1622, and further Norman documentation shows how it changed down to 1634. The collectors got their 8d./l. fees and 12d./l. for the costs. In 1616, the *commissaires des tailles* got this s./l. for the costs; they, in turn, were responsible for paying these

61. BN, NAF 200; Mallet, *Comptes rendus.*
62. AD Calvados, 4 C 392; 4 C 393.

costs. The collectors lost 2d./l. to the *greffier des affirmations* in
1621 and the final 6d./l. to the second *commissaire des tailles* in
1624. They received a new 6d./l. in 1626, and in 1630, the king
added a new 2d./l. to bring them back up to 6d./l. again (indicating
that he had sold 2d./l. of the amount given to them in 1626 to
someone else).[63]

There were other local costs as well. The parish roll for Dournazac in the Limousin, for 1623, gives the following list: 6d./l. each
to the *greffier, commissaire des vivres,* sergeant of the parish, and
collectors; 8d./l. to the guards of the petty seals; 4d./l. to the *greffier
des affirmations;* 2 *sous* for the seal; 1 l. 6s. for the verification of
signatures on the roll (to the *greffier*); 1 l. 12s. for the *bordereau*
(to same); bringing of the *quittances* from the receiver, 2 l. 10s.; six
payments of 2s. 6d. to the *greffier,* 15 s. The entire process was
repeated for the *taillon,* the *crue,* and two special levies, of 14 l.
and 9 l. 18s., for the marshals Epernon and Schomberg. The *commissaires des tailles* got 12d./l. on everything. In this case the parish
paid a surtax of some 5 percent for special costs totally unrelated
to the *droits aliénés;* they had to pay for services rendered, such as
the affixing of the seals.[64]

The *droits* were sold at the *denier 10,* or ten times their annual
value. The sales were handled by *traitants,* and often the same individual bought all the offices in a given jurisdiction and then resold
them. For example, in Picardy, André Le Sellier, controller general
of the *bouettes des monnaies de France,* bought all of the offices of
commissaires des tailles in 1625.[65] These *droits* were hereditary.
The officers were forced to buy them, and the king made it clear
that he would sell them to a third party if the given officer did not
buy them.

A clear example of this practice was the sale of 2d./l. to the receivers of the *fouages* in Brittany in 1624–26.[66] The letters of creation specifically stated that the *droit* was separate from the office
and could be bought by any outsider. A lawsuit involving the receiver general of Brittany, Guillaume Martin, and Nicolas Vauguin,
who had lent Martin 13,160 l. (of 23,160 l. needed) to purchase
this *droit,* determined that Vauguin was entitled to a proportional

63. AD Marne, C 2492–2494.
64. AD Haute-Vienne, C 145.
65. AD Somme, C 1702.
66. ADLA, B 74, fol. 187.

split of the *droit* in question, rather than the even division demanded by Martin. In the case of certain bishopric receivers, the 2d./l. was purchased as late as 1633, by a new occupant of the office.[67] There can hardly be better proof that the *droits* were a form of forced loan or *rente*.

The king made this point even clearer in February 1634, when he abolished the *droits aliénés* and converted them into 8 million l. worth of *rentes sur l'Hôtel de Ville de Paris*. These *rentes* were to be paid by a special surtax to be levied in place of the *droits*, which had been 12.75 million l. in 1634, excluding the portion of the cavalry surtax earmarked for the officers. Bercé claims that "by this partial bankruptcy, the superintendants of finances hoped to diminish the diversion of the *tailles* for the (personal) profit of the officers."[68]

If that was the case, the government could certainly count on public support for an end to the *droits*, as this anonymous complaint of 1636 shows:

> and if one can see the cessation of useless and superfluous expenses, the payment of pensions and *gages* of the officers newly created since the beginning of this reign, with all of the small ("menuz") *droits* introduced as surtaxes to the *tailles*, [these *droits*] invented solely for the ruin of the people.[69]

The *cahiers* of the Estates of Normandy, as we have seen, echoed these sentiments. In addition to their general criticism of the *droits*, they protested the creation of specific ones, such as the 12d./l. of the *greffiers* in 1629 or the 6d./l. of the *élus* added in 1627.[70] The Estates also requested the elimination of all new offices and *droits*, with reimbursement to be conducted at the *denier 14* and all previous payments made to the officers deducted from the principal owed to them. The king refused.

As one might expect, the special *rentes* of 1634 were handled by a *traitant*. The central *commis* for receiving the money, Nicolas Drouin, received the lion's share of the 54,566 l. levied in the *élection* of Châlons during 1636 for *rentes* and a cavalry surtax, but one wonders how much the officers got. Drouin was listed on doc-

---

67. Collins, "Taxation in Bretagne," chap. 7.
68. Y.-M. Bercé, *Histoire des Croquants* (Geneva, 1974), 70.
69. Ibid., 737.
70. De Beaurepaire, *Cahiers*, arts. 11 and 13 of *cahier* of 1627.

uments of 1638 as having taken in only 3.5 million l.—part of this money was also used to pay for cannons.[71]

Drouin had other problems as well; Bercé notes that Drouin could not even find his assistants in Guyenne in 1635, and adds that the local *élus* had, on their own authority, eliminated the special *droits* surtax from the commissions of the *tailles* sent to the parishes.[72] The king began selling new *droits* (paid at the *denier 14*) as soon as the old ones were abolished. In contrast to the old system these *droits* were sold on a parish basis, rather than as a percentage surtax on the *tailles*. There could therefore be no question of the *droits* increasing as taxes went up or as new *droits* were created; the king could thus fix the rate of interest, an issue that had proved to be a sore point with the earlier method. In Normandy in 1636 each parish in the *généralité* of Caen paid 279 *sous* to a variety of officers.[73] The new *droits* were estimated at 3.27 million l. for the kingdom in 1638.[74]

There was no uniform fashion of conducting the levies at this time, however, so there was considerable local variation in the manner of raising the *droits*. In Normandy the parish of St-Ouen-de-Breuil raised its *droits* as an integral part of the *grande crue* in 1645, there mixed in with many military levies. The village roll also specified percentage *droits* of 4d./l. for the *greffier* of the rolls of the *tailles* (levied on the *tailles* alone), 2d./l. on the levy for troop subsistance (to the same), and 1d./l. to the officers of the *élection*. The parish collector got his 6d./l. in addition to all these sums.[75] By way of contrast, at St-Martin-les-Melles in Poitou, the 1642 roll listed *droits* of 5 l. 14 s. for the *élection* officers, 6 l. to the *commis* for making the roll, 7 *sous* for the seal, and 47 l. 4 s. (6d./l.) for the collector.[76] The local inconsistencies in the method of listing the *droits* make it impossible to know their precise size in the 1640s, or the extent to which they were underpaid.

The issue of underpayment of *droits* and of *gages* was a critical one in the 1630s and 1640s because of the partial bankruptcies of 1634 and 1648 and the government's penchant for trying to bal-

71. AD Marne, C 2498, fol. 174v; BN, Ms. Fr. 18490.
72. Bercé, *Croquants,* 361. He adds, "Popular detestation was aimed particularly at that part of the *brevet* of the *tailles* called the *droits aliénés.*"
73. AD Calvados, 4 C 394.
74. BN, Ms. Fr. 7736.
75. AD Seine-Maritime, C 2108.
76. AD Deux-Sèvres, C 511.

ance its books by paying the officers less than their due. While we have considerable information about the upper-level officers, we know quite little about the *foule* of petty officers created solely to sell them *droits*. One interesting glimpse at this world is offered by the records of the *élection* of Figéac, which list the officeholders in the 1630s. In 1630, we find the following list of those receiving payments for *droits:*[77]

Office	Owner
Commissaire des vivres	Claude Charlot, *secrétaire du roi*
Greffier ancien	Germain Courtin
alternatif	Pierre Martin, "conseiller au Parlement de Bordeaux"
triennal	Jehan Jacquelin, *trésorier général des bâtiments du roi*
Maitre clerc ancien	Samuel de Colom, receiver of *tailles,* Figéac
alternatif	Jehan Dugué, master of accounts, Paris
triennal	Pierre Robineau, *trésorier général de la cavalrie légère*
Garde de petit scel	Anthoine de la Porte, *viguier* of Figéac, *conseiller du roi*

By 1633, the offices of *greffier* had been sold, the old and triennial to Bernard Daribat, the alternative to Louis Morineau. Such sales raise the critical question of who held the *droits* at any given time? In Brittany, for example, in 1632 and 1633 there were sales of both offices of receiver of the *fouages* of Léon, both receivers at Fougères, one receiver at St-Brieuc, a receiver general, a controller general, and both offices of *trésorier de France.*[78] Of the twenty-six offices of the direct tax system in Brittany, nine changed hands in 1632–33; this turnover was unprecedented in the first sixty years of the seventeenth century. If one could establish such a pattern elsewhere in France, it might indicate a change in the identity of those holding the royal debt in 1632–33. The pattern at Figéac indicates that powerful figures such as Martin (a Parlementaire)

77. AD Gironde, C 4832.
78. ADLA, B 77.

and Dugué (a master of accounts) were replaced by smaller fry like Daribat and Morineau. Did people such as Martin and Dugué buy these *droits* (perhaps at a discount), speculate in them (given that they were fully paid in the early years), and then dump them on locals such as Daribat?

Such questions lie at the center of the issue of the profitability of the *droits*. Those who purchased *droits* early in the game, such as the *greffiers* of 1621, would have collected substantial sums. Those who purchased *droits* created from the original 2 *sous* of the collectors would have made out best of all, since these *droits* were always levied on all direct taxes, including other *droits* and surtaxes. Many officers, however, had to pay for these latter privileges; in 1633, for example, the king issued a *traité* allowing the *greffiers* and master clerks of the *élections* to collect their *droits* on the other *droits* in return for a payment of 6 million l.[79]

The *droits* were sold on a mandatory basis in Brittany as early as the 1620s (although the king had trouble enforcing this). In the early 1630s, the king ordered *traitants* to collect the share of recalcitrant officers from their *gages* and other *droits*.[80] After 1634, all *droits* were sold on a mandatory basis. The *élection* officers claimed that they had paid 60 million l. for the "confirmation of an imaginary *droit* or attribution of a fictitious supplement" in the period 1640–48, and officer resentment at the forced sale of *droits* was clear in 1648. It was general policy to pay *gages* and *droits* at threequarters, or half, or three-eighths of their face value in the 1640s; in fact, the treasurers of Bourges remonstrated that they were paid nothing at all from 1640 to 1643.[81]

Those who bought *droits* in the early 1620s probably made a very nice return on their investment, but those who purchased such *droits* after 1629 lost substantial amounts of money. Such losses were particularly severe for those who bought *droits* in the 1640s. Yet, given the endemic and epidemic proportions of nonpayment of taxes in the late 1630s and 1640s—that is, the complete breakdown of central authority over the tax system of the parishes—one must wonder if local officials did not, in fact, collect their own *droits* and *gages* in spite of royal prohibitions.

All calculations of the profitability of the *droits* for the officers

79. BN, Ms. Fr. 18205, fols. 178–80.
80. Collins, "Taxation in Bretagne," chap. 7.
81. BN, Ms. Fr. 18510, fol. 388.

must also consider the other party, the king, and his calculations of his own profit on the sales. Perhaps the king made long-term calculations reflecting the money paid for the *droits* and the money paid out to their owners, and he may have sought to achieve some sort of balance between the two. The overall situation between 1616 and 1633 would lend itself to such an interpretation because of the existence of such a (rough) balance, but the situation would have been much different after 1633.

How much did the king make from the sales? It is impossible to make much more than a guess because the *droits,* like new offices, were sold by *traité.* As we have seen in Chapter 2, the claim of the *élection* officers to have paid more than 200 million l. to the king from 1624 to 1648 is somewhat inflated, and their total includes new offices as well as *droits.* The sale of the *droits aliénés* was worth more than 80 million l. at the *denier 10,* for those *droits* created before 1634. This figure excludes the likely payments for the right to levy the *droits* on the *droits:* for example, the 6 million l. paid by the *greffiers* and master clerks in 1633 for that purpose. If one accepted the *denier 10* as the criterion for the proposed levy of 1634, then the amount paid was about 140 million l. This total excludes the sale of offices, not only in the *élections,* but in the indirect tax administration, judicial system, and municipalities.[82]

The other aspects of this issue are the role of the *traitants* and the difference between their prices and the money received by the king. Most of the *traités* agreed to by the royal council in 1633 included rebate clauses of 12–25 percent. Thus, even if we accepted the 140 million l. figure just cited, we would have to deduct a substantial amount for the fees of the *traitants.* Most of the extraordinary revenue of the period 1621–34 came from the officers, with direct tax increases merely representing interest payments on the capital thus raised. After the partial bankruptcy of 1634, the direct tax increase of 1625–34 reverted to the king, and he added on new increases for himself. The secret payments of the monarchy, recently estimated at 10.5 million l. per year in the period 1625–29

82. BN, Ms. Fr. 18205 is a list of *traités* signed in 1633. As noted in Chapter 2, Françoise Bayard has shared her ideas on this point with me, as well as providing me with a copy of her article on the issue of *traités:* "Fermes et traités en France dans la première moitié du XVIIe siècle," *Bulletin du Centre d'Histoire Economique et Sociale de la Région Lyonnaise* 4 (1975): 45–80. On the sale of offices and *droits,* one first looks at R. Mousnier, *La Vénalité des Offices* (Rouen, Paris, 1945, 1971) and at the articles of Georges Pagès cited in the bibliography.

and 19.8 million l. per year in 1630–34, must have come primarily from money raised through the officers.[83]

The sale of the *droits* and their abolition in 1634 had very important consequences for French administrative development. The *droits* increased taxation very rapidly after 1620, yet the king received the increase only in the form of lump sum payments from the *traitants*. It is likely that the king received more money than was paid out, but direct tax revenue did not reach him in the normal manner. When more money was needed in 1634, the king raised taxes a lesser amount, but he eliminated the *droits,* thus regaining his share of the great increases of the 1620–33 period. The problem with this method of operation is self-evident: it alienates those who are supposed to collect the taxes. When the tax administration itself is no longer reliable, a new method must be found to collect the money.

Yet the cooperation of local officials, as is always the case, was essential even for the new system to work. The king therefore coopted some of the original tax administration into the new system. In the 1640s, the intendants apportioned the *tailles* with the help of two or three treasurers in each *généralité;* while this disenfranchised the other twenty or so local officers, it did not totally exclude the entire apparatus.

The final issue was, of course, money. The 1640s and 1650s were a period of experimentation: could one largely dispense with the old apparatus, taking in only small elements, and yet still collect the taxes? The answer was no. The *non-valeurs* of the 1640s and early 1650s were staggering (see Chapter 4), in some cases, 100 percent. Under Colbert, a more effective compromise was reached, leaving real power to the intendants, without completely alienating the old officers. As noted in Chapter 2, the latter were often more concerned with their investments than political power, so solidification of the former pacified them.

Revenues from Direct Taxation, 1595–1645

Now that we have some idea where the money came from, let us turn to the issue of the money itself. Following the method used

83. R. Bonney, "The Secret Expenses of Richelieu and Mazarin, 1624–1661," *English Historical Review* 91 (1976): 825–36.

in the first section of this chapter, we will examine one province, Champagne, and then discuss the system as a whole. The first stage in the general discussion will be a look at several other *généralités*, notably Caen and Rouen, while the total system will be treated at the end. This procedure is necessary because while we have fairly continuous figures for Champagne, those for the system as a whole are more fragmentary.

Direct taxation was extremely heavy during the Civil War of the 1589–98 period. The gradual end of the Civil War reduced direct taxation by more than 50 percent, on paper, but the amounts collected are another matter. During the period 1590–95, the king assessed slightly over 650,000 l. for the *tailles* and about 660,000 l. for wages of troops each year in Champagne.[84] It is unclear how much of this money was paid, but in other provinces the portion of the assessment actually reaching the king was erratic and, in certain cases, very small.[85]

In 1597, the king seems to have given a small measure of tax relief, asking only 1,256,577 l. from the province.[86] This sum included payments of 460,000 l. to the Central Treasury and 456,000 l. to the war treasurer. Once again, however, one must be quite wary of proposed levies; the *non-valeurs* must have been substantial. As has been noted in Chapter 2, Henry IV was forced to remit unpaid taxes for the period prior to 1599 in all of France (an action taken in 1602). Serious tax relief can be seen first in 1599. In 1598, the *taille* itself is unknown, but the great *crue*, the one used to pay the troops, was 266,000 l. This amount represented something of a reduction from previous levels but not real relief. The following year the *tailles* were 609,000 l., but the *crue* was only 42,000 l. Sully notes in the margin that the original figure was 192,000 l. but that 150,000 l. had been taken off due to the poverty of the people.[87] In 1600, this policy continued, as the *tailles* dropped to

84. AD Marne, C 2489, fol. 12 (1591), fol. 24v (1592), and fols. 65v–66 (army in 1593), and so on.

85. AD Haute-Vienne, C 551, shows no returns for Limoges in 1594 (perfectly believable in light of the Croquant rising). Permézel, *La politique financière de Sully*, has figures on nonpayment in one parish from 1597–1601. Local documents for Bourges, Brittany, Caen, Châlons (here from the papers of Sully, dealing with the garrison tax of 1599, noting a reduction of 50,000 *écus*, "due to the poverty of the people," AN, 120 AP 16), Lyon, and Limoges all indicate heavy nonpayment prior to 1600.

86. AD Marne, C 2490.

87. AN, 120 AP 16; BN, 500 Colbert 15; BN, 500 Colbert 289.

520,000 l. and the *crue* was only 87,000 l. (Sully's figure; the treasurers cite a figure of 75,000 l.). In 1602, relief continued with *tailles* of 542,000 l. and a *crue* of 42,000 l. Thus tax relief of some 670,000 l. was given in the drop from the figures of 1597–1602.[88]

This period of tax relief ended in 1603, when taxes went up to a more normal level. The new level lasted for about twenty years; in part, the levelling was a reflection of the extremely effective administration of Sully, under whom taxation all over France was very stable. On the other hand, expenses were also quite stable; the general peace of the period 1603–20 was the source of this stability. The immediate source of increase in 1603 was the abolition of the *pancarte* (established, as we saw in Chapter 2, by the Assembly of Notables of 1596–97). Public works projects added further supplements in 1604–5. The *crue* of 1608 was divided among four expenses: (1) garrisons (39,000 l.); (2) the replacement of the *pancarte* (30,000 l.); (3) the Seine-Loire Canal (18,000 l.); and (4) bridges (12,000 l.). Another 10,000 l. was added for the dredging of a local river in 1609.[89]

Table 18 shows the movement of taxation in Champagne from 1602 to 1634. As we can see, the level of direct taxation was very stable from 1604 until 1620. If we take the years 1609–14 as an index of 100, then direct taxes had no movement at all in this period (1604–20). A small increase starts in the early 1620s, when the index, only 98 in 1620, rises to 114 in 1621, but the index remains between 107 and 111 from 1622 to 1626. The serious jump begins in 1627. The connection between this date and the chronology of the Protestant problem can hardly have been fortuitous.

Yet the king was taking new forms of money from the direct tax levies. The *droits aliénés* provided substantial revenues without raising taxes, because the ones sold before 1621 came entirely from the old 2s./l. collection costs and fees. If we take the 1620 level of direct taxation as our base, about 15 million l. in the *pays d'élection,* then the s./l. sold to the *commissaires des tailles* in 1616 and the 4d./l. sold to the guards of the petty seal in 1618 would have produced about 10 million l. in additional revenue between 1616 and 1619. The 6d./l. sold to the *greffiers* in 1620–21 would have

88. AD Marne, C 2490, fols. 123 and ff. Published by A. Chamberland as "Le budget de la généralité de Châlons en 1602," *Revue Henri IV* 3(1908):144–87.
89. AD Marne, C 2490–2491.

been worth 5 million l., while the 10d./l. to the *greffiers des affirmations* and sergeants added 8.35 million l. to the king's coffers (minus the money taken off the top by the *traitants*). These early *droits* were sometimes listed among the local charges—in 1622–23, for example—but after 1624 they disappeared from the *brevets*. Taxes thus went up slightly to cover the annuity payments on these new *droits* of 1621–23. In 1624, the creation of a second *commissaire des tailles* did not change matters much because the s./l. came from the sergeants (abolished) and the parish collectors. The *droits* started to jump again in 1627, just as the taxes did.

The figures for 1627 and 1628 cited in Table 18 are undoubtedly too low because of military surtaxes. The garrison *crue* of 1629, for instance, was noted by the king in the *brevet* as a reduction in this tax, when, in fact, it had gone up from a listing of 91,600 l. in 1628 to 103,200 l. in 1629. Clearly, a military surtax, which post-dated the *brevet*, was added to the levy of 1628.[90]

After 1624, however, the situation becomes so complex that one must hesitate to cite specific figures. The *droits* were levied in their year of creation, but they were levied proportionate to their date of creation (again, their function as *rentes*): a *droit* created in February, for example, would be paid at five-sixths its full value during the year in which it was created. If the officers did not buy the *droit* immediately, the *traitant* collected the interest for the first year.[91] The issue of levying *droits* on each other is even more complicated. As it was created, each new *droit* was either for everything existing at that time or, as in the case of *droits* given to the receiver of the *taillon* in 1629, for specific levies. The question is: when were the *droits* created in, say, 1621, also levied on those *droits* created in 1629 or 1630? The complaint of the Estates of Normandy in 1629 indicates the king was following just such a policy in 1628–29, and we also know that *traités* were given for this purpose in 1631, 1632, and 1633.[92] However, the obvious doubling on the principal of the *taille* alone indicated by the *brevets* of 1634 makes one wonder how this process was handled from the beginning; that is, starting in 1624.

90. AD Marne, C 2494, fol. 211, noting the reduction for the kingdom was 1 million l.
91. BN, Ms. Fr. 18205, fol. 180, fol. 230v. Examples in Collins, "Taxation in Bretagne," chap. 7.
92. BN, Ms. Fr. 18205. BN, Ms. Fr. 18479, fols. 121 and ff.

Table 18. *Direct Taxation in Champagne, 1602–34*

Year	Total Levy (in 000 l.)	Mallet	Index (1609–14 = 100)	Mallet Index
1602	638.2	212.1	90	72
1603	675.2	243.0	95	83
1604	696.0	256.9	98	88
1605	698.0	322.2	98	115
1607	720.2	315.9	101	108
1608	698.5	289.7	99	99
1609	709.5	304.5	100	104
1610	709.5	293.0	100	100
1611	709.5	293.1	100	100
1613	710.6	315.9	100	108
1614	710.6	293.0	100	100
1620	693.8	180.8	98	62
1621	808.1	250.1	114	85
1622	794.4	216.9	112	74
1623	828.1	178.9	117	61
1624	755.7	141.3	107	48
1625	755.7	143.0	107	49
1626	791.2	136.5	111	47
1627	832.6	54.4	117	19
1628	872.5	56.7	123	19
1629	953.7	99.8	134	34
1630	1166.1	197.8	164	66
1631	984.8	210.6	139	72
1632	1148.8	111.1	162	38
1633	1224.9	180.6	173	62
1634	1538.4	95.6	217	33

Sources: 1602–5, 1608–11, 1621–33, AD Marne, C 2490–2499. 1620, BN, Ms. Fr. 16623, fols. 190–230; 1634, BN, NAF 200; 1607, 1613–14, Y. Durand, *Cahiers de doléances du bailliage de Troyes* (Paris, 1966), 40, checked on originals in AD Marne, C 2657.

The figures in Table 18 are no more than an educated guess at what was happening from 1627 until 1634. The 833,000 l. of 1627 is without question too low, as is the 872,500 l. of 1628. The figures include, where possible, the extra levies mentioned (the 70,000 l. for the fort razing at La Rochelle, the 10,000 l. or so for officer reimbursement, both in 1629) under the assignation problem, but one must be wary here of ad hoc military levies in a frontier prov-

ince. The individual parishes also had the right to levy money for
their own needs, with official permission, and those amounts are,
by and large, not included. The pattern is unmistakable, steadily
up after 1626, with the index going from 111 in 1626 to 134 in
1629, 164 in 1630, 173 in 1633, and 217 in 1634. These figures
are undoubtedly too low as a representation of *projected* levies, but
they also do not reflect *non-valeurs*. How much money actually
came in? We simply do not know. Given the lack of information
about *non-valeurs* in the late 1620s and early 1630s, they were
probably not an overwhelming problem. In the 1640s, when they
become quite serious, we have abundant information about them
from many sources. The only figures from this period are from
Caen, where the *non-valeurs* of 1629 were 19.6 percent. This was
a year of pestilence in some areas of western France, and one must
wonder if that had an effect. Nonetheless, *non-valeurs* in the range
of 20 percent could have been general in this period (1627–33).[93]

After 1634, one is in never-never land. The receiver general of
Champagne, as we have seen, wrote in August 1639 that he had
not received a penny from the *élection* receivers; this is hardly a
statement to inspire confidence in proposed tax levy figures. Excluding *non-valeurs* and staying with proposed taxes, we find the
brevets listed the following tax burdens: 1637—1.99 million l.;
1640—2.06 million l.; 1643—2.66 million l. The local charges
were estimated at 739,000 l., and the regional ones at 265,000 l.
in 1640.[94]

The overall increase in proposed taxes was thus 121 percent
from 1620 to 1634, and about 60 percent from 1634 to 1643. (The
increase in terms of *livres* would therefore be slightly greater in the
latter period.) The main jump occurred between 1627 and 1633,
with a second one in 1634–36. Again, the amount actually received
did not follow this progression, especially after 1634. For a clearer
picture of what happened in the 1630s and 1640s, we must look at
other provinces and the kingdom as a whole.

Normandy, particularly Lower Normandy, the *généralité* of
Caen, is another well-documented province. Table 19 provides
some figures for both Rouen and Caen in the period 1597–1640

93. M. Caillard, "Recherches sur les soulèvements populaires en Basse-
Normandie (1620–1640)," *Cahiers des Annales de Normandie* 3 (Caen, 1963): 23–
153.
94. BN, Ms. Fr. 7736; BN, Ms. Fr. 18490.

Table 19. *Direct Taxation in Normandy, 1597–1640 (in 000 l.)*

Year	Caen	Rouen	Total	Non-valeurs in Caen
1597	1,253[a]	1,935	3,188	
1599	1,150	2,096	3,246	165
1600	1,082[b]	1,989	3,071	32
1601	1,088			16
1602	963			0
1604	997			1
1605	1,012			1
1606	1,017			12
1607	989[c]	1,826	2,815	0
1609	1,021[d]	2,108	3,129	6
1610	1,012			5
1612		1,841		
1613	970			
1617	1,016			
1618	1,016			
1619	1,010			
1620	1,040	1,838	2,878	
1622	1,027[e]			
1624		1,838		
1625		1,854		
1626		1,854		
1629	1,072			210
1631	1,075			
1632	1,102			
1633	1,150			
1634	2,214[f]	3,943	6,157	
1635	2,294			1,470
1636	2,175[g]			
1637	2,782			
1638	3,199			1,855
1639	2,799			1,162
1640	2,171[h]	2,883		
	Alençon	2,097	7,151	
1643	2,614[i]	3,525		
	Alençon	2,543	8,682	

Sources: 1597   A. Chamberland, "La répartition de la taille en 1597," *Revue Henri IV* 2(1905–6): 82–85.

1599   BN, 120 AP 16 (garrison tax only), also for 1600.

1599   BN, 500 Colbert 16, fols. 65 and ff. (*taille* only).

1600   BN, 500 Colbert 289 (*taille* only).

1600–10   L. Romier, *Lettres et chevauchées du bureau des finances de*

Table 19. (continued)

	Caen sous Henri IV (Rouen, 1910), app. Romier omits *élection* charges, so 120,000 l. has been added for each year to make up for their absence.
1612	AD Seine-Maritime, C 1379.
1607	BN, Ms. Fr. 16626, fols. 73–82 (cited figure from Romier).
1609	AN, 120 AP 17 (cited figure from Romier).
1613	Extrapolation of figure for *élection* of Valognes, by A. Lefebvre and F. Tribouillard, "L'élection de Valognes de 1540 à 1660," *Annales de Normandie* (1973): 216.
1617	Ibid., 220 (extrapolation).
1618	AD Calvados, 4 C 393 (also for 1619).
1620	BN, Ms. Fr. 16624, fols. 319–59v (Caen), 249–317v (Rouen).
1622	AD Calvados, 4 C 393.
1624	AD Seine-Maritime, C 1438. (Also for 1625–26.)
1629–43	M. Caillard, "Recherches sur les soulèvements populaires en Basse-Normandie, (1620–1640)," *Cahiers des Annales de Normandie* (1963): 23–153, figs. from pp. 130, 132.
1634	BN, NAF 200.
1643	Ibid.
1640	BN, Ms. Fr. 18490 and Ms. Fr. 7736.
1636–40	M. Foisil, *La révolte des Nu-Pieds* (Paris, 1970), 62–92.

[a]This figure excludes both military surtaxes and *non-valeurs*.

[b]AN, 120 AP 16 and BN, 500 Colbert 289 give a total of 1,040,000 l.

[c]BN, Ms. Fr. 16626, gives 975,000 l.

[d]AN, 120 AP 17, gives 1,118,000 l. for Caen. The figures for both Rouen and Caen in this document seem a bit high.

[e]From this point on, one must add in the *droits aliénes*. All figures before 1622 need a 10 percent surtax (mostly paid to the collectors); those of 1622 would need 17.5 percent; those of 1629, more like 32.5 percent.

[f]Here we begin to get into a quagmire. Foisil gives very different figures for the period 1636–40 from either Caillard or the archival citations I have. Caillard gives 1.9 million l. for 1634 for Caen. His other figures exclude the *droits*.

[g]In 1636–40, Foisil gives the following figures: 1636—2.3 million l.; 1637—1.4 million l.; 1639—2.4 million l.; 1640—1.65 million l. (Figures for Caen only.) She also notes extra levies of 80,000 l. in 1636, 1.0 million l. in 1637, 1.43 million l. in 1638, and 713,000 l. in 1639.

[h]Caillard gives 2,594,000 l. for Caen in 1640.

[i]Caillard gives 3,233,000 l. for Caen in 1643.

(the new *généralité* of Alençon, in full extent in 1638, is included for 1640). As in Champagne, a measure of tax relief occurs at the end of the League wars. There is an end to the extra military levies and, in Caen, a reduction in the regular taxes as well: they drop from 1.25 million l. in 1597 to 1.15 million l. in 1599 and 1.08 (1.04 according to Sully) million l. in 1600. In Rouen, however, the regular taxes stay about the same, going up slightly in 1599, and back down in 1600 to about the level of 1597 (1.99 million l. as opposed to 1.94 million in 1597).[95]

Following the pattern noted elsewhere, the *non-valeurs* are considerable in 1599: they were 164,561 l. (about 15 percent) in the

95. BN, 500 Colbert 16; BN, 500 Colbert 289; AN, 120 AP 16.

généralité of Caen. From 1601 to 1610, however, the taxes were fully paid: total *non-valeurs* in Caen for eight of these nine years (the figures for the ninth are missing), were only about 40,000 l. in a total collection of 9.2 million l. (0.4 percent).[96]

Reinforcing the pattern noted in Châlons and Lyons, the level of direct taxation was quite stable from 1603 until 1620. In Caen the receipts fluctuated between 0.96 and 1.11 million l., while in Rouen they stayed between 1.83 and 2.11 million l.[97] All these figures exclude the costs of collection, or 10 percent. Of that cost, 1.67 percent (4d./l.) was going back directly to the king for the repair of buildings until 1618, when this 4d./l. was sold to the guards of the petty seal. In 1618, as we have seen, the actual collection costs, 12d./l., were sold to the *commissaires des tailles*. A total of 50,786 l. was levied to pay them in the *généralité* of Caen in 1618; thus we can say that the king also obtained a further 507,860 l. (minus *traitant*'s fees) from Caen in 1616–17. If the usual 65:35 split for Rouen and Caen held up in that year, then one can estimate the king obtained another 943,000 l. from the *généralité* of Rouen in 1616–17.[98]

Once we pass 1620, however, the *droits* begin to bite into the principal of the levies. The figure listed for Caen in 1622, 1.03 million l., does not include a 17.5 percent surtax for the *droits*:[99]

commissaires des tailles	12d./l.
collectors	6d./l.
guards of the petty seal	4d./l.
greffiers des affirmations	2d./l.
greffiers and master clerks	8d./l.
receivers of the *tailles*	4d./l.
hereditary sergeants (newly created)	6d./l.
	42d./l. (17.5 percent)

6s./parish for preparing the rolls (2s./roll)

96. L. Romier, *Lettres et chevauchées du bureau des finances de Caen sous Henri IV* (Rouen, 1910), app.

97. AD Seine-Maritime, C 1379 and C 1438; AD Calvados, 4 C 392 and 4 C 393.

98. In addition to the archival sources, see A. Lefebvre and F. Tribouillard, "L'élection de Valognes de 1540 à 1660," *Annales de Normandie* 21 (1973): 208–33.

99. AD Calvados, 4 C 393.

This surtax represents a 7.5 percent increase in taxation (the pre-1620 level of the surtax being 10 percent).

As has been noted, the two *généralités* divided the province's tax burden on a 65:35 basis. The general tax burden of France was usually apportioned among the provinces/*généralités* in a fairly similar manner; the fact that Rouen and Caen were part of the same province made their relationship all the stronger. Thus while we have no figures for Caen from 1623 to 1628, the figures for Rouen in 1624–26, showing taxes of 1.87 million l. (as opposed to 1.84 million l. in 1620), lead one to suspect that Caen continued to pay about 1.05 million l. per year in the 1620s. The figure for 1629, 1.08 million l., reinforces this conclusion.

These figures, however, leave out the *droits,* so they leave out the substantial increases. The figures cited by Caillard for the 1630s also exclude the *droits,* so the huge increase he indicates in 1634 is really nothing of the sort: it is simply the king reclaiming his taxes. The jump of 66 percent in direct taxes from 1633 to 1634 merely indicates that the *droits* surtax now went to the king. As we have seen for Châlons, the *droits* surtax there was about 84 percent in 1633; if we add such a surtax to the figures for Caen, we would get direct taxes of 2.12 million l. for 1633, and the figure for 1634 would be a *reduction.* The sharp break of 1634 is therefore a break in the position of the officers, not in the level of taxation. The huge increase in *non-valeurs,* up from 19.6 percent in 1629 (which I suspect is unusually high for the pre-1634 period) to 64.1 percent in 1635, is due not to an increase in taxation but to the dissatisfaction of the officers. The increases of the period 1637–39 and the periodic exorbitant levels of the 1640s *do,* however, represent substantial tax increases. The *non-valeurs* of 1637–50 are due both to officer dissatisfaction and to abnormally high levels of tax assessment.[100] (*Non-valeurs* are discussed at length in Chapter 4.)

The records of two other *généralités,* Lyon and Bordeaux, are also sufficient for us to have a long-term picture of direct taxation between 1600 and 1634. In Lyon the annual levy was some 662,000 l. from 1604 to 1607 (index 100) and only 649,000 l. from 1608 to 1610 (see Table 7). The regular levies in 1617 were 678,000 l., with an additional 77,000 l. for *étapes:* a total of

---

100. Caillard, "Soulèvements populaires en Basse-Normandie," and M. Foisil, *La révolte des Nu-Pieds* (Paris, 1970), give figures for *non-valeurs.* See Chapter 4, below.

755,000 l. (excluding parish surtaxes), an index of 114.[101] Save for years of high military surtaxes, such as 1622 and 1623 (index values of 122 and 124), the annual levies remained stable from 1618 to 1626, at an index value between 101 and 108. As in Champagne, there was a sharp jump in 1627, up to 820,000 l. (124) and high taxation in 1628 and 1629. In 1634, the proposed levies were 1.57 million l., plus the 6d./l. of the collectors: an index value of 243.[102]

In Bordeaux, regional records indicate levies of about 1.16 or 1.17 million l. from 1600 to 1609.[103] The introduction of *élections* led to much higher taxation for their suppression in 1611, and military campaigning cost 330,000 l. in 1615–16. In 1615, the king's entry into Bordeaux cost the *généralité* 108,000 l. In 1620, Bordeaux's taxes were 1.43 million l; in 1623, the *taille* alone was 901,956 l., indicating a total levy of some 1.3–1.4 million l. In 1629, the *taille* was 839,073 l., to which one must add the *droits* and the *crue*. In 1633, the total levies were about 2 million l., while the proposed amount for 1634 was 3.3 million l.[104] This last figure may have been an error, since it included the 2s./l. of the *commissaires des tailles,* who appear not to have existed in the *généralité* of Bordeaux (in the *pays* of Quercy, they were abolished in return for payments of some 42,000 l. in 1620 and 1621).

The *généralité* of Bordeaux also has a second set of figures that are virtually complete for the period 1600–33: the *états au vrai* for the *élection* of Figéac.[105] Here we see a pattern similar to that of the kingdom as a whole, with local variations reflecting both the special situation of the *généralité* of Bordeaux (and the introduction of its *élections*) and the ambiguity of Figéac's location in a small *pays d'Etats,* Quercy. The *états au vrai* for 1600–1603 show the magnitude of the *non-valeurs* of 1597–99: nominal levies of 27,414 l.

---

101. AD Rhône, 8 C 32, fol. 107, noting that 412,105 l. for the *taille* in 1618 was the same as in 1617; fol. 112v shows the *crue* of 205,000 l. to have been the same in 1618 as in 1617; fols. 61v and ff. on *étapes.*

102. AD Rhône, 8 C 32 to 8C 47, covering 1617–29. Figure for 1634 from BN, NAF 200.

103. AD Gironde, C 3809 and 3810, citations from 1605, 1607, 1609.

104. AD Gironde, C 3819 on troop levy of 1615–16 and cost of royal entry; C 3990, *commission des tailles* for Bigorre, *commission* of Rhodez, 1633, of Haut-Rouergue, 1633, of entire *généralité* of Bordeaux, 1634. *Commission* of Rhodez for 1633 notes that the 10d./l. were sold on the basis of 901,956 l. 5s. 4d., which would be the figure for the *taille* in the year of their creation, 1623.

105. AD Gironde, C 4832.

in 1600; 21,327 l. in 1601; and 18,115 l. in 1602 to cover the shortfalls of 1597–99. In each case the listed amount is probably the outstanding arrears, so that the levies were 6,087 l. in 1600, and so on. The Estates of Quercy composed with the king for 8,115 l. in 1603, to cover the arrears.

The regular levies dropped from about 53,000 l. (1600–1603) to 46,000 l. from 1604 to 1608. New local expenses, such as the shift of the governor of Quercy's *état* onto the three *élections*/districts (and thus off the Central Treasury budget) and the debts of the *pays* of Quercy raised Figéac's taxes to between 55,000 and 58,000 l. from 1609 to 1610. Basic taxes in Figéac remained about 58,000 l. until the early 1620s, again quite similar to the situation in the kingdom as a whole. Yet local issues played a dramatic role in the area and show us how taxes could jump sharply in a given *élection* even during a time of overall, nationwide tax stability. In 1611–12, for example, Figéac (along with the rest of the *généralité*) had to pay for the suppression of the *élus:* 12,133 l. for their abolition; 14,539 l. for the *gages* of the suppressed *élus;* 6,100 l. to Marie de Medicis and Marguerite of Valois for their acquiescence in the abolition. There were military levies of 6,549 l. in 1620 (of 26,000 l. in Guyenne) and perhaps some 15,000 l. (not listed on the *état au vrai*) as Figéac's share of the 330,000 l. levied in 1615–16. The *élection* somehow escaped its share of the cost of the king's entry to Bordeaux in 1615; when the treasurers of France discovered the error, however, Figéac had to contribute 10,973 l. in 1620 as its share. In 1620–21, Figéac also had to pay 133,060 l. to abolish the *commissaires des tailles*. In 1620, total direct taxes were 84,500 l. (plus any costs of parish collection), an increase of some 24.7 percent over 1619 and of nearly 50 percent over 1608, at a time when nationwide tax levels were quite stable.

The early 1620s show the local situation at its most chaotic. The levies in 1621 continued high (81,351 l.), but there was a decline in 1622 (to 71,144) and a lower level in 1623 (75,178 l.). In 1624, the figure rose to 81,998 l. and there was a peasant rebellion in the Quercy aimed at the elimination of the *élus* (recreated in 1621 but not serving in Figéac in either 1622 or 1623). The following year the *élection* of Figéac had to pay 81,232 l. in regular taxation and an additional 21,568 l. to three of the newly instituted *élus*—Dufour, Dupuy, and Reynal, "pour les pertes et ruines par eux suffertes en leurs biens dans led. pays en l'année 1624." Here we can see the problem with using general figures to explain such matters as local tax revolts. In a period, 1605–24, during which general French direct taxation went up little (10 percent at most), the direct taxes of Figéac increased from about 46,000 l. to about 81,000 l., a jump of nearly 76 percent. In Figéac, the levies of the late 1620s and early 1630s were less of an increase than elsewhere because the area had already seen its taxes jump so sharply between 1605 and 1624, and particularly after 1619.

The Figéac records are somewhat confused in the late 1620s and 1630s because they do not seem to be complete with respect to the *droits aliénés*. Thus the *état au vrai* for 1631 or 1633 lists *droits* of some 7,500 l., yet the levy to replace the *droits* in the *généralité* of Bordeaux in 1634 gives a figure of 63,637 l. for Figéac, and such amounts were elsewhere less than the annual value of the *droits* themselves.[106]

The congruity of the extensive information on these four *généralités* makes it easier for us to piece together the somewhat sparser information for the kingdom as a whole. There are some isolated figures for the period 1597–1634. The documents from the 1634–47 era are largely illusory, so, while they are cited here, one cannot really take them seriously, except in understanding what the government was trying to get out of the system.

The *répartition* of the *tailles* of 1597, published by Albert Chamberland, provides a good documentary base from which to begin our estimate of French revenues from direct taxation in the first half of the seventeenth century.[107] This account shows direct tax levies of about 18 million l., of which 17 million l. are to be levied in the *pays d'élection*. Chamberland cites evidence from the *généralités* of Bourges, Bordeaux, and Châlons supporting the accuracy of the central documents. Further research establishes its accuracy for Brittany and Tours as well.[108]

There are discordant notes in Tours, Brittany, Poitou, and Châlons, however, and all include extra military levies. An "état des

106. AD Gironde, C 3990, *commission des tailles*, 1634, noting additional levy of 1,401,094 l. (of 13,800,000 l. in the kingdom) for the replacement (that is, levied in place of, for the king's own benefit) of the *droits aliénés* of the *généralité* of Bordeaux.

107. A. Chamberland, "'La répartition de la taille en 1597," *Revue Henri IV*, 2:82–85 and "Le budget de 1597," *Revue Henri IV*, 1:15–20.

108. AD Ille-et-Vilaine, C 2645, fol. 8 (Brittany); BN, 500 Colbert 41, fol. 85 (Tours).

levées faites" for the *généralité* of Tours coincides almost exactly with Chamberland's document, but several special levies added to the *état* do not appear on the central account. The king levied 82,535 l. to repay his creditors for war loans; 40,500 l. for two-thirds of another loan repayment; 45,866 l. for the s./l. of the *turcies* (levees); 245,100 l. as a surtax for the army in Brittany; and 60,000 l. for the victuals of the army in Picardy: a total of 474,971 l. 16s. 8d. more than the regular levies (a 26.5 percent increase).

In Châlons the official *brevet* for the *crue* lists 435,000 l., the same amount as Chamberland's central account.[109] Yet the total revenue of the province (direct taxation only) is listed as 1,256,577 l. on the *état du roi*. This indicates a surtax on the *crue* of 213,504 l. (20.4 percent).[110] In Brittany the regular taxes are much as Chamberland lists them, but there is a garrison tax of 120,000 l./month that is not listed.[111] In Poitou the province had to provide 30,000 twelve-ounce loaves of bread to Marshal Schomberg's army; the cost of the bread (190,000 l.) was divided on a two-thirds:one-third basis between Poitou and Touraine (which was a 7.44 percent increase for Poitou).[112]

In addition to the regular direct taxes cited in the central document, other, mainly military, surtaxes were levied in 1597. Much of the proposed money was not collected, however, because of the inability of the peasantry to pay it. As we have seen, the *non-valeurs* of Caen were 15 percent in 1599; they were undoubtedly more in 1597. In the Limousin nothing was collected in 1594 due to a revolt. In 1598, the unpaid taxes there were 257,000 l. They dropped to 44,000 l., 51,000 l., and 63,000 l. in 1599–1601, respectively. If the taxes of 1598 were the same as those of 1597, the *non-valeurs* would have been about 19 percent.[113]

In the *généralité* of Lyon the unpaid taxes were 135,000 l. in 1597: 12 percent of the proposed levy.[114] Châlons received massive tax relief in 1599 because of the poverty of its inhabitants. The figures from the *généralité* of Amiens must also be discounted because the Spanish held Amiens for part of the year,

109. AD Marne, C 2489, fol. 443v.
110. AD Marne, C 2490.
111. AD Ille-et-Vilaine, C 2645, fols. 8 and 159.
112. BN, Ms. Fr. 3558, fols. 104–5.
113. AD Haute-Vienne, C 551; AN, 120 AP 13.
114. AN, 120 AP 13. Permézel, *La politique financière de Sully,* app.

and heavy military campaigning in the surrounding area probably led to something like total nonpayment of the regular taxes. In Brittany several local *fouage* receivers lost their offices because they could not pay what was due the central receiver for the province.[115] In Berry, despite heavy remissions for taxes in 1598 and 1599, total remission eventually had to be granted for all pre-1600 levies.[116] Later the king spread this ruling to the entire country, for all arrears antedating 1598.[117]

The figures for 1599 and 1600 indicate substantial tax relief. Direct taxes dropped about 6 percent from 1598 to 1599, from 17 to 16.1 million l., and a further 9.8 percent in 1600, going to 14.5 million l.[118] If we say that the special military levies, which were about 15–25 percent in the areas for which we have figures, and the *non-valeurs*, which were roughly 12–20 percent, cancel one another out for 1597, then taxes did indeed drop from 1597 to 1600. (One problem here, though, is that *non-valeurs* relate to the regular taxes, but we know nothing about the *non-valeurs* of the extra levies.)[119]

This new, lower level of direct taxation, roughly 14.5–15 million l. per year, lasted from 1603 until 1620. One must add the 10 percent collection surcharge to come up with a reasonably accurate estimate of 16–16.5 million l. per year of regular direct taxation. Some extra levies were charged in this period, such as the local parish impositions cited earlier for Berry, and perhaps certain military expenses in specific local areas—for example, in Brittany for the dismantling of the fort at Douarnenez in 1617–18.[120]

Starting in 1620, however, the *droits* begin to change matters. As we have seen, the sale of the 12d./l. in 1616 and the 4d./l. in 1618 raised substantial amounts of money (about 10 million l.)

115. ADLA, B 68, fols. 140–43 on *fouage* receiver of St-Malo, who owed 6,809 l. 10 s.; fols. 146v–150v, *fouage* receiver of St-Brieuc, who owed the king 17,162 l. 12 s. from the taxes of 1601.

116. AD Cher, C 984, fols. 19v–20.

117. J. R. Major, "Bellièvre, Sully, and the Assembly of Notables of 1596," *Transactions of the American Philosophical Society*, new ser. 64 (1974): 3–31, discusses this action.

118. One must add 10 percent for the costs of collection at the parish level (although 1.67 percent went back to the king for "repair of demesne buildings").

119. The extra levies were often collected by the troops, who did not account for them in the normal fashion. This problem is discussed in detail, for Brittany, in Collins, "Taxation in Bretagne," chaps. 5, 6, and 8.

120. BN, Ms. Fr. 22311, fols. 267–69.

and, to a certain degree, this money came indirectly from the direct taxes. The *droits* sold between 1621 and 1633, however, were a different matter. They affected direct taxation immediately, yet they did not affect the portion of the money going to the king. Here again, the sale of the *droits* was basically an anticipation of revenue coming from the direct taxes. Year in, year out, from 1621 to 1633, the sale of *droits* on the direct taxes added something like 10 million l. to the king's receipts (more later in the period, less in the beginning). This amount excludes the substantial revenues obtained from the sale of offices in the direct tax administration and the sale of other offices and other *droits* (the latter were sold to officers in the salt tax and indirect tax administrations as well).

The effect on direct taxation was gradual; there was a slow increase beginning in 1621, picking up speed after 1627. The net result is seen in Table 20. Direct taxes levied for the king declined by 11 percent between 1620 and 1634, while the amount actually levied went up more than 100 percent, from 16.45 million l. in 1620 to a proposed 33.22 million l. in 1634.[121] As Mallet documents, the king's receipts at the Central Treasury dropped heavily in the late 1620s, a reflection of higher local and regional charges, much of that increase being the result of the creation of new offices. The creation of eight *trésoriers* in each *généralité* between 1621 and 1629, for example, would cost the king about 350,000 l. in new *gages* each year.

Once we get past 1634, the central documents, even the regional proposed revenues, are of little use. There are a number of copies of one document from 1640 showing that direct taxes were 39.6 million l. in 1636, 40.8 million l. in 1637, 39.0 million l. in 1638, 45.7 million l. in 1639, and 43.7 million l. in 1640. Some copies show local charges of 9.8 million l. for 1640 and regional charges of 4.2 million l.[122] Caillard and Foisil show that *non-valeurs* in Caen were 58 percent in 1638 and 40.5 percent in 1639 (Caillard), and that much of this money remained unpaid as late as 1643 (Foisil).[123] In June 1643, the intendant of Alençon complained that the *élection* of Mortagne had paid only 1 percent of its taxes.[124]

121. BN, Ms. Fr. 16622, 16623, 16624 for 1620; NAF 200 for 1634.
122. BN, Ms. Fr. 7736 and Ms. Fr. 18490, the former somewhat more complete.
123. Caillard, "Soulèvements populaires," and Foisil, *Nu-Pieds.*
124. R. Mousnier, *Lettres et mémoires adressés au chancelier Séguier* (Paris, 1964), 2 vols., I, 520. 5,000 of 460,000 l.

Table 20. *Direct Taxation in France, 1597–1643, Selected Years (in 000 l.)*

Généralité	1597	1599	1600	1607	1609	1620	1634	1640	1643
Paris	1,384	1,415	1,265	1,385	1,342	1,427[a]	3,231	3,813	5,392
Soissons	593	635	497	505	489	526	1,362	1,425	1,607
Amiens	321	261	261	280	289	290	1,003	1,209	1,177
Châlons	1,043	650	566	655	645	636	1,500	2,064	2,280
Orléans	1,197	1,175	1,100	1,086	1,033	1,118	2,333	2,669	3,574
Tours	1,795	1,736	1,511	1,319	1,356	1,444	2,909	3,417	4,576
Poitiers	1,611	1,536	1,353	1,330	1,285	1,401	3,031	3,358	3,903
Limoges	1,361	1,271	1,432	945	1,024	1,184	2,522	2,116[b]	2,707[b]
Bourges	623	609	521	508	470	515	1,201	1,295	1,761
Moulins	710	626	614	602	576	617	1,300	1,611	2,043
Riom	981	983	788	781	801	858	1,973	2,117	2,979
Lyon	1,080	713	623	602	590	641	1,572	1,688	2,212
Bordeaux	1,194	1,222	1,222	1,168	1,173	1,431	3,330	5,257[c]	6,815[c]
Rouen	1,935	2,096	1,990	1,826	2,108	1,838	3,943	4,980[d]	6,069[d]
Caen	1,253	1,150	1,041	975	1,118	1,040	2,214	2,171[d]	2,614[d]
Total	17,081	16,078	14,784	13,967	14,299	14,966	33,424	39,190	49,709

Sources: 1597: A. Chamberland, "La répartition de la taille en 1597," *Revue Henri IV* 2 (1905–06): 82–85; 1599: AN, 120 AP 16; BN, 500 Colbert 16; 1600: AN, 120 AP 16; BN, 500 Colbert 289; 1607: BN, Ms. Fr. 16626, fols. 73–82; 1609: AN, 120 AP 17; 1620: BN, Ms. Fr. 16622, 16623, 16624; 1634: BN, NAF 200; 1640: BN, Ms. Fr. 18490 and Ms. Fr. 7736; 1643: BN, NAF 200.

Notes: The figures for 1597, 1599, 1600, 1607, 1609, and 1620 should be increased by 10 percent for the costs of collection. In the first five of these years the parish collectors would get five-sixths of this money, the king one-sixth. In 1620, various new officers would get three-fourths and the parish collectors one-fourth. The figures for 1634, 1640, and 1643 are proposed levies. In 1643, for example, the intendant of Limoges wrote to chancellor Seguier that many parishes were paying nothing (as had been the case in 1642). The figures for 1597 are also suspect, due to nonpayment (I would estimate it at 15 percent in 1597). All figures exclude military surtaxes.

[a]Paris—the 1620 figure is for 1622.

[b]The *élection* of Saintes was removed from the *généralité* of Limoges and given to that of Bordeaux in the 1630s; the figure for Limoges in 1640 (and in 1643) is therefore based on a smaller area than the earlier ones.

[c]Bordeaux—the figures for 1640 and 1643 are for the combined *généralités* of Bordeaux and Montauban, the latter established in the mid-1630s.

[d]Rouen and Caen—the figures for 1640 and 1643 include all the taxes of the new *généralité* of Alençon in with Rouen. In fact, one *élection* of this *généralité* was taken from the *généralité* of Caen

The intendants lamented their inability to collect the taxes; they universally protested the uncooperativeness of the regular officers and the collusion of the officers in nonpayment of taxes. Rouergue and Gascony paid only a third of their taxes from 1642 to 1644 and required remission of past due sums in 1642 and 1644. In the Lyonnais, prisons were jammed with parish collectors; in the Orléanais, three parishes near Montargis had not paid any *tailles* in four years (1643); at Aurillac, by November 1643 only two of ninety-six parishes had drawn up rolls; at Conches, in July 1643, the king had gotten only 50,000 l. from 1642 and a mere 11,000 l. (of 380,000 l. owed) for 1643.[125] The *pays d'Etats* made up some of the slack. For example, in Brittany, the king received the regular taxes (1.1 million l.), the Estates' grant (1.5 million l.), and revenue from expedients such as the sale of *fouage* exemptions (778,000 l. in 1638).[126] Unlike the *pays d'élection,* the *pays d'Etats* actually paid their taxes in the 1640s.

Despite the abundance of documents on the period 1634–54, one cannot even begin to venture a guess as to how much money was really coming in. The problem pointed out by Bercé, that those parishes within easy access of the troops paid large taxes, while isolated ones may have paid little, also warps our figures after 1633. The 1630s also involve certain special gimmicks, such as the forced loan of 20 million l. started in 1637, the sale of *affranchissements* (tax exemptions) in Brittany, and, most important of all, the money collected by the troops themselves.

The overall movement of French direct taxation in the *pays d'élection* between 1597 and, say, 1647 can be outlined as follows. There was a sharp reduction in direct taxation, about 15 percent, from 1597 to 1600. Tax relief seems to have been general from 1600 to 1602, with a small increase again in 1603, in part due to the abolition of the *pancarte*. From 1603 to 1620, one has almost total stability, at a level of 16–16.5 million l. per year, including the collection costs and fees. This total excludes levies made at the local level, either for parish purposes (church repair, and so on) or special military ones.

In the 1620s, the intermittent wars against the Protestants raised taxes in certain years, such as 1621 and 1627–28, by means of military surtaxes. The main levies continue to be for a principal of

125. Porshnev, *Soulèvements,* piece 74. Mousnier, *Lettres,* I: 511–58.
126. Collins, "Taxation in Bretagne," chaps. 5–8.

about 14.5–15 million l. Unlike the 1603–20 period, however, this 1621–33 period saw a drastic increase in the surtax for the *droits*. The percentage levied for the *droits*, 10 percent at the start, 51 percent in 1634 (proposed), rose even faster than it appears, because the *droits* began to be levied on each other. Thus while the *droits* of 1634 were supposed to be a surtax of 51 percent, they in fact represented one of 88 percent.

Direct taxation probably increased by something like 20 percent between 1620 and 1627, and again by 66 percent from 1627 to 1633–34. The king received less and less of this money directly from the collection; both the *droits*, taking huge chunks out (46 percent for 1633), and the new offices, inflating the local and regional charges, severely cut the money paid in to the Central Treasury. The receiver of the *parties casuelles*, however, became a major focus of money. The direct tax system alone provided at least 10 million l. per year, on average, from its officers from 1621 to 1633.

After 1633, money went directly to the king. The 30–34 million l. levied annually in the early 1630s moved into the high 30s and low 40s after 1635. Normal *non-valeurs* for the period 1627–33 were probably not higher than 10 percent, thus a collection of 27–30 million l. But the *non-valeurs* of the late 1630s and 1640s, often exceeding 50 percent for entire *généralités*, would reduce collections for that period to less than those of the earlier one. So, while the amount supposedly levied went up sharply in the period 1636–47, the amount collected may have gone down.

The complications of the 1640s boggle the mind. The regular direct taxes are in the 40–45 million l. range, yet one also has enormous special levies, such as the one for winter quarters raised throughout the 1640s. Starting in 1642, the intendants have the authority to levy the taxes on their own, although they lose some of this power in 1646, and have a back-and-forth struggle with the regular officers all through the Fronde. The king also levies some of the *tailles* by means of *traité* after 1642, and the rebates to the *traitants* may have gone as high as 50 percent: in other words, the *traitant* paid the king half of the money assessed to a given area, and then set out to collect in full. As we have seen, the *non-valeurs* were often 50 percent or more, so a 50 percent rebate would break everyone just about even.

The enormity of the fines levied on the receivers general by the *Chambre de Justice* of 1661—Bordeaux, 600,000 l.; Rouen,

400,000 l.; Tours, 500,000 l.; Caen, 200,000 l.; Poitiers, 600,000 l. and 150,000 l.—leads one to suspect that the central government had some suspicions about the honesty of regional bookkeeping. As for the central officials, one must agree with Julian Dent, when he writes, "[I]t is clear that the whole central financial administration was involved on a permanent basis in conspiracy to commit fraud." [127]

It is likely that a great deal of money was levied on the countryside in the 1640s, much of it by soldiers who did not account for how they spent it, but it is also likely that many parishes, particularly those in more isolated areas, paid little or nothing at all.[128] In the Limousin, for example, most of the parishes had not even apportioned their taxes for 1649 as late as January 1650.[129]

The great issue here, of course, is just the problem posed by such inequitable distribution of collection between parishes: who paid the money? The tax increases of the 1627–33 period put a sharp strain on the French peasantry, and the added increases of 1636–38 seem to have overwhelmed them. Two major factors in this inability to pay heavier taxes were the distribution of the tax burden within the villages themselves and the sharp jump in land rents in most of France after 1640 or so. Pay the rent or pay the taxes? This question must have faced many French tenant farmers after 1635 or 1640. Clearly, the landlord would urge the peasant to pay the rent, and one must remember that tenants paid taxes on their share of the crop, even if the landlord was a noble.

Higher taxes, higher rents, economic recession—this was a staggering blow to the French peasantry. While the Fronde is, of course, a series of uncoordinated revolts by various groups, it is also the political symbol of the near complete collapse of French society in the late 1640s and early 1650s. The pressures of the Thirty Years' War changed not only French administration but the French economy and French society as well. In Chapter 4, we will see how those changes came about on the individual level.

127. On the fines, D. Dessert, "Finances et société au XVIIe siècle: à propos de la Chambre de Justice de 1661," *Annales E.S.C.* 29 (1974): 847–81, list in appendix. J. Dent, *Crisis in Finance* (New York, 1974), 83.

128. Bercé, *Histoire des Croquants,* has many examples. See also, chap. 4, below.

129. BN, Ms. Fr. 18510, fols. 427–28v.

4. Direct Taxation at the Village Level

Dividing the Tax Burden

The revolts of the seventeenth century are often held to have been caused by overtaxation. As we have seen in Chapters 1 through 3, the amount of taxation did rise substantially after 1616 and, more severely, after 1625. Undoubtedly the revolts in Normandy (1639), the Southwest (endemic), and in the *pays d'Etats* (around 1630) were all related to or caused by taxation. Yet our knowledge of the overall movement of taxation does little to help us understand the day-to-day dynamic of the situation. The fact that overall direct taxation rose by 100 percent from 1625 to 1634 tells us nothing about the burden of the typical peasant, nor does it provide much enlightenment on the relationship between taxation and economic decline.

The rapid increase in taxation after 1625 also brought with it another scourge: the presence of large numbers of troops in the countryside. Gaston Roupnel has vividly described the devastation caused by troops in Burgundy, where some villages have never recovered their pre-1634 population levels.[1] Similarly, we have seen that the taxes in Champagne could not be collected because the troops of the king ruined many villages. We will return to this problem, but it is worth citing the opinion of Yves-Marie Bercé, chronicler of the southwestern revolts, in this context: "But the heaviest, the most constant ordeal with which the war weighed down the village communities, was the housing of troops."[2]

To understand how the presence of troops was so closely interrelated with the increase in taxation, we must turn to the manner

1. G. Roupnel, *La ville et la campagne dijonnaise au XVIIe siècle* (Paris, 1929), 69.
2. Y.-M. Bercé, *Histoire des Croquants* (Geneva, 1974), 57.

in which the money was raised. By examining the repartition process, we can understand how the system worked bureaucratically on the local level and, most importantly, what direct effects it had on the peasants.

There were several steps in the division or repartition of the total direct tax burden. After the Royal Financial Council decided how much money was needed for a given year, the total sum was divided among the *généralités*. This division was usually based on the previous year's split, with a strong persistence of the old medieval percentage rates (those rates existed because the original direct tax was apportioned on the basis of men-at-arms). For example, Normandy contributed about 20 percent of the total direct tax levies in the sixteenth century, and just under 20 percent in the early seventeenth century. This percentage declined slightly, to about 18 percent, in the 1640s. Other areas showed similar consistency on a long-term basis, but there was some short-term adjustment for specific contingencies (local harvest failures, troop movements in a given area).

The council sent the *brevet de la taille* (see Table 21), or proposed levies, to the treasurers in each district; the treasurers were to receive it in the spring, but the timetable was followed properly only under Sully (for 1609, for example, they got it in June 1608), although in certain later years, such as 1633, it was followed with reasonable promptitude. The treasurers divided the amount for their district among the *élections;* this repartition was based on the previous year's amounts and on any changes the treasurers had noticed during their obligatory tours of inspection (*chevauchées*). They returned the *brevets* to the council, or, more specifically, to the *commission des tailles* of the council, which, in turn, combined them into the official preliminary statement—the *état du roi*. This statement was returned to the treasurers in November (again, only Sully followed the timetable with great success). The treasurers would then communicate the amounts due to the officers of the *élections,* the *élus,* who would make any adjustments necessary for changes made since the first repartition.[3]

The repartition within the parishes is very difficult to follow. Most sources claim that it was done among the parishes by the *élus,* based on the *brevet,* and that the parishes then made the apportion-

3. D. Buisseret, *Sully and the Growth of Centralized Government in France* (London, 1968). See, as an example, AD Cher, C 984, fol. 105, 1612 *commission des tailles* for Bourges.

Table 21. *Local Charges in Provins: The* Election *Budget, 1622*

Receipts	Amount	Expenses	Amount
Equivalent	126	Seven *élus*, three controllers	3,648
Taille	12,647	*Gages* increase, to same	1,109
Postal	118	Two *élus*	600
Pont Neuf	312	Inspection tours of *élus*	525
Constabulary	1,220	*Avocat du roi*	130
Taillon	3,065	*Procureur du roi*, three-fourths	56
Garrisons	10,290	*Greffier*	35
Bridges	55	Receivers	1,309
Taxes of receivers	33	*Taxes* of receivers	33
Total	27,866	3d./l. to receiver, on garrison tax	130
		d./l. to receiver	73
		Triennial payer of presidial	200
		Lt. *criminel* of presidial	400
		Constabulary	1,698
		Triennial payer of constabulary	125
		Rentes	1,429
		Roads and bridges	1,604
		Shipment of money to regional office (Paris)	150
		Epices, to Chamber of Accounts	856
		New *épices*	60
		Drawing up account	80
		Total	14,251[a]
		To regional bureau account	13,615

Source: BN, Ms. Fr. 16623, fols. 1–148v, *généralité* of Paris.
[a]Figures rounded to nearest *livre*.

ment themselves, following the previous year's roll. The rolls I have examined are all dated very close to the term of the collection. For instance, the roll for the first term of the direct taxes in the parish of Lanvaudan in Brittany for the year 1635 was drawn up in December 1634.[4] This timing would indicate a last-minute assessment, which was done after the *état du roi* for the given area had been prepared and promulgated. While changes in the assessment for districts, *généralités, élections,* and even parishes were done proportionately (*au sou le livre,* in the phrase of the day), such an

4. AD Morbihan, B 2782.

approach was not the case within the parishes themselves. We will return to this point later, but we must emphasize that while increases in taxation were proportional with respect to royal administrative districts, they were *not* proportional with respect to individual taxpayers.

The actual division of the tax at the parish level was done by the parishioners themselves: the codes of the seventeenth century specified two men for parishes contributing less than 900 l., four for those paying more. In fact, the peasants seem to have appointed whatever number pleased them, varying from two to six in the rolls I have examined. The sixteenth-century system had been to have separate men assess and collect the tax, but Henry IV changed that practice in 1600. He felt that the assessments would be more accurate if those who assessed were also responsible for the collection. As the ordinance of March 1600 put it: "[this reform is] a proper means of preventing them [the assessors] from cotisizing the poor and 'mediocre' for more than they can pay, in fear of having to advance their taxes."[5]

This repartition at the parish level was the source of many, if not most, of the complaints against the tax system.[6] The peasants had a wide variety of problems to overcome in order to draw up their roll for the direct taxes. Mousnier suggests that because so many of the peasants could not read, it was easy for the clerk who assisted them to falsify the rolls.[7] After 1616, the *commissaires des tailles* further complicate the situation. In the case of Dournazac in the Limousin, the *commissaire* was a powerful local taxpayer, Martial Garreau, who was also a *procureur*. Garreau, his son, and another relative, Pierre, the local *greffier*, paid a combined 49.6 l. in taxes on their property and *métairies* in 1623 and 85.0 l. in 1630: 8.4 percent and 9.9 percent, respectively, of the parish's total. The roll itself was compiled in Garreau's house on both occasions. Did these men protect themselves and their farmers? As for the literacy of the collectors themselves, none of the peasants involved on any

5. "Edit de mars 1600," in *Règlements rendus sur le fait des tailles* (Rouen, 1710). See also, "Règlement des finances du 19 janvier 1599," *Revue Henri IV* 1 (1905): 189–90. J.-P. Charmeil, *Les trésoriers de France à l'époque de la Fronde* (Paris, 1963), 151–53, shows the similarity of the system of these two *règlements* and that laid out by the Code Michau of 1629.

6. This is the pattern suggested by the papers of the Cour des Aides of Rouen, series C, AD Seine-Maritime.

7. R. Mousnier, *La Vénalité des Offices* (Rouen and Paris, 1945, 1971), 149.

roll signed his name. In Normandy the richer two of the peasant collectors made complicated marks, while the poorer two were signed for. This example follows the normal path toward literacy seen elsewhere in France.[8]

A problem more serious than illiteracy, as the Limousin example suggests, was the intervention of local landlords on behalf of their farmers. While this intervention was illegal, the constant reiteration of the prohibition in the *règlements* on the *tailles* is clear proof that the interference of landlords was endemic to the system.[9] The nobles' greatest solicitudes were reserved for their large farmers and *métayers*, since these men and women were usually among the richest peasants in the village and their taxes were very high. The nobles sought to have them exempted from the *tailles* for the revenues obtained from the *métairie* but not those from other sources. In 1614, the nobles of the Orléanais wrote in their *cahier* to the Estates General:

> First, in that which concerns their farms and *métairies*, which are so excessively charged and "foullez" with *tailles* and salt taxes that they [the nobles] cannot obtain but small revenues from their lands, which leads to great loss and damage [to them] . . . By this very just complaint and remonstrance, the said nobles supplicate very humbly to Your Majesty that in the future no farmers or *métayers* will be subject to and highly levied for the said *taille*, salt taxes, and other subsidies because of the lands and farms they hold of nobles ("gentilshommes") but only for what they should pay in their own names ("porter de leuf chef").[10]

The *cahiers* of Angoumois, Beaujolais, and Troyes for the proposed Estates General of 1649 contained similar requests. The nobles of Beaujolais complained that their farmers were assessed so highly that they (the nobles) had to pay the *tailles*.[11] The nobles of Angoumois protested that "against their rights and privileges, they are being constrained indirectly to pay them [the *tailles*] in that

8. R. Mandrou, *De la culture populaire en France aux XVIIe et XVIIIe siècles* (Paris, 1964). In the late seventeenth and eighteenth centuries, this was one of the most literate regions in France.

9. R. Mousnier, *Fureurs Paysans* (Paris, 1967), 40 and ff.

10. Y. Durand, ed., *Cahiers de doléances de la noblesse des gouvernements d'Orléanais, Normandie et Bretagne* (Nantes, n.d.), 75. Similar complaint from Normans, 99.

11. J.-P. Gutton, "Le cahier de doléances de la noblesse de Beaujolais aux états généraux de 1649," *Revue Historique* (1975): 115.

their farmers are cotisized." [12] Nor were these protests misleading; in almost every case (indeed, for every case in the rolls examined here for which such information is given—as a margin note on receipt of payment), the landlord paid one-half of the *taille* for his *métairies*. Nonetheless, the exemptions of the landlords—their half of the income from the holding was not taxable—were a considerable advantage, and there is no evidence that landlords paid any of the taxes of their lessees (that is, of those renting land for a cash payment, rather than sharecropping by equal shares). The more important point is that direct taxes competed with land rents, and that higher taxes meant more difficulty in collecting rents. This relationship was particularly true of cash resources, because both landlord and king sought to obtain the peasant's cash. For example, in Brittany landlords introduced, in the 1620s, the practice of substantial cash entry fees for leases. These fees were often specified by *coin* as well as by amount (thus 20 *écus* or 50 *pistoles,* not simply 60 pounds).[13] Higher *tailles* competed both with entry fees and, after 1635 or so, with sharply higher rents.

If there were disputes about the *tailles,* the parish could take an appeal to the *élus,* from whom there was no appeal for amounts less than 5 l. The exclusion clause effectively meant that most of the taxpayers in France had no right of appeal: in the rolls for the period prior to 1635, about 65–70 percent of the taxpayers paid less than 5 l. This was a considerable problem, because the *élus* were notorious for the protection of their friends and relatives, and for their general corruption. Their favoritism was so evident that the *taille* for the home parishes of all *élus* was set by the treasurers of France.[14]

Nor were the *élus* immune to pressure from powerful landlords;

12. Y. Durand, R. Mousnier, and J. Labatut, *Deux Cahiers de la Noblesse* (Paris, 1965), 88. Similar complaint from Troyes, 151.

13. AD Loire-Atlantique, G 244–45, papers of the Cathedral chapter of Nantes, provide many examples. For the tithes of Asserac, the entry fee began in 1622; for the tithes of Cambon, it started in 1633 (specified as fifty *écus* to be paid in *quarts d'écu*); for the tithes of Doulon, it started in 1628 as one "pistole d'Espagne"; for those of St-Erblain, it was six *écus* in *quarts d'écu* in 1617, four *pistoles* in 1629. Of the twenty-two parishes for which we have clear figures, five had a "denier à Dieu" (entry fee) by 1614, fifteen had one established between 1615 and 1630, and the two others began in 1645 and 1648.

14. Bercé, *Histoire des Croquants,* 75. E. Esmonin, *La taille en Normandie au temps de Colbert* (Paris, 1913), 180–90, gives examples. Again, they are supported by the papers of the Cour des Aides of Rouen.

such pressure could come from the highest sources. In January 1627, Cardinal Richelieu himself wrote to the *élus* of Thouars:

> Messieurs, ne pouvant que je n'affactionne les interests de mon nepveu de Pont-de-Couche à l'esgal des miens propres, je vous fais ceste lettre pour vous prier de soulager les habitans des paroisses qui luy appartiennent, deppandants de vostre eslection au département des tailles, autant que vous y sentirez convies par leur pauvreté et ma recommendation, vous asseurant que, là où j'auray le moyen de recognoistre le favourable traictement que vous leur départirez en ceste occasion, je m'y porteray avec autant de bonne volonté comme je demeure.[15]

One can well imagine the effect of such a letter on the humble *élus* of Thouars.

Protests against the system were constant throughout the early seventeenth century; this protest was strongest against the *élus*. In 1614, for example, the nobles of both the Orléanais and Normandy demanded a reduction in the number of *élus* from the current levels to two per *élection*, and of the treasurers of France from ten to two per *généralité*. The nobles also complained of the inequitable repartition of the *tailles*; laying the blame on the *élus*, the nobles wrote:

> but the corvées, pensions, presents which this quantity of *élus* receives makes it such that the excessive taxes levied for Your Majesty ruin some and the gratifications taken by the *élus* ruin the others, a fact that the nobility recognizes as only too true in all its parishes, and it is constrained to supplicate very humbly and in all affection Your Majesty to suppress the *élus* and reduce them to the above-mentioned number [two/*élection*], with a *procureur*, as there was formerly in each *élection*, without re-imbursing them, given the profits they have made in their said charges.[16]

The reforming agents, intendants (pre-1634) and *commissaires départis*, found the *élus* wanting as well. The *Chambre de Justice* of 1607, for example, imprisoned Gilles de Chevancy, *élu* of Mortain in Normandy.[17] In the mid-1640s, the treasurers at Bourges complained that the *élus* there raised their *gages* from the first monies collected in the period 1640–42.[18]

15. P. Grillon, ed., *Les papiers d'Etat de Richelieu* (Paris, 1977), vol. 2, papers of 1627, piece 16.

16. Durand, *Cahiers . . . d'Orléanais*, 109.

17. BN, Ms. Fr. 16627, fols. 226v–373, papers of 1607 Chambre.

18. BN, Ms. Fr. 18510, fol. 387.

The detestation of the *élus* was one symptom of the extraordinarily complex network of social relations in seventeenth-century rural France. One element in the nobles' resentment of the *élus* was precisely that the *élus* could aid their tenants in battle with the local tax bureaucracy, whereas the nobles frequently could not. This disadvantage was not so much true of the more powerful local noble families, who frequently had clientage ties to the local officer clans, as it was true of the medium-sized nobles, precisely those most sharply affected by the higher tax rates.[19]

Village Tax Rolls in the *Pays d'Election*

To understand how this process worked, we must go to the tax rolls themselves. Here we enter into the most bewildering thicket of all. While quite interesting in themselves, the rolls do not provide the full information we seek. This inadequacy will become clear as we proceed, but we must first examine a few of the tax rolls before we turn to such problems as multiple rolls and nonpayment (*non-valeurs*).

Very few tax rolls are available for northern France in the period prior to the Fronde. The information from the eighteenth century, which is quite voluminous, is of little value because of the considerable changes that took place in the interim. Similarly, one must be extremely wary of any rolls dated after 1625 as an indicator for the period 1600–1624, or for any rolls from the 1640s (because of the high level of *non-valeurs*). The nonpayment of taxes reached epidemic proportions after 1634, so one must cast a cautious eye indeed on information after that date (and prior to 1661).

Pierre Goubert has published some of the only information taken from tax rolls, but his documents date from the very end of the seventeenth century. In his monograph on the Beauvaisis he cites a role for the village of Cuigny-en-Bray, with 115 taxpayers. A local notary pays 254 l., an enormous sum, while, at the other end of the scale, 47.8 percent of the taxpayers contribute less than 5 l., and 62.6 percent, less than 10 l. Yet Goubert states that a typical *haricotier* (small farmer) paid about 20 l.[20] A similar ex-

19. J. Dewald, *The Formation of a Provincial Nobility, The Magistrates of the Parlement of Rouen, 1499–1610* (Princeton, 1980).

20. P. Goubert, *Beauvais et le Beauvaisis* (Paris, 1960), 153.

ample from La Bellière in Normandy shows that community to
have paid 904 l. in 1698, of which two taxpayers, both farmers for
"sieurs de . . . ," paid 150 l. and 110 l., respectively. Three others,
also farmers of "sieurs de . . . ," paid 53 l., 49 l., and 48 l. If we use
a quartile distribution, based on the size of the contributions, we
find that the top quartile paid 68 percent of the taxes, while the
bottom one paid about 2.5 percent.[21]

Jean Jacquard, in his work on the area south of Paris between
1550 and 1670, provides similar evidence. He shows large farmers/
métayers to be paying over 100 l. per year and, in one case, 310 l.
(in 1662). Jacquard settles for an approximation of 150 l. per year
for a large farmer.[22]

How representative are these figures? Let us take some examples
from several provinces in different parts of the kingdom: Poitou,
Guyenne, and the Limousin in the Southwest; Beaujolais and Forez
in the Southeast; and Normandy in the Northwest. We can compare the small samples from these provinces with a large one from
Brittany. The examples from the *pays d'élection* span the period
1596 (St-Laurent-d'Oingt) to 1649 (Aveize). Four of the rolls—
Augé and St-Martin-les-Melle (both 1642), Aveize and St-Ouen-de-
Breuil (1645)—present only proposed levies and they are from a
period of extremely high *non-valeurs*, so one must be wary of viewing their figures as actual levels of tax payment. The figures from
Brittany are from a special system, whose peculiarities will be de-
tailed in a moment, but they offer a useful counterpoint to the
French examples.

In most cases the rolls contain only the names of those assessed
and their cotisation, but some rolls list professional classification.
Others have indications as to the amount actually paid, and that of
St-Ouen lists the land rented and owned by each individual. Using
the southwestern rolls and those from the *généralité* of Lyon, we
will look at the general distribution and differentiation by professional status. The Breton rolls will demonstrate the general distribution in a system of lower taxation, as well as the prevalence of
women on the rolls and the instability of the villages and towns for
which we have multiple rolls.

The parish of St-Martin-les-Melle is some 55 kilometers south-

21. P. Goubert, *The Ancien Régime* (New York, 1969, 1973), 121.
22. J. Jacquard, *La crise rurale en Ile-de-France, 1550–1670* (Paris, 1974), 381.

Table 22. *Tax Distribution (Assessments) in Three Southwestern Parishes (Percentage Assessed to Quartile)*

Parish (Year)	I	II	III	IV
St-Martin-les-Melle (1642)	67.6	22.7	8.2	1.5
Augé (1642)	81.0	12.5	5.0	1.5
Farguerolle (1607)	74.1	16.2	7.4	2.3[a]

Sources: St-Martin-les-Melle (AD Deux-Sèvres, C 511); Augé (AD Deux-Sèvres, C 145); Farguerolle (AD Gironde, C 4821).

[a]The roll at Farguerolle was expressed in *sous*, *deniers*, and fractions of *deniers*, with each *sou* representing a given level of assessment (in 1630, 3 l.) In my notes I listed those individuals assessed for less than one *denier* as a single category, and that category has arbitrarily been assigned a total contribution of nine *deniers* (one-half *denier* each). This amount is probably too high, thus the slightly higher figure for the fourth quartile.

west of Poitiers; it lay in the *élection* of St-Maixent (see Table 22). In 1642, it was assessed for 1,986 l. of principal and 60 l. of surcharges. There were ninety-four taxpayers, thus an average assessment of 20.7 l., quite similar to Goubert's figure. The median, however, was only 10 l. One finds a strong division between the two largest groups of peasants with the village: the *labourers* (twenty cotisations, of which eight were partnerships) were assessed for 1,020 l. (52 percent of the total); the *journaliers* (nineteen) were assessed for only 102 l. (5.2 percent). Every *laboureur* was assessed for 20 l. or more, nine of them for more than 50 l. No *journalier* was assessed for more than 16 l., and only four were assessed for 10 l. or more. The local elite, those assessed for 50 l. or more, consisted of nine *laboureurs*, a notary, a clothier, a draper, and a merchant (see Table 23).[23]

Here we see patterns that will remain constant throughout all the rolls. The distribution will be sharply skewed: at St-Martin the top quartile was assessed for 67.6 percent of the taxes, the bottom one for 1.5 percent. At Augé the respective figures in 1642 were 81 percent and 1.5 percent; at Farguerolle, in the Bordelais, in 1607, they were 74.1 percent and 2.3 percent.[24] Augé's roll also contains some information on professional status, and we again find the *laboureurs* at the top of the heap: thirteen of the fourteen richest taxpayers, assessed for 1,449 l. Of Augé's 277 taxpayers, eight

23. AD Deux-Sèvres, C 511.
24. AD Gironde, C 4821 (Farguerolle).

Table 23. *Tax Distribution by Occupation in St-Martin-les-Melle, 1642*

Description	Assessments (in l.)
Laboureur with consorts	30; 61; 72; 85; 91; 130
Laboureur with nephew	80
Laboureurs	20 (two, together); 20; 20; 20; 27; 28 (2); 32; 40; 44; 54; 58; 68
Widow of *laboureur* with consorts	40
Sergeants	0.5; 1; 4; 6 (royal sergeant)
Journaliers	0.5; 1; 2; 3; 3; 3; 3.5; 4; 4; 4; 4.25; 5; 5; 6.5; 7.5; 10; 10; 10; 16
Weaver and consorts	25; 25
Weaver	0.5; 7; 10; 37
"Fouthier"	2
"Boutier" and son (merchants)	40
"Bouthier"	25
Clothier	0.5; 4; 4; 9; 52 (2)
Carder	21
Carpenter	5; 9
Medical doctor	3.5
Notary	14; 30; 50
Merchant	1; 1; 7; 12; 15; 18 (2); 20; 22; 25; 25 (2); 50
Draper	75
Stonecutter	0.2
Blacksmith	9 (2)
Tailor	1; 8
Serge maker	0.05
Unknown	0.05; 0.2; 0.2; 0.2; 2; 8; 9; 15; 15 (dame); 16 (consorts); 18; 25; 40

Source: AD Deux-Sèvres, C 511.

were assessed for 100 l. or more and fourteen others for 50–100 l.; however, 149 people were assessed for less than 5 l. Collectively, this 54 percent of the population was assessed for only 7 percent of the taxes.[25]

Three rolls from the *généralité* of Lyon reinforce this image of a highly skewed tax distribution. In the case of two of the rolls, those of St-Laurent (1596) and Chassigny (1647), we know that the

25. AD Deux-Sèvres, C 145 (Augé).

money was actually collected; for Aveize (1649), we know only the assessments. Some of these assessments were quite large—two over 100 l. and nine others for 50–99 l. Very few people on the roll of Aveize are identified by professional classification, but among those singled out, *laboureurs* are assessed at 84.2 l. (fourth highest in the village) and 66.1 l. Yet the classification is not so strict as in Poitou, for we also find *labourers* assessed for as little as 10 s. 9 d. One group is singled out: the "chapitre des grangiers et fermiers." This landless group of thirty-two (in a total of 131) were to pay only 49.15 l. (1.9 percent), and four of their number were assessed for over half this amount. The poorest twenty-eight *grangiers* (day laborers; literally, barn workers) thus were assessed for less than 1 percent of the taxes.

The roll at Chassigny is for a special tax to alleviate the 1646 arrears of Lyonnais parishes damaged by a hailstorm. The payments ranged from 1 s. to 13.4 l. This latter figure would translate into a regular burden of some 75–100 l. Once again we find a special chapter for "fermiers et grangiers"; and again they are desperately poor. Eleven of the sixteen members of the group paid 3 s. or less; collectively, they paid 3 l. 12 s., 2.7 percent of the total, yet they were 27 percent of the group.

The roll at St-Laurent, which dates from 1596, contains margin notes as to actual payments. Most of the taxpayers had fully acquitted their obligations, which ranged from a high of 38.8 l. to a low of 10 d. In all three Lyonnais rolls the highest quartile paid a disproportionate share, ranging from 66.5 percent at Aveize to 74.0 percent at Chassigny (see Table 24). The lowest quartile paid between 0.9 percent (Aveize) and 1.9 percent (St-Laurent).[26]

Village Tax Rolls in Brittany

When we switch from France proper to Brittany, we find that the individual cotisations are much smaller because of the nature of the Breton direct tax system. The highest quartile paid less than in France; the other quartiles, notably the third and fourth, much more (in percentage terms, although not in real terms).

The Breton tax system did not include the *taille* or the adjuncts

26. AD Rhône, 3 C 20 (Chassigny, 1647), 3 C 39 (St-Laurent-d'Oingt, 1596), 3 C 15 (Aveize, 1649).

Table 24. *Tax Distribution in Nine French Parishes, 1596–1649*
         (Percentage Assessed to Quartile)

Parish (Year)	I	II	III	IV
St-Laurent-d'Oingt (1596)	71.8	20.0	6.3	1.9
Farguerolles (1607)	74.1	16.2	7.4	2.3
Dournazac (1623)	69.4	22.5	7.5	0.7
Dournazac (1630)	68.5	22.7	7.5	1.4
Augé (1642)	81.0	12.5	5.0	1.5
St-Martin-les-Melles (1642)	67.6	22.7	8.2	1.5
St-Ouen-de-Breuil (1645)	72.3	18.5	7.7	1.5
Chassigny (1647)	72.1	19.4	7.2	1.3
Aveize (1649)	66.5	24.4	8.3	0.9

Sources: St-Laurent (AD Rhône, 3 C 39); Farguerolles (AD Gironde, C 4821); Dourna-zac (AD Haute-Vienne, C 145); Augé (AD Deux-Sèvres, C 145); St-Martin (AD Deux-Sèvres, C 511); St-Ouen (AD Seine-Maritime, C 2108); Chassigny (AD Rhône, 3 C 20); Aveize (AD Rhône, 3 C 15).

to it (the *droits,* for example). The *fouage* was fixed at 7 l. 7 s.m. (Breton money, of which 5 s. = 6 s. t.) on a fixed number of hearths (*feux*), plus various additional taxes—the *taillon,* the constabulary tax, and a tax for the Estates. In addition, there was a separate roll for the garrison tax, which varied from 75,000 l. under Henry IV to a high of 106,000 l. in the early 1640s. The total came to about 14.25 l./*feu,* or some 475–500,000 l. Most towns were exempt, but some important ones paid the *fouage* and others had specific parishes that were not exempt. This burden, the same in absolute terms as it had been in the late fifteenth century, doubled in 1643, with the introduction of the *fouage extraordinaire.*[27]

Our sample includes fifteen *fouage* rolls, dating from 1558 to 1672. The 1558 roll covers a lower assessment per *feu,* but all of the others deal with the basic sum of 10.45 l./*feu* (that is, the *fouage* and its adjuncts but not the garrison tax) except for the rolls of Masserac. The rolls of Masserac, Loc Eguiver, and Carhaix (1668 roll) also exclude the assessments for the *fouage extraordinaire,* which would double everyone's tax burden.

In Table 25, we can see the tax distribution in ten Breton parishes. The share of the top quartile varied from 51.2 in Muzillac

27. J. Collins, "Taxation in Bretagne, 1598–1648" (Ph.D. diss., Columbia University, 1978), chap. 5.

Table 25. *Tax Distribution in Ten Breton Parishes, 1558–1672*
(Percentage Assessed to Quartile)

Parish (Year)	I	II	III	IV
Masserac (1665)	63.9	21.5	10.3	4.3
Lannion (1641)	61.9	22.0	10.9	5.2
Carhaix (1603)	61.0	25.3	10.8	3.0[a]
Audierne (1616)	60.9	20.2	12.8	6.1
Loc Eguiver (1672)	58.9	20.3	13.3	7.4[a]
Carhaix (1668)	58.2	21.4	13.8	6.7[a]
Langourla (1652)	56.6	25.9	12.8	4.8[a]
Assérac (1620)	55.0	22.0	14.6	8.5[a]
Lanvaudan (1634)	52.1	26.9	16.9	4.1
Muzillac (1558)	51.2	31.4	14.1	3.4[a]
St-Nicolas of Nantes (1586)	78.0	15.1	5.9	1.0[b]

Sources: Masserac (AD Loire-Atlantique, G 440); Lannion (AD Ille-et-Vilaine, papers of A. de la Borderie, series E); Carhaix (AD Finistère, 2 E 1501–1603, 2 E 1502–1668); Audierne (AD Finistère, 16 G 1); Loc Eguiver (AD Finistère, 125 G 2); Langourla (AD Finistère, 1 F 1640); Assérac (AD Loire-Atlantique, G 348); Lanvaudan (AD Morbihan, G 853); Muzillac (AD Morbihan, B 2782). St-Nicolas (AM de Nantes, GG 744).
[a]Rounded figures do not add up to 100%.
[b]This is not a *fouage* roll, as are the others, but a poor relief assessment, not bound, as was the *fouage*, by custom. In that sense it is not comparable to the others.

(1558) to 63.9 percent in Masserac (1665). The median of the nine seventeenth-century rolls is 58.9 percent for the first quartile, as against 71.8 percent in the nine French parishes. The share of the other quartiles is higher, the difference most striking in the bottom quartile.

There are two reasons for the differences. First, Breton assessments were much lower than those in France. At Audierne, for example, 196 of 235 taxpayers (1617) paid less than 1 l. and the median contribution was 7 s. Indeed one taxpayer at Augé was assessed for more than the entire parish of Audierne.[28] In Carhaix the roll of 1668 indicates regular *fouage* payments of 11 *sous* or less for 256 of the 452 taxpayers (56.6 percent).[29] At the other end of the scale the richest Breton taxpayers paid very little—for example, at Masserac, in 1665, the top assessment for the regular

28. AD Finistère, 16 G 1. The 1616 roll at Audierne was published by D. Bernard, "Role des fouages à Audierne en 1616," *Mémoires de la Société des Antiquaires du Finistère* 38: 158–66.
29. AD Finistère, 2 E 1501.

levies was only 8.5 l. (this amount would have meant 17 l. for regular levies and the *fouage extraordinaire*).[30]

The second factor involved in Brittany, at least in the western
part of the province, was the unique Breton system of landholding
known as the *domaine congéable*. T. J. A. Le Goff has shown that,
in the eighteenth century, this system kept its *tenuyer*'s taxes quite
low because the land continued to belong to the (tax-exempt) noble
landlord. The *tenuyer* was not, strictly speaking, a tenant in the
same way in which a *métayer* was a tenant, so he was taxed at a
special, lower rate.[31] The one Breton parish clearly outside the geographic range of this system, Masserac, is that with the distribution
closest to the French model, and its variance from that model could
easily be explained by the lower overall assessments. That the lowest quartile paid more (in percentage terms) in Brittany than in
France says nothing about its relative well-being. The individual
members of the lowest quartile paid only 1 or 2 *sous* a year in all
of the parishes in Brittany; their higher percentage of the total al-
lotment can be explained by the proximity of the median contribution (usually 10 or 11 *sous*) to their assessment. (In France the
median contribution ranged from 3 l. to 10 l.)

The most instructive of the Breton rolls are those of Masserac,
in the Vilaine valley, covering the years 1665–68. While the distribution of the tax burden was somewhat more skewed than in other
Breton parishes, Masserac shared several important elements not
only with Breton villages but with French ones as well. First, it had
a substantial number of households headed by women: 19 percent
of the taxpayers were women. These women were often quite poor:
they paid only 7 percent of the taxes. We can see in Table 26 the
percentage of women taxpayers in eleven sample parishes (five in
France, six in Brittany). The percentage of women was highest in
Carhaix (1603), 24.4 percent, while their contribution was highest
in Langourla, 18 percent.[32]

The women on these rolls are not defined as carefully as one
might wish. Some are identified as widows, but others are listed
solely by name. The roll of Lannion (1641) shows us the different
ways of listing women:[33]

30. AD Loire-Atlantique, G 440.
31. T. J. A. Le Goff, *Vannes and Its Region* (Oxford, 1981).
32. AD Finistère, 1 F 1640, for Langourla, 2 E 1501, for Carhaix.
33. AD Ille-et-Vilaine, series E, special subseries for papers of A. de la Borderie.

Marguerite Le dautec	30 shillings
Jacquette Le mogueron, vefve de Penhuel	2 shillings
Janne Le Moullec, vefve de deffunct Claude Hue	5 shillings
La vefve de Herve Berthou	1 shilling
La veufve de feu Jan Le Moign à présent compagne espouse de (left blank)	5 shillings
Marie Queraulen et son gendre	5 shillings
Martin Auti, marij espoux de Catherine Le Rueult	3 shillings
Yvon Bodeveur et Janne Bizich, sa femme	10 shillings

On the other rolls one might find " 'X' et sa femme." What is one to make of such distinctions? It is likely that Marie Queraulen was a widow, yet no such distinction about her is made. In other rolls widows were listed as " 'Y', veuve de 'X' "; why, in some cases, do we not have their own names at Lannion? We must therefore be very careful in dividing widows from single women on the basis of information from the rolls. For example, using the simplest classification system—counting only those identified as widows or with children living with them—one would find that twenty-eight of the forty-six women on the 1641 Lannion roll were widows, eighteen were single women. The widows were somewhat better off; they could be found fairly evenly divided among the quartiles, albeit with the largest group in the bottom quartile (eleven). Among the single women, ten were in the bottom quartile, four in the third.

This pattern repeats itself in most other cases. At Lanvaudan, six of the seven single women were in the bottom quartile, but the widows were more evenly split among the quartiles: 1; 4; 7; 3.[34] The situation in France was much the same. At Dournazac, the 1623 roll shows at least fifteen women and twelve other households described as the "heirs of 'X'." The fifteen women included ten from the fourth quartile, two from the third, and three from the first (all widows).[35] Five of the fifteen women remained in 1630: nine of ten disappearances were from the fourth quartile.

The substantial presence of women on the rolls is due both to majority laws—in most cases, one had to be twenty-five to rent land—and to the presence of a large number of (presumably young

34. AD Morbihan, B 2782.
35. AD Haute-Vienne, C 145.

Table 26. *Women Heads of Households in Five French and Six Breton Parishes*

Parish (Year)	% of Women	% of Women's Contribution
Carhaix (1603)	24.4	16.6
Langourla (1652)	21.0	18.5
Masserac (1665)	19.0	7.0
Audierne (1617)	14.7	11.3
Lanvaudan (1634)	14.2	10.0
St-Ouen-de-Breuil (1645)	14.0	10.0
St-Laurent-d'Oingt (1596)	13.6	6.3
Lannion (1641)	10.5	7.8
Chassigny (1647)	10.0	4.4
Dournazac (1623)	9.5	4.1
St-Martin-les-Melle (1642)	7.4	3.4

Sources: Carhaix (AD Finistère, 2 E 1501); Langourla (AD Finistère, 1 F 1640); Masserac (AD Loire-Atlantique, G 440); Audierne (AD Finistère, 16 G 1); Lanvaudan (AD Morbihan, G 853); St-Ouen (AD Seine-Maritime, C 2108); St-Laurent (AD Rhône, 3 C 39); Lannion (AD Ille-et-Vilaine, series E); Chassigny (AD Rhône, 3 C 20); Dournazac (AD Haute-Vienne, C 145); St-Martin (AD Deux-Sèvres, C 511).

or fairly old) single women in the villages. The first case is neatly demonstrated in the 1695 lease of the *métairie* of Coudray, near Nantes, in which Perrine Bouteiller signs "tant pour elle que pour Pierre Bouteiller son frère" on a lease made out to her and her husband (Jan Luneau, *laboureur à boeufs*). Pierre promised to approve the contract when he turned twenty-five.[36] The second case concerns a group to whom we will shortly turn: those who disappeared from the rolls each year. There were a considerable number of women in this group, as we shall see; they were often the single women.

These single women usually clustered at the bottom of the roll. Yet women as a group, taking the single women and widows as a mass, often controlled significant parts of the village's land. The one roll for which we have both the land distribution and the tax assessments, that of St-Ouen-de-Breuil (1645), illustrates this phenomenon (see Table 27).[37]

We can see that women owned 35 *acres,* of the 208.5 *acres* pos-

36. AD Loire-Atlantique, H 275, côte 2.
37. AD Seine-Maritime, C 2108.

Table 27. *Women on the Tax Roll of St-Ouen-de-Breuil, 1645*

Description	Assessment	Land Owned	Land Rented
Widow and son	78.45 l.	10	
Widow and son	101.85		40
Widow and son, *cordonnier*	22.8		4
Widow and son, *batteur en grange*	12.7	1	
Widow and son	4.05		
Widow	81.5	14	
Widow	48.9	10	
Widow			
Widow			
Widow			
"Pauvre femme"	2.0		

Source: AD Seine-Maritime, C 2108. Land in Norman *acres*. 1 Norman *acre* = 1.37 English acres.

sessed by those listed on the roll. They farmed another 44 *acres*, giving them control of about 8.5 percent of the village's land. They were 14 percent of the taxpayers (eleven of seventy-eight) and paid just under 10 percent of the taxes. While one can argue that here (and elsewhere) it was the widows who made up the economically important element among the women, there is no reason to gainsay the economic role of these widow-farmers. While their control of the land could be short-lived, because sons would take over the holding when they reached twenty-five, it was nonetheless control. For every widow whose son took over the farm, there was another new widow who now ran the family enterprise. This assumption of management was particularly important in maintaining the continuity of a family's holding.

The other large group of women, the single women often clustered at the bottom of the roll, introduces us to another large social group whose existence is strongly implied by the rolls: the itinerant poor. If we return again to Masserac, we find that, in 1665, there were 208 taxpayers (with 92 different surnames). The average contribution was only 1 l. 3 s., the median just under 10 s.; 64.4 percent of the taxpayers paid less than 1 l. In 1666, we find that sixteen of the 208 taxpayers (7.7 percent) have disappeared; by 1668, forty-five of the original 208 were neither on the roll nor replaced by a widow or other heirs. While some of these people died, most of them probably simply moved.[38] They did not drop off the roll due to poverty, since the roll lists individuals who did not pay any tax.

This pattern is repeated in all cases of multiple rolls. Thus, at Audierne, 10 percent of the taxpayers of 1617 were gone in 1619 (excluding nine known deaths); two other taxpayers had had their assessments reduced to nothing due to poverty. Indeed most of the rolls clearly list even those who were exempt, such as the keeper of the town clock and winner of the *papegault* at Carhaix or Henry Baillec of that town, "exempte à cause de la foll."[39] In St-Ouen there is a list of twelve *feux inutiles* (those not paying). For all cases of multiple rolls, we have 5 to 7 percent of the taxpayers disappearing each year, excluding those succeeded on the roll by heirs.

The annual disappearance of 5 to 7 percent of the local taxpaying population demonstrates the likely existence of a large rural underclass, wandering the countryside, selling its labor. The identity of the missing ones makes this clear: they are overwhelmingly from the poorest groups in the village. At Carhaix, for example, fourteen of the seventeen missing taxpayers had paid 1 l. or less; these fourteen people, 5.3 percent of the population, had paid less than 1 percent of the taxes. At Audierne, the missing twenty-four (10 percent of the taxpayers) had paid only 6.7 percent of the taxes. The missing thirty-three people (including the known dead) had been replaced by nine heirs and thirty-nine new villagers. The thirty-nine new people (15.1 percent of the taxpayers) paid only 9.4 percent of the taxes.

The figures suggest that there were two societies in rural France: the stable, sedentary society of traditional historiography and an itinerant society of semiproletarians, moving from village to village, selling their labor or perhaps renting a *bordage*. We have seen, in the rolls from the *généralité* of Lyon, that the "grangiers et fermiers" made up the bottom quartile of the parish, and we will see in a moment that there was a similar group in St-Ouen-de-Breuil. Those who disappeared from year to year tended to come from this group more than any other. The itinerants probably stayed within

38. P. Goubert, *Beauvais et le Beauvaisis* (Paris, 1960), indicates that 2.5 to 3.0 percent of the heads of household might die in a given year. This figure would leave us with 2.0 to 4.5 percent of the taxpayers as migrants each year.

39. AD Finistère, 2 E 1502.

their own *pays,* and many may have returned to their original villages. As Masserac we have the case of Benjamin Hadet, assessed for 2 s. in 1665, not on the rolls of 1666 or 1667, and paying 1.5 s. in 1668. Many of these itinerants were women; one might hypothesize that they were young women, working outside of their family home to save money before marriage.[40]

The pattern of disappearances is clear in Masserac: 21.6 percent lost between 1665 and 1668; in Audierne, 10 percent between 1617 and 1619; in Carhaix, 6.4 percent from 1603 to 1604; and Lannion, 75 percent between 1641 and 1651 (using a sample of 100 taxpayers). This matter is not simply a Breton one, as the example of Dournazac, in the Limousin mountains, illustrates. There we have rolls from 1623 and 1630; 44 percent of the taxpayers disappeared for reasons unknown to us. We will return to this issue in a moment, but first let us examine the rolls of Dournazac in greater detail.

Dournazac

The rolls date from 1623 and 1630; thus they straddle the great jumping-off point in increase, which we have dated, using regional and central documents, to the period 1625–30. The roll of 1630 is, in fact, two rolls combined into one: a roll for the *taille, taillon,* and associated charges, and a second one for the garrison tax and the *droits aliénés* (here called the *petits droits*). The garrison tax was 146 l., the *droits* 210 l. In addition, certain other *droits* were listed separately on both rolls. The parish had to pay 4d./l. to the *élus,* 9d./l. to the receivers, 3d./l. to the controllers, and small fees for the carrying of the commission for the *bordereau,* for the four *quittances* (receipts), for the seals, and 8d./l. for the collectors. The total for the *droits* of the officers was about 275 l., plus another 28.3 l. for the collectors. The *droits* thus took about 32 percent of the total, or 35 percent if the collector is included.[41] These are precisely the amounts indicated by the documents from Champagne, for that entire *généralité* (see Chapter 3).

40. AD Loire-Atlantique, G 440. J.-P. Gutton, *Domestiques et serviteurs dans la France de l'ancien régime* (Paris, 1981), 80, indicates that most female servants at Lyon in the eighteenth century came from the countryside. They stayed six or eight years, earning their dowry to take home.

41. AD Haute-Vienne, C 145.

The overall movement of taxation in Dournazac is slightly sharper than in France as a whole. The parish contribution rose from 589 l. in 1623 to 862 l. in 1630: a jump of 46 percent. The general increase for this period, based on provincial figures from Normandy and Champagne, was about 35 percent. The figures from Dournazac give us some idea who paid the great increases of the period 1625–30 and thus a clearer view of the real grievances against the system (see Table 28).

Starting with the distribution pattern, one finds it quite similar to the parishes examined earlier. The individual cotisations are somewhat different, lower than the excessive (and probably imaginary) rates of the 1640s (at Augé and St-Martin-les-Melles) and much higher than the privileged Breton villages.

We can see what we now call "bracket creep." The percentage of those assessed for more than 10 l. jumps from 43.3 to 57.6, an increase of 33 percent. The biggest loss is in the group paying 5–10 l.; clearly, they have moved into the next bracket. This question of bracket creep is quite different from that of the quartile distribution. While the overall distribution remained about the same, the individual assessments went up sharply.

It is not as easy as one might expect to explain the total increase, because we must contend again with the question of disappearance of taxpayers. Between 1623 and 1630, 70 of the 158 taxpayers of 1623 disappeared from the rolls, leaving no clear heirs (widows or children with the same surname). Another 7 people died but were succeeded by their widows or children. In other words, 49 percent of the people disappeared, and 44 percent did so for reasons unknown to us.

The identity of the lost parishioners is not surprising: the top three quartiles retained just over 60 percent of their members while the bottom quartile lost over 60 percent of its members. While there are few descriptions of occupation, of the seven people identified in 1623 as *bordiers*, very small sharecroppers, only one is left in 1630. A similar pattern prevailed in Brittany, where the disappearances at Carhaix (1603–4), Audierne (1617–19), and Masserac (1665–68) took place disproportionately within the bottom quartile of the taxpayers.

The holdovers among the richest taxpayers at Dournazac paid a much larger sum in 1630 than in 1623; their average contribution went up by 75–100 percent. This general figure, however, masked

Table 28. *Tax Distribution in Dournazac, 1623 and 1630*

Payment	Number of Taxpayers 1623	Number of Taxpayers 1630	% of Taxpayers 1623	% of Taxpayers 1630	Contribution in l. 1623	Contribution in l. 1630	% of Contribution 1623	% of Contribution 1630
Under 1 l.	59	50	37.3	29.8	14.3	18.2	2.4	2.1
Under 5 l.	54	63	34.2	37.5	134.5	169.2	22.8	19.6
Under 10 l.	28	24	17.7	14.3	186.6	178.8	31.6	20.7
10 l. and over	17	31	10.8	18.5	254.9	496.7	43.2	57.6

	Tax Distribution by Quartile			
	Contribution in l.		% of Contribution	
Quartile	1623	1630	1623	1630[a]
I	410.3	590.5	69.3	68.5
II	133.0	195.3	22.5	22.7
III	44.3	64.5	7.5	7.5
IV	4.4	11.8	0.7	1.4

Source: AD Haute-Vienne, C 145.
[a]Rounded figures do not add up to 100%.

substantial individual variation. The tax roll also does not fully reflect the tax burden of some of the most important parishioners. In all cases for which the margin notes exist, the owner of a piece of land and the *métayer* split the actual payment of the taxes, even though only the *métayer*'s name appeared on the roll. In one case, that of Marsalle de Lasche, it was the *métayer* who appeared in the margin, while de Lasche appeared on the roll. In 1630, we have the case of Jehan de Lasche, merchant; he paid 4 l. of the *taille* of his *métayer*, T. Bussière, out of a total of 7 l. 4 s. When we examine the assessments against the land owned by local notables, we get an idea of their domination of the village. The totals of Table 29 include not only the assessment against the landlords in their own names but those against their *métayers*.

The concentration of the wealth is greater than in Brittany, perhaps because our source, the tax roll, deals with much larger sums of money here than in Brittany. Both the total village assessment and the average assessment are much higher in the French villages than in Brittany. The correlation between average contribution and percentage of the total paid by the top quartile in Brittany is not

Table 29. *Contributions of the Ten Largest Landlords in Dournazac, 1630*

Taxpayer	1630	(1623)
Heirs of M. de Lasche	76.25	(54.6, de Lasche himself)
Sieur Vitelle	38.75	(17.25)
Martial Garreau, the elder	35.7	(16.35)
G. de Merguier	32.6	
A. de Mouguibir	28.6	(17.95)
Pierre Garreau	25.45	(22.25)
Sieur Defayolles	23.9	
M. Deschamps	18.7	
Jehan de Lasche	15.0	(16.5)
Martial Garreau, the younger	13.55	(10.85)
Total	308.5	(155.75)
Percentage of parish total	35.7	(26.5)

Source: AD Haute-Vienne, C 145.

Note: It is possible that Defayolles or Vitelle was on the roll in 1623 under an actual name. The roll is not consistent in identifying people: Pierre Garreau appears both under that name and as the sieur de Maulmont. While internal evidence enables me to make the connection for Garreau, the absence of such information does not mean Defayolles or Vitelle was not present in 1623 under a Christian name.

extremely high, $r = 0.30$, but it is of some significance. (This correlation was done using nine rolls, excluding those of Muzillac—because it is from the sixteenth century—Asserac—because it is not for an entire parish—and the second of the closely paired chronological rolls of both Carhaix and Audierne.)

The increase for the seven holdovers among the landlords is only 49.5 percent, just slightly more than the 46 percent for the village as a whole. Matters are not so simple, however, as the figures for certain taxpayers indicate. The Garreau family, for instance, had a new holding assessed for 15 l. in 1630; their old holdings were assessed for 49.55 l. in 1623 and only 60.1 l. in 1630, an increase of just over 20 percent. Is this relatively favorable treatment for their *métayers* due to the family positions, particularly that of *commissaire des tailles?* One also finds, however, that the original holdings of the village elite do not see their taxes rise precipitously— that is, much of the increase in their tax burden was due to new *métairies*.

Dournazac seems to have been a relatively normal or average

parish. The overall increase in taxation from 1623 to 1630 is about the same as for the country as a whole. The number of people who disappeared, about 6 percent a year (excepting known deaths), seems to have been typical. The tax distribution was relatively normal, with the top quartile paying about two-thirds of the taxes; indeed, if anything, this figure is too low for France as a whole (excluding favored Brittany and Burgundy).

The rolls are more complicated than these simple generalizations make them appear. The question of the quartile distribution, for example, leaves glaring gaps in our understanding of village life in the area of the *taille personnelle*. As we have seen for Dournazac, many times the most important taxpayers appear on the roll in a subsidiary role, and, if one does not have margin notes of payments, they do not appear at all in the area of the *taille personnelle* if they are nobles, exempt officers, or exempt bourgeois.

Despite these problems of interpretation, the tax increases, in absolute terms, were paid by a relatively small minority of the peasantry, simply because that minority, the richest 25 percent, paid two-thirds to three-quarters of the direct taxes in any case. This minority dominated village life, holding most of the land, either in lease, from a still more powerful group, or in ownership. The large-scale peasant entrepreneurs could be powerful individuals, or those like Estienne Reyes of Dournazac, who paid 17 s. in his own name in 1623 but paid 10.35 l. in 1630: 8 l. 16 s. as the *métayer* of the sieur Defayolles and 1 l. 11s. in his own name.

This village elite, a combination of local notables—the Garreaux, for example, were a *procureur* and a *greffier,* as well as *commissaire des tailles*—and the most important peasants, remained fairly stable within the village. The remainder of the population, the vast majority, found a very hard living. There was tremendous instability and mobility at the bottom of this group. This mobility was, at least in part, economic, and one must agree with Robert Mandrou when he states that "mobility . . . was one of the great social features of the time."[42] One might classify these people as a sort of rural proletariat, a group of landless laborers, wandering the countryside, selling their labor. The annual disappearance of 5 to 7 percent of the taxpayers is a constant from Carhaix (1603–4),

42. R. Mandrou, *Introduction to Modern France, 1500–1640* (New York, 1975), 209.

to Audierne (1617–19), to Dournazac (1623–30), and to Masserac (1665–68). As noted earlier, a disproportionate number of these people came from the bottom quartile. At Carhaix, for example, seven of the seventeen who disappeared were from the bottom quartile, the other ten from the third (four) and second (six): all but two of these people paid 15 s. or less. Another member of the bottom quartile, Henry Ballec, went mad and received an exemption in 1604.

Because the roll is so well kept, we are also able to use Dournazac to illustrate some of the other issues raised in this chapter. Women played a major part in the tax structure, but it is difficult to define precisely the extent of their contribution. In 1623, there were three widows and eleven other women; thirteen other contributors were described as the heirs of "*x*"—one of these was a widow, but there is no information on the identity of the others. A further ten cotisations were assigned to husband and wife units: in Farasse, "Jehan Marcouty et sa femme," or, in Fargeas, "Leonard Deboubourg, dit le cousy, et Marguerite Defargeas, sa femme." In 1630, there were four widows, seven other women, ten heirs of "*x*," and ten husband-wife units.

In the roll of 1623, there were fifteen women clearly heading households; ten were from the fourth quartile, two from the third, and three from the first. They were 9.5 percent of the taxpayers but paid only 4.9 percent of the taxes. The husband-wife teams paid an additional 4.1 percent of the taxes; they were 6.3 percent of the contributors. Only five of the fifteen women appeared again on the roll of 1630; of the heirs, eight of eleven were missing; only two of the ten husband-wife teams had completely disappeared, but in one case the holding was in the hands of heirs, and in another, only the woman remained. Nine of the ten women in the fourth quartile in 1623 were gone by 1630.

The most important woman in the village may not have been on the roll: there was a listing for *métairies* owned by the dame de la Vye in both Las Vergnias and La Rougerie. In 1630, the first holding was apparently held by another owner, the sieur Tournon, while the second remained in her hands. The taxes on the two *métairies,* assessed to the *métayers* on the rolls, were 12.2 l. in 1623; the remaining one was assessed at 9.4 l. in 1630.

In 1630, eleven women would be only 6.5 percent of the taxpayers; they paid 5 percent of the taxes. Including all the heirs raises their number to twenty-one (12.5 percent) and their contribution to 14.5 percent. This latter figure is high precisely because the richest taxpayer in the village, Marsalle de Lasche, had died between 1623 and 1630; the assessments of his heirs were 76.25 l. in 1630—44.65 in their own names (counted in our total) and 31.6 l. for their *métayers* (excluded in our total). If one excludes the de Lasche figure, the percentage would drop to 9.4, similar to that of 1623.

All these data hide a bewildering variety of individual evolutions. If we confine ourselves to those on both rolls, we find specific cases such as that of Marguerite Boyassaud. In 1623, we find only the mention of the heirs of Aymerie Garabeuf, assessed at 10.8 l.; in 1630, Marguerite, his widow, was assessed at 14.6 l. Another woman, Marguerite Dupuyrovy, was assessed with her children for 5.45 l. in 1623, and with her *métayer* for 4.5 l. in 1630. Such a listing certainly implies that this peasant women owned her own parcel of land. Yet a third Marguerite, wife of Jehan Defayollas, was assessed with her husband, a *cordonnier*, for 3.95 l. in 1623; widowed, she paid 4.6 l. in her own name in 1630.

There are other curious changes between the two rolls. What does one make of the listing for Pierre Reytier, "dit gasnyant," assessed for 2.2 l. in 1623, an assessment against him and his wife, Catherine Lapot. In 1630, there was no mention of Catherine, and "gasnyant," true to his name, was now assessed for 16.15 l. Had Catherine died in the interim? Was her absence from the roll an oversight? (The latter possibility would be unlikely.) Does this change represent an alteration in her position in the household? One strong possibility is that Pierre and Catherine had been assessed together as hired laborers in 1623, thus the low rate; in 1630, they held a tenancy, thus the higher tax, which was listed only in his name (the usual practice in Dournazac).[43]

The information from 1630 is somewhat different from that of 1623. Five of the eleven women were in the fourth quartile, two in each of the others. If we take all four categories that included women (and count Catherine Lapot), we would find that the distribution among the four quartiles was 7, 6, 9, and 9. This finding would indicate that women played a major role in the local econ-

---

43. Local practice, both on tax rolls and on leases, varied sharply with respect to listing women. It was least common in the south of France.

omy; the evidence of the two years also implies that this role was played selectively. There seem to have been two distinct categories of women: the very poor, and those integrated into the mainstream local society. This poor group were among the poorest of the poor: while women made up only 9 percent of the taxpayers, they were 25 percent of the fourth quartile, and 36 percent of those who disappeared from the fourth quartile were women.

These poor unfortunates at the bottom of village society were precisely those accused, in contemporary accounts, of fomenting the popular revolts against taxation.[44] This possibility seems quite unlikely: rather, they were the shock troops of other, more powerful forces. Although these people must have been desperately poor, all of them assessed at a few miserable *sous* each year, their propensity for revolt against an increase in their assessment from 6 s. to 14 s. (the respective dividing lines between the fourth and third quartiles in 1623 and 1630), would seem rather limited. The great problem with these people is that they were less stable than the others, less tied to the individual village, and that they tended to have other grievances as well. Mandrou is quite right when he states that these revolts "were far more complex than a simple struggle between rich and poor."[45]

The notables and the second tier of the peasantry had serious grievances against the tax system, too. We get some idea of how dangerous this process was, when we consider that two of the ten largest taxpayers in the parish were Martial Garreau and Pierre Garreau, sieur de Maulmont, *greffier,* and that Martial Garreau, the younger, also contributed substantially. Martial Garreau, the elder, in addition to being the local *procureur,* was the *commissaire des tailles.* We can see the complexity of their interests in the village in Table 30, which lists the parcels associated with the name Garreau for both 1623 and 1630.

The rolls raise some interesting questions. What is the relationship between the three *notable* Garreaux and peasant farmers such as Jehan and Bartholomew Garreaux, or the widow Marguerite Garreau? She had been married to Pierre Lachaud, perhaps a relative of Leonard Lachaud, the *métayer* of Martial Garreau the younger. She is gone by 1630, but we find Jehan and Bartholomew

44. R. Mousnier, *Fureurs Paysans* (Paris, 1967), for some contemporary descriptions.

45. Mandrou, *Introduction to Modern France,* 103.

Table 30. *Holdings of the Garreau Family of Dournazac, 1623 and 1630*

Taxpayer	Assessment	
	1623	1630
P. Redon, his land and that he works for M. Garreau (elder)	3.65	
P. Marchat, *métayer* of M. Garreau, same holding as Redon		8.2
J. and B. Garreau	3.5	5.75
J. and B. Garreau, as *métayers* of L. Deschamps		11.1
G. Garreau, *métayer* of M. Deschamps		7.45
J. de la Garnoudye, "dit petit," *métayer* of M. Garreau (elder), each pays half		2.5
J. Defargeas, *métayer* of M. Garreau, elder	7.7	
J. Virolle, *métayer* of same, same piece each pays half		8.0
P. Garraud, *métayer* of P. Garreau	7.7	
J. Chantaveu, *métayer* of same, same piece		8.0
M. Garreau		15.0
F. Garreau, miller of M. Garreau, elder	0.2	0.35
L. Barbeaux, *métayer* of M. Garreau, elder	5.0	
L. Vervier, *métayer* of same, same piece		4.5
L. Boissard, *métayer* of M. Garreau, elder	4.2	4.15
J. Defargeas, *métayer* of M. Garreau, young	5.15	7.1
M. Garreau, young,		4.0
and P. Garreau	5.55	2.8
Métayer of P. Garreau (unnamed in 1623; L. and J. Valladier in 1630)	8.35	10.5
L. Lachaud, *métayer* of M. Garreau, young	2.15	
Petit Defargeas, *métayer* of same, same piece		2.45
Marguerite Garreau and her children (widow of L. Lachaud)	0.1	

Source: AD Haute-Vienne, C 145.

have prospered, assessed for 5.75 l. in their own names (as against 3.5 l. in 1623), and now *métayers* of L. Deschamps, and assessed as such for 11.1 l. Just below them, one finds Guillaume Garreau, as *métayer* of M. Deschamps, paying 7.45 l. Was the success of this group of Garreaux related to their last name? Were they, in fact, relatives of the *notable* Garreaux? Again, we know not.

It is little wonder that popular revolts against royal taxation seemed to have the collusive support of local notables: these were the people paying the tax increases. The tenants of the local landlords, and, to a lesser extent, the landlords themselves, particularly in areas dominated by *métayage,* were the ones truly affected by rising taxation. It also affected the middling and poor peasants, but it did so more indirectly. They were subject to tremendous pressure from the united local elite, and undoubtedly many "spontaneous" acts of violence against the royal tax collectors were, in fact, urged or even abetted by the leading citizens of the towns and villages involved. While one must agree with Bercé and Mousnier that the seigneurs were a major force behind the tax revolts, and the entire seigneurial apparatus one of taxation's chief obstacles, the large loss of revenue was the key motivation for the seigneurs. Their "privileges" and "honor" were also considerations, but their land rents were very severely affected by struggles with the tax collection system.[46]

These popular tax revolts, much like grain riots, were a part of ordinary French political discourse.[47] The village or town elite encouraged a public demonstration against the excessive level of taxation. These demonstrations could take many forms: nonpayment of taxes, failure to draw up tax rolls, abuse of royal officials, and open revolt. The revolts were a very complex affair, however, because the lowest level of the peasantry had grievances against more than the tax system.

The revolts usually began as dissatisfaction with *indirect* taxes and then broadened to include underlying grievances against direct

46. This is particularly the position of Mousnier, perhaps most explicit in part 1 of *Fureurs Paysans.* Bercé, *Histoire des Croquants,* 146, claims the landlord defended primarily "the honor of his land and the liberty of the *pays.*"

47. The issue of revolts and grain riots as political discourse is much discussed for the eighteenth century in the works of George Rudé, Charles and Louise Tilly, and E. P. Thompson.

taxes. The indirect taxes hit closer to the livelihood of the poor: the taxes on hides that touched off a tanners' revolt in Caen, the threat of the *gabelle* that threatened the livelihood of the salt producers of the Cotentin, or the new transit taxes that inflamed the transportation workers of the Southwest. What made rural outburst against specific indirect taxes into vehicles for the expression of long-term discontent against direct taxes was the cooperation of the local elites. The extreme dependency of the poor on the landlords and, more immediately, on the upper stratum of the peasantry itself, made it quite unlikely that the poor peasants would get involved in any long-running disturbance that did not have the sanction of part or all of the local elites. As is often the case, the members of the lowest classes were singled out for punishment at the end of the revolt. Bercé points out that while many nobles sympathized with and even encouraged tax revolts, only marginal nobles had any active role in them.[48] Many great nobles also got half or more of their annual income from royal pensions generated by the taxes, so they had rather mixed views about taxation.[49] The great failure of the French tax system in the 1630s and 1640s was that it alienated local elites. Without their support the monarchy could accomplish nothing.[50]

To what extent did the most important taxpayers dominate the life of villages such as Dournazac? Much the same pattern can be found in the Ile-de-France, with bourgeois buying up land and renting the various parcels to peasant *métayers*. In Dournazac the two hamlets whose taxes went up most sharply had new *métairies* in 1630.[51] The one factor that makes cases from the Limousin and Poitou difficult to judge is the use of the *parsonu* system, the local name for the *frèrêches* so common in the fifteenth century. This communal renting approach existed at Dournazac, Augé, and St-

---

48. Bercé, *Histoire des Croquants,* on the 1630s opposition to transport taxes; M. Foisil, *La révolte des Nu-Pieds* (Paris, 1970), on the *gabelle* threat in the Cotentin.

49. J. P. Labatut, *Les ducs et pairs de France au XVIIe siècle* (Paris, 1972). BN, Ms. Fr. 21479, fols. 101v–3, pensions list from 1636; BN, 500 Colbert 106, 1609 pensions.

50. E. Asher, *The Survival of Feudalism in the France of Colbert: The Resistance to the Maritime Classes* (Berkeley and Los Angeles, 1960).

51. AD Haute-Vienne, C 145. At La Gratte, Gabriel Merguier added two *métairies,* assessed at 14.6 and 18 l., respectively.

Table 31. *Tax Distribution in St-Ouen-de-Breuil, 1645*

Tax Bracket	% of Taxpayers	% of Taxes Assessed[a]
Under 10 l.	28.2	2.0
Under 20 l.	16.7	4.9
Under 50 l.	28.2	18.3
Under 100 l.	12.8	20.3
100 l. or more	14.1	54.4
By Quartile		
I		72.3
II		18.5
III		7.7
IV		1.5

Source: AD Seine-Maritime, C 2108.
[a]Rounded figures do not add up to 100%.

Martin-les-Melles. The largest *laboureurs* are often accompanied by partners (*parsonus*), so the largest scale peasant farmers are often not merely family units acting alone but coalitions of families.

St-Ouen-de-Breuil

The final tax roll, from St-Ouen-de-Breuil in Normandy, is the richest in terms of information, but it comes from a very unreliable period. As we shall see, the rate of nonpayment of taxes in Normandy in the 1640s was extremely high, often 75 percent or more. The roll of St-Ouen dates from 1645, so we must be extremely wary of accepting the figures given as the amounts actually paid. The roll does, however, show us taxation at its most outrageous level, and it provides some general idea of the balance of taxation in one of the richest areas in France.

The roll from St-Ouen lists two major taxes—the *taille* itself, for 1800 l., and the combination of all other levies (*taillon*, provost, garrison tax, and so on), 1869 l. for a total of 3669 l. This amount is considerably more than the figure for 1665, which is 2109 l.[52] The number of hearths in the village dropped from seventy-eight

52. AD Seine-Maritime, C 2108.

utile (paying) and twelve *inutile* (nonpaying) in 1645, to seventy-two and nine in 1665. The individual cotisations are much higher than any of our other rolls, as we can see in Table 31.

The earlier categories make little sense, although it is worth noting that sixteen of the twenty-two taxpayers contributing less than 10 l., paid less than 5 l., and seven less than 1.5 l. The top 5 percent, in this case four people, contributed 26.2 percent of the taxes, which is more than the combined contribution of the 73 percent of the villagers who paid less than 50 l.

One of the most interesting parts of the roll is its description of the villagers. Each cotisation is listed with the taxpayer's name, occupation, and landholding. Landholdings are divided between land rented and land owned. As one might expect, those paying less than 10 l., with three exceptions, neither owned nor rented land.

There are 924 Norman *acres* (1 Norman *acre* = 1.37 English acres) listed on the tax roll, of which 208.5 (22.6 percent) are owned by the listed taxpayer. The remaining 77.4 percent is owned by persons unknown. The largest holding is that of Guillaume Morisser, owner of 40 *acres* and farmer of 20 more; he also pays the most in taxes, 275 l. Only two others hold 20 *acres* or more, Denis Follerfan, *laboureur* and owner of 26 *acres* (paying 143 l.), and Robert Le Roux, owner of 20 *acres* (paying 143 l.). The largest taxpayers are primarily important renters, as we can see in Table 32. Nine of the eleven largest taxpayers (assessed for more than 100 l.) rented some land.

These eleven individuals, four of whom own no property, collectively possess 58.5 percent of the land owned by those who appear on the village tax roll, and they rent 69.3 percent of the other land. Altogether, these eleven people control 67 percent of the land of the village, yet they pay only 54.4 percent of the taxes.

While these richest individuals paid too little, everyone else paid too much. Table 33 shows that the upper quartile paid 72.3 percent of the taxes, even though it controlled 79.8 percent of the land; this ratio is misleading. If we take those members of the quartile not included in the list of the eleven richest members of the parish, those assessed for more than 100 l., we find that they control 12.9 percent of the land but pay 17.8 percent of the taxes.

We can see that the village elite dominated the land distribution, and that the other groups were systematically discriminated against

Table 32. *Lands Rented and Owned by the Eleven Largest Taxpayers of St-Ouen-de-Breuil, 1645*

Name and Occupation	Owned Acres	Rented Acres	Assessment
Guillaume Morisser, *laboureur*	40	20	275 l.
Jean de la Rue and sons, *laboureurs*	14	66	245
Jean Gonfreville[a]		120	244
Denis Foucault and son, *laboureurs*		80	198
Adrien Verdier and son, *laboureurs*[b]	12	15	195
Robert Rualt		60	163
Ollivier Collette and sons	4	50	153
Denis Follerfan, *laboureur*	26		143
Robert Le Roux	20		143
Jean Doury, *laboureur*[c]	6	45	133
Widow of Pierre Le Roux and son	___	40	102
Total	122	496	1,994 l.

Source: AD Seine-Maritime, C 2108.

[a]Gonfreville also owned 50 l. of *rente*.

[b]The roll states "tenant à fieffe," a Norman leasing arrangement explained in J.-B. Voysin de la Noiraye, *Mémoire sur la généralité de Rouen en 1665*, ed. E. Esmonin (Paris, 1913).

[c]Doury was a collector.

Table 33. *Land Distribution in St-Ouen-de-Breuil, 1645*

Quartile	Land Owned	Land Rented	Total	% of Land[a]	% of Taxes
I	175.5	561.5	737	79.8	72.3
II	31	100	131	14.2	18.5
III	2	49.5	51.5	5.6	7.7
IV	0	4.5	4.5	0.5	1.5

Source: AD Seine-Maritime, C 2108.

Note: Land in Norman *acres*, 1 Norman *acre* = 1.37 English acres.

[a]Rounded figures do not add up to 100%.

in the tax assessment. We can also see how poor the latter were: only three of the nineteen members of the bottom quartile even rented land, and the richest member of this quartile, assessed at 6.1 l., rented 3 of the 4.5 *acres* tilled by the entire group. The upper quartile owned 84.2 percent of the land possessed by those appearing on the roll, the upper two quartiles 99 percent. The poorer 50 percent of the population controlled only 6.1 percent of the land.

Each *acre* is assessed at about 4 l., yet the assessors do not judge all *acres* to be the same. There is a particularly marked difference between owned land and rented land: owned land is assessed an average of 7.2 l./*acre*, while rented land is assessed at about 3 l./ *acre*. It is a measure of the tax relief accorded to those listed in Table 32 that their owned land is assessed at about 2.5 l. per *acre* and their rented land at only 6.2 l. per *acre*. There are also substantial qualitative (at least one must assume they are qualitative) differences in assessment per *acre;* normally, the greater the acreage, the lower the per *acre* tax. Jean Gonfreville, for example, pays only 244 l. on his 120 rented *acres* and his 50 l. *rente*. Although this assessment may seem an inequity, and almost surely was an inequity, larger holdings probably had greater amounts of waste land.

There are several ways of determining the weight of taxation for the parishioners of St-Ouen. If we follow the estimates of Jean Meuvret, allowing a yield of 15 Parisian *setiers* per sown *hectare* (based on sowings of two hectoliters per hectare), we accept a crop ratio of just over 7:1.[53] In fact, this small area of Normandy may have exceeded that figure, perhaps reaching 10:1, double the normal French yield. According to the *intendant*'s report of 1665, rents in this area were 20 to 24 l. per *acre*.[54]

The added burden of taxation competed directly with land rents. If we take the largest renter, Jean Gonfreville, renting 120 *acres,* we find him paying 244 l. 12 s in taxes. His rent, at the figures cited by the intendant, would be between 2,400 and 2,880 l.; one would suspect the lower figure in 1645, because there was some rent inflation in western France from 1645 to 1665. If we take his sown holdings, assuming he uses the three-field system common in the

53. J. Meuvret, *Le problème des subsistences à l'époque de Louis XIV* (Paris, 1979).
54. J.-B. Voysin de la Noiraye, *Mémoire sur la généralité de Rouen en 1665*, ed. E. Esmonin (Paris, 1913).

area, he would sow 21.9 ha. in wheat and rye and the same area in barley and oats. If we take the best case, wheat and barley, and prices normal for the period, 8 l. to 9 l. for wheat and perhaps 5 l. for barley, we find Gonfreville's income to be about 3,200–3,500 l. from the sale of these grains. This figure allows for tithe and seed (about 20–23 percent if we follow Meuvret) but does not include food for his family and workers or the wages of the workers. If the rent is 2,400 l., Gonfreville has only 800–1,100 l. left, of which 245 l. goes in direct taxes. If there are a few slight variations in the rent or the yield, Gonfreville would find himself with less than 500 l. to pay his workers and feed everyone. He must rely on other sources of income (rental of his plow teams, the 50 l. *rente,* incidental income from poultry, or other sources) to make ends meet.

Jean Quereville and his son, farmers of eight *acres,* fare still worse. They would net only 50 l. or so from the sale of grains, after paying their rent and taxes. This amount would not feed the two of them alone. While such calculations are fraught with danger, they show that direct taxes alone could equal as much as 25 percent of the ground rent. One must add to this figure the *gabelle;* in the 1640s, an average family would have paid about 10 l. for it. In addition there were the *aides* and other taxes. Together these taxes offer a full picture of the king's new conflict with landlords and rich peasants. By the late 1630s and 1640s, there can be little doubt that royal direct taxation equalled some 15 percent or more of ground rent, and that all royal taxes reached perhaps 25 percent of such rent. By way of contrast, the figure for St-Ouen-de-Breuil in 1665, a reduction of 42 percent in comparison with 1645, would equal less than 10 percent of ground rent.

Resistance to Direct Taxation

This competition with ground rents led to the most serious problem of the tax system in the 1630s and 1640s: nonpayment. One of the great weaknesses of central documents from this period is that they are often the representation of wishful thinking, and they bear little relation to actual revenues. They represent proposed revenues, or "hoped-for" revenues, not in any sense money actually collected. The extent of the problem has been documented for certain areas, such as Normandy, but here we will try to present new materials and an overall picture.

Starting in the *généralité* of Caen, Caillard gives the following figures for 1635, 1638, and 1639:[55]

	Proposed tax in 000 l.	Receipts in 000 l.	Nonpayment in percent
1635	2,294	826	64.1
1638	3,199	1,344	58.0
1639	2,799	1,667	40.5

Lefebvre and Tribouillard show that the *élection* of Valognes had a shortfall of 32.6 percent in 1636, while Caillard gives the shortfall as 82.1 percent in 1641. The *élection* of Avranches still owed 34,083 l. of its 1641 *tailles* as late as March 1644.[56]

Madeleine Foisil provides the following figures for the percentage of nonpayment in the parishes of the *élection* of Coutances as of 9 June 1640:[57]

Percentage of nonpayment	Number of villages
100	82
95–100	28
90–94	23
85–89	15
80–84	7
70–79	7
65–69	1

In other words, more than half of the parishes had paid nothing at all, and none had paid more than a third of its taxes. As Foisil shows, while the least imposed parishes sometimes paid quite little, the general pattern was one in which the parishes assessed for the most paid the lowest percentage.[58]

In the *généralité* of Châlons there is the statement of the receiver general in August 1639 that he had not

55. M. Caillard, "Recherches sur les soulèvements populaires de Basse-Normandie (1620–1640)," *Cahiers des Annales de Normandie* 3 (1963): 132.

56. Ibid.; A. Lefebvre and F. Tribouillard, "L'élection de Valognes de 1540 à 1660," *Annales de Normandie* 23 (1973): 208–33.

57. Foisil, *Nu-Pieds*.

58. Ibid. Foisil's data carry this implication, but she does not agree with this interpretation of it.

up to the present received anything from the [*élection*] receivers of the said *généralité* because of the ruin and desolation of the said province brought about both by the raids of the enemy and the armies and men of war that His Majesty has been forced to maintain here for the past four years, and by the plague ("maladie contagieuse") with which it [the province] has been afflicted, in such manner that most of the villages are deserted and the bourgs, which were made up of two and three hundred hearths, are reduced to 30 or 40, and in such extremity that they live only on barley bread and are constrained to hide themselves in the woods.[59]

He asked to resign his post but was refused.

In the small southwestern *élection* of Lomagne, encompassing 156 parishes, 71 parish collectors were imprisoned in January and February 1637. The royal sergeants filled out 120 reports in this *élection* between 1636 and 1638. The Armagnac area as a whole required the use of sergeants 1,398 times during this period to collect its taxes.[60]

The situation all over France was so bad in the early 1640s that the amount of money actually collected went down. In the *généralité* of Bourges the treasurers wrote to the king in 1643 with a request to cut the share of the area from 1.9 to 1.1 million l. They divided this 1.1 million l. among the king (600,000 l.), the officers (300,000 l.), and the *rentiers* (200,000 l.). The king did not receive his money in 1643, nor did the rentiers: can one say the nonpayment of 1643 for the *généralité* of Bourges was 100 percent?[61]

The neighboring *généralité* of Moulins owed the king 8.4 million l. in 1654. Nonpayment of the *tailles* was 5.4 million l., and a further 3 million l. was owed for the *gabelle*. This amount represented nonpayment of at least one-third for the entire period and more than 50 percent for 1653. The *traitants* who had loaned the king money against the *tailles* wanted 100,000 l. for the period 1649–52, 300,000 l. for 1653, and 600,000 l. for the advance payments made for the surtax of winter quarters for the troops in 1654. They had given up on the money they were owed from 1647 to 1648.[62]

For the *généralité* of Limoges, the nonpayment reached 570,517

59. AD Marne, C 2499, fol. 176. Cited in M. Pelicier, *Inventaire sommaire des archives départementales de la Marne*, series C (Châlons, 1898), 77–78.

60. Bercé, *Histoire des Croquants*, 95 and ff.

61. BN, Ms. Fr. 18510, fol. 387.

62. Ibid., fol. 477.

l. in 1647, 734,903 l. in 1648 (despite a remission by the king of one-fifth of the direct taxes), and 1,560,000 l. of 1,913,000 l. assessed for 1649.[63] In this report by the treasurers, dated 20 January 1650, the levels of nonpayment are 24 percent, 34 percent, and 82 percent for the three years in question. The worst situation is that of 1649, since the treasurers also state that many of the parishes have not even apportioned that year's taxes. This situation reflects the fact that many isolated parishes paid little or nothing at all in the 1640s, while the parishes accessible to the royal army often gave most of their taxes to it, rather than to the regular royal agents.[64]

The army was a two-edged sword, because its relations with the general population, always bad, could get only worse when it was charged with collecting the taxes. The *doléances* of the villages and chastellanies of the bailiwick of Troyes at the Estates General of 1614–15 are a long litany of abuse at the hands of troops.[65] Gaston Roupnel cites, among other examples, the case of Saulx-le-Duc, a common halting stop for the army, whose population was greater in 1636 than in 1921.[66] René Pillorget supplies very similar stories about Provence, another major troop movement area.[67] Bercé gives the case of a Poitevin village in which the costs of collecting 400 l. were 2,000 l. He also cites a letter of chancellor Séguier, in 1644, stating that the troops who had collected taxes in the Southwest, had kept everything, leaving the receiver general at Bordeaux with no money.[68] As he says, in the 1640s the royal tax system had entered a vicious circle. Money could not be obtained from the taxpayers without recourse to violence, but the use of troops to collect taxes alienated the peasants even further and did little to improve the cash flow problem because the army usually kept what it collected.[69]

Nonpayment was hardly a new problem. In the late sixteenth

63. Ibid., fols. 427–27v.
64. AD Haute-Vienne, C 146, for Limousin examples. Bercé, *Histoire des Croquants,* has many examples.
65. Y. Durand, *Cahiers de doléances du bailliage de Troyes pour les Etats généraux de 1614* (Paris, 1966).
66. Roupnel, *La ville et la campagne dijonnaise.*
67. R. Pillorget, *Les mouvements insurrectionnels en Provence de 1595 à 1715* (Paris, 1975).
68. Bercé, *Histoire des Croquants,* 107.
69. Ibid., 117–18.

Table 34. *Nonpayment of Taxes in the Limousin, 1643–45*

| Parish | Taille | | Taillon | | Subsistence | | All |
	Assessed in l.	Paid in %	Assessed in l.	Paid in %	Assessed in l.	Paid in %	Paid in %
Le Dorat	2,775	82.1	218	72.9	1,246	76.9	80.1
Dinsac	1,660	92.5	130	70.8	747	38.7	75.6
St-Genest-Oradour	1,850	74.8	145	74.5	832	43.3	65.5
Bellac	5,200	60.7	480	42.5	1,340	75.7	62.3
Châteauponsac	3,542	73.1	620	64.5	7,876	54.5	60.5
Javardat	450	47.8	34	52.9	203	80.3	57.6
Oradour-s-Glane	6,000	23.7	475	26.1	2,700	31.6	26.2
Moulisme	2,100	27.2	165	25.5	945	22.4	25.7
Isle-Jourdain	2,000	28.9	158	28.5	900	18.0	25.7
Luchapt	3,780	12.7	298	50.3	1,707	43.1	23.6
Breuil	4,600	22.6	363	44.9	2,070	21.6	23.5
St-Martial	2,000	13.4	158	24.7	900	23.7	17.0
Mortemart	1,600	5.3	126	24.6	720	10.6	7.8

Source: AD Haute-Vienne, C 146.

century, it had reached considerable proportions. In the *généralité* of Lyon, for example, the nonpayment of 1597 was about 200,000 l. (18 percent); in that of Limoges, it was 257,000 l. in 1598 (19 percent), 44,000 l. in 1599, and 63,000 l. as late as 1601.[70] In Caen, it was 164,561 l. (15 percent) in 1599 and 15,000 l. in 1601.[71] The figures for the 1590s suggest a collapse of the system then, and the massive shortfall of the 1640s indicates an even more complete dislocation during that period.

Table 34 shows the problems of some Limousin villages in the period 1643–45. The figures indicate two clusters of villages: Bellac, Châteauponsac, Le Dorat, Oradour-St-Genest, and Dinsac, close to the main Poitiers-Limoges road, paying between 62.3 and 80.1 percent of their taxes; Mortemart, Breuil, Oradour-sur-Glane, and Javardat, in or close to the Monts de Blond, paying 7.8, 23.5, 26.2, and 57.6 percent of their taxes, respectively. These two clusters dramatize the effects of being accessible (or inaccessible) to the

70. AN, 120 AP 13.
71. L. Romier, *Lettres et chevauchées du bureau des finances de Caen* (Rouen, 1910), app.

troops. The figures for Châteauponsac demonstrate the tragedy of an immediate army presence: its share of the subsistence (for winter quarters of the troops) was disproportionately high, and it paid the highest real amount of taxes among the villages.

One must conclude from this information, taken from all over France—Normandy, the Loire valley, the Massif Central, Champagne, the Southwest—that tax evasion was so rampant in the 1630s and, especially, the 1640s, that revenues declined sharply. All the chilling tax figures from the 1640s are mere imagination; they have little foundation in reality. The harsh reality of the situation was that certain villages, such as Saulx-le-Duc or, perhaps, Châteauponsac, were within reach of the troops and no one, or virtually no one, had paid all (or even close to all) of their taxes. The troops therefore had a legitimate reason to extort money from any village in which they stopped.

Because the troops did not turn over this money, the monarchy went through what amounted to a general bankruptcy in the 1640s and 1650s. One of the major reasons for the failure of the tax system to provide the money necessary for the war effort, aside from the obvious great cost of the war, was that the king alienated precisely those people he needed to collect the money.

The king's key mistake at the local level was to alienate people like the Garreaux of Dournazac. They were the ones on whom local order depended. The king knew this, and one must see the punishment of local elites as justifiable in the case of revolts, even if there was little direct evidence against them. As Porshnev, Mousnier, Bercé, and others have shown, these people fomented revolts, encouraged them, sometimes even directed them.[72] While one is hard put to prove such charges, the tax rolls and even the *cahiers* speak clearly to the point. The taxes and tax increases were paid almost exclusively by large landowners and their farmers. The nobles were perfectly correct in saying they paid taxes indirectly; every time village taxes went up, the taxes of the *métayers* rose highest of all, in absolute terms. These men dominated village life; they farmed the largest share of the land. They had to pay the taxes. Clearly, it was in their interest to reduce royal taxes, and it was in the interest of their landlords as well.

---

72. Mousnier, *Fureurs Paysans;* Bercé, *Histoire des Croquants;* B. Porshnev, *Les soulèvements populaires en France avant la Fronde* (Paris, 1963).

What is more, the landlords clearly recognized the precise relationship between ground rents and taxes. As the First President of the Parlement of Normandy put it, in addressing the Estates in November 1566:

> In the second place, while the *tailles* and other *crues* that the prince demands for his subvention are levied directly on those of the Third Estate, nonethless, those of the Church and the Nobility pay them indirectly, which can be seen from a familiar example.
>
> How many *laboureurs* are there holding in farm the heritages and possessions of ecclesiastics and gentlemen, *laboureurs* who pay 60 l. and 80 l. of *tailles*, who, without the said farms, would pay 100 *sous*? Does not this charge come in direct diminution of their farm rents ("fermages")? *Voilà*, thus their [the nobles and clergy] particular interest in assisting at the Estates.[73]

One cannot place a specific figure on the relationship between royal direct taxes and ground rent, but 10 percent would be a typical maximum. It makes little sense to talk about contributions per hearth when it is obvious that land is worth considerably more in some areas than in others. In Normandy, for example, the very high crop ratios made it possible to have very high taxation. Normandy revolted not because it paid so much in relation to others; indeed its share of direct taxes declined in the seventeenth century. It revolted because taxation grew too heavy for local conditions to bear. These conditions were greatly worsened by plague and poor harvests in the late 1630s and early 1640s, but those elements only worsened a situation that was bad from the outset.[74]

Royal direct taxation was not a factor in the immediate starvation of the peasantry; peasants did not generally choose between starvation and paying their taxes. Most of the peasants paid so little to the tax collector that it could have made little difference in their daily lives to pay twice as much. This rule was not true during the period 1635–50, however, when very poor peasants were taxed at 5 l. or even 10 l. They simply could not afford such levels, and they probably refused to pay them. Even here, however, one is not likely to find peasants choosing between starvation and paying their taxes. The one great exception to this point—and it is an important

73. C. de Robillard de Beaurepaire, *Cahiers des Etats de Normandie, règne Charles IX* (Rouen, 1878), *cahiers* and documents of 1566.

74. This is also the conclusion of Foisil, *Nu-Pieds,* and Caillard, "Soulèvements."

exception—was the peasant whose village was occupied by troops. The troops could and did drive peasants to starvation, especially in years of dearth, as around Paris in the time of the Fronde.[75]

The most important effects of overly heavy taxation were long-term ones. The little savings of the peasants just above the *bordier* level, paying 5 or 6 l. per year in taxes, were eaten up by the tax increases of the 1630s and 1640s. These increases cut very sharply into their discretionary income, much more so than into their subsistence income. In many cases this drop in discretionary income led directly to recessions in consumer-oriented sectors of the economy, such as the wine trade.[76] The recession in the wine trade, in turn, severely affected the ability of the peasants of the West and South to pay their taxes. The collapse of the wine trade did lead them down the path to starvation.

The higher echelons of peasant society were very harshly affected by rising taxes. They must have had to retrench—to cut back on capital investments in the middle of the seventeenth century. There are no figures for such investment in the 1640s, but the general decline of the French economy after 1640 may have its roots in this loss of resources among the richer peasantry. Their lack of investment would have led to loss of job opportunities for the poorer peasants, and the latter's condition would have worsened.

It is particularly interesting to note the timing of the tax increases of the seventeenth century. The first great increase, from 1625 to 1635, seems to have been paid by the peasants. As Le Roy Ladurie has pointed out, taxation declined in real terms between the reigns of Louis XII and Henry IV and the Regency of Marie de Medicis.[77] The increases of the period 1625–30 or so could easily have been taken from the greater income of the peasantry. Even the further jump of 1630–34 could well have been handled by the peasantry, particularly with support for the king from local elites. The alienation of these elites in 1634, and the new tax increases of the late 1630s and early 1640s, led to massive nonpayment of taxes. In the 1640s, another phenomenon enters this complex equation: rapidly increasing ground rents.

75. On the price effects, J. Meuvret and M. Baulant, *Le prix des céréales aux Halles de Paris*, vol. 2 (Paris, 1960–61), 19.

76. J. Collins, "Les impôts et le commerce du vin en Bretagne au XVIIe siècle," *Actes du 107e Congrès National des Sociétés Savantes* 1 (1982): 155–68.

77. E. Le Roy Ladurie, *Les Paysans de Languedoc* (Paris, 1966).

Jean Jacquart has shown the substantial rent increases near Paris during the 1640s and 1650s, and the work of Venard shows the bourgeoisie buying up land and then consolidating its holdings during this period.[78] Rents also rose sharply in Brittany during this period, especially in the region of Nantes.[79] New groups, most particularly the bourgeoisie, were also involved in rural investment. At Valets, near Nantes, the *dîme* (tithe) is farmed by a merchant in 1643; at St. Luc, a silk merchant is the lessee of the tithes in 1660. Elsewhere one finds the rector replaced by a notary.[80] In each case the lease price rises substantially (an average of more than 15 percent).

The peasants could not afford higher rents, more rigorously collected tithes, and higher taxes. The ruling classes apparently felt the peasantry to be keeping too much of its own production, and each group within the ruling classes—king, clergy, and nobles—sought to increase its own share of the surplus value produced by the peasants. The bourgeoisie and the officer class sought their share of this wealth by allying with both the nobility and the king.

The complexity of this conflict over the production of the peasantry goes a long way in explaining the complexity of the Fronde. Returning to Mandrou's point that social revolts or tax revolts were not simple rich versus poor outbursts, one can see several layers of unrest in midseventeenth-century France. There is an obvious conflict between the landlords and the king: landlords want higher rents, the king wants higher direct taxes. This situation leads to a split within the nobility, because many nobles receive royal pensions, and many of those who receive royal pensions give pensions to lesser nobles in their turn. Reduced tax receipts mean less frequent payment of pensions. Conversely, for those nobles, especially at the middle level (which is to say, the dominant notables of local society), whose income derives primarily from the land, higher taxes are an unmitigated disaster.

The clergy find themselves split along similar lines, although clerical opposition to the king was probably stronger than opposi-

78. J. Jacquart, *La crise rurale en Ile-de-France, 1550–1670* (Paris, 1974); M. Venard, *Bourgeois et paysans au XVIIe siècle* (Paris, 1957).

79. Collins, "Taxation in Bretagne," chap. 9.

80. AD Loire-Atlantique, G 245, fol. 106 (Valets), vol. 277v (St-Luc). At St-Erblain, when the rector, Ysaac Moreau, lost the lease on the tithes in 1625, it was to Noel Bernard, merchant, "comme plus offrant," at 250 l. (the previous price had been 170 l.), plus an entry fee of 4 *pistoles* (fol. 294v of G 244, lease of May 1629).

tion within the nobility. The clergy has to pay higher *décimes,* and it finds its tenants harshly taxed. As landlord, it opposes direct tax increases. There is also the problem of the tithe, since higher direct taxes make the tithes that much more overbearing.

The bourgeoisie were in a particularly difficult position. The officers relied on royal authority to make the most of their investments, and many bourgeois families had close ties to officers (either immediate or collateral relatives among the officers). But the bourgeoisie owned substantial amounts of land and was heavily involved in the collection of tithes.

The peasantry were the most compromised of all, because their income was attacked from all sides. The majority of the peasant revolts against taxation took place in the period 1624–40 (within the 1598–1648 period), so most of them antedate the sharp upturn in rents. The revolt that does come after the increase, the *Bonnets Rouges* of Brittany (1675), was aimed at the landlords. This exception is somewhat misleading, however, for Breton direct taxation was quite light and its seigneurial regime very heavy. The contemporaneous urban revolt, the *Papier Timbré,* was aimed against royal indirect taxation, which was a heavy burden on Breton towns.[81]

The major antitax revolts ended around 1640 probably because the effectiveness of the central government in collecting its direct taxes also declined at that time. Simple nonpayment of taxes sufficed after 1640. In the late 1640s and early 1650s, at the village level, the available information would suggest that the royal bureaucracy simply ceased to function. The aggressive reinstatement of royal authority in the late 1650s and early 1660s was largely a response to the nonpayment of taxes, and the concomitant collapse of royal authority, in the immediately preceding period. Tax relief, clear by the time of Colbert (but possibly antedating his administration), was a necessary condition for the restoration of royal authority and power.

One extra element in this complex situation was the shortage of coinage during the period, especially after 1635. As we know from estate inventories, the peasants had their savings in goods and tools, not in cash. Thus, 10 or 20 l. was a considerable sum of hard

81. J. Tanguy, "Les révoltes paysannes de 1675 et la conjoncture en Basse Bretagne au XVIIe siècle," *Annales de Bretagne et des Pays de l'Ouest* 82 (1975): 429–42.

cash for such a family, even if its total resources were up to the task.[82] The poorer peasants would have had to borrow from the village notables to come up with hard coins, as opposed to *billon* (copper pennies) that made up what little store they had. This problem was far more serious than it first appears, since it was precisely the borrowing for small sums to pay taxes (both direct and indirect) that often cost peasants their land. Jacquard and Venard have shown how frequent this phenomenon was in the Parisian region, and there is little reason to suspect it was less pronounced elsewhere. In Normandy, for example, the number and value of coins minted at Rouen declined sharply after 1620 or so, and Foisil sees a distinct connection between that decline and the revolt of Nu-Pieds.[83] In general, however, the eastern and central provinces suffered from the most severe coinage shortages.

The tax rolls and other financial documents of the early seventeenth century show France to be a society in turmoil: large numbers of itinerant laborers, constant consolidation of landholdings and the means of production by the richer elements of the society, severe pressure from all elements of the ruling classes against the peasants, and illiquidity of the assets of the latter. The king got an ever-increasing share of the production of the peasantry between 1620 and 1634, but it is not at all clear he got more after the latter date. The nonpayments of the 1640s show that local notables had powerful means at their disposal to make sure the process of transfer of surplus production to the king did not go too far.

France was a country of local notables. Many of these people were noble, but many, perhaps most, were not. It was a very hierarchical society, even within the ranks of the lowest classes. As the tax rolls show, the peasantry included a wandering mass of individuals who lived by their labor and had considerable geographic mobility. There was a certain concentration of the means of production into fewer hands: the roll of St-Ouen-de-Breuil, with 14 percent (eleven) of the taxpayers controlling 67 percent of the land,

---

82. J. Meuvret, "Circulation monétaire et utilisation économique de la monnaie dans la France du XVIe et du XVIIe siècle," *Etudes d'Histoire Economique* (Paris, 1971). The king was aware of this problem. In a letter cited in a case before the Chamber of Accounts of Brittany, Henry IV referred to the "manquement de fonds que se trouveroit en quelques endroits de nostre dite Royaume et spécialement en nostredite province de Champagne" (AD Loire-Atlantique, B 73, fol. 187v).

83. Foisil, *Nu-Pieds,* relying on the work of F. Spooner, *L'économie mondiale et les frappes monétaires en France* (Paris, 1956).

is one indication of this concentration. At the other end of the scale, the poorest members of society were pitiable indeed; one marvels that contributions of one day's wages or two days' wages were deemed beyond their means. Yet the rich at St-Ouen, who owned or rented 67 percent of the land, paid only 54 percent of the taxes. Even paying as little as they did, the poor and mediocre (to use the term of the day) may have paid more than their fair share.

These poor were in no position to revolt alone; they needed the leadership and support of those directly above them. The tax roll of St-Ouen shows this network, as does that of Dournazac. At St-Ouen the land was monopolized by nontaxpayers, at Dournazac the richest peasants rented from landlords and the poorest peasants rented tiny strips from the richer peasants. This Dournazac roll shows several cases of rich peasants living on the *métairie* of some-one like Martial Garreau, while their tiny holding is occupied by a *bordier.*

It was the Garreaux and people like them, together with their noble and peasant allies, who ran rural France. Not only does the Garreau clan own much of the village (at least 8 percent), but they monopolize local offices, such as *greffier, procureur,* and, perhaps most important of all, *commissaire des tailles.* In both 1623 and 1630, the tax roll was drawn up in the house of Martial Garreau. The absence of a tax roll at Dournazac in 1650 could not have been possible without the open collusion of Garreau or his successor.

One cannot explain the conduct of a Martial Garreau by saying he, a bourgeois, was the ally of the monarchy against the power of the nobility. He was also not simply a local opponent of central power. He derived considerable benefit from his ties to the central power, but he also had the same grievances against it as his fellow local landlords did. Garreau was a man with his fingers in several pies, and we must accept him and those like him for what they were. Seventeenth-century France has medieval and feudal elements in it, like the *frèrêches* of the Limousin and the nobles seeking to protect their tenants, but it also has the major elements of capitalist beginnings—the concentration of the means of production and a large class of landless, itinerant laborers.

The fragmentation of the Fronde period is representative of the fragmentation of French society in the middle of the seventeenth century. There are economic classes that do not conform to the later distinctions of the capitalist period, but there are also traditional

groups or orders. Loyseau and his modern proponents, notably
Mousnier, see this society too much in terms of an ideal setting that
did not exist in this period, if it had ever existed. To see seventeenth-
century France as a conflict between aristocracy and monarchy is
as short-sighted as the view that the revolts before the Fronde were
evidence of massive class struggle. The tax rolls indicate that
France was not a nice, sedate, compartmentalized, geographically
static society; rather it was a society with an overwhelming number
of transients. Those transients were symbolic of the upheaval of the
period, one of ill-defined social distinctions and unusual political
and economic coalitions. The Fronde is so confusing because it is
so simple: everyone is unhappy with the status quo, so they revolt.
But everyone is unhappy for different reasons, so the coalition of
revolters must change constantly.

At the village level these coalitions pitted peasant against peasant in some ways, such as the drawing up of the tax roll, but they
united all in an effort to reduce the level of taxation. It would
be interesting to know if the compromise reached by the nobility, bourgeoisie, and king in mid-century included tax relief for
the farmers of the landlords. Would one find a lower portion of
taxes being paid by farmers and *métayers* of the nobility and bourgeois landowners (especially office-owning bourgeois) after 1655 or
1660?

The revolts before the Fronde were caused by taxation, but they
were fundamentally caused by the political and economic constellation of France in the first half of the seventeenth century. Society
and the national economy were in great flux between 1600 and
1635, and each group sought to obtain an advantage in a period of
transition. For the peasants, the internal divisions among the *laboureurs,* the middling peasants (those paying, prior to 1625, 5 or
10 l. a year in taxes), and the itinerant poor made any kind of long-
term cooperation impossible. Class warfare would have pitted the
bordiers against the *laboureurs* and the local bourgeoisie, not the
peasants against the landlords. The massive increases in royal direct taxation after 1625 upset the delicate balance of French society
(as well as the equally delicate French economy). Open revolt was
the peasants' form of political discourse. Their revolts highlighted
the problem, and their passive resistance made their point effective
in the long term.

The police, to use the term in its seventeenth- and eighteenth-century sense, was in the hands of the local notables, noble, bourgeois, and peasant alike. They were the public authority. The Fronde demonstrated to the Crown that the undermining of their public authority—the real, tangible public authority—was the undermining of its authority as well. While the intendants could collect the taxes and run the country even though they ignored the treasurers and officers at that level (remembering here that the intendants coopted some of the treasurers and that they were themselves taken from the same social grouping), they could not run the country without the help of people like Martial Garreau.

Conclusion

One of the defining characteristics of the so-called absolute monarchy was its ability to tax without seeking consent. In France the king never succeeded in doing this throughout the kingdom—provinces such as Brittany voted their taxes right down to the Revolution—but he did raise most of his tax money through seemingly arbitrary means. As we have seen, these means were less arbitrary than has often been thought to be the case. The simplest, most effective check on the king's power to tax arbitrarily was the peasants' refusal to pay. In the late 1630s and 1640s, this refusal to pay reached staggering proportions and it served as a major impediment to the extension of the king's power.

The limits of royal power were set, to a large degree, by the amount of money at the king's disposal. It is in this sense that one must understand the evolution of Richelieu's statement that finances are the sinews of the state. He followed the ideas of Montchrétien, who wrote that "it is impossible to make war without men, and to have men without money." Bouthillier, viewing things from a narrower perspective than did the Cardinal, wrote to him that "finances are the sinews of war." In the context of 1639, war was the primary cause of expense, so Bouthillier was accurate. But Richelieu was certainly correct in understanding the general power of the state to be limited by the state's ability to raise money to pay for itself.

This process of raising money to pay for the state had two key elements. First, the state assessed and collected, by means of indirect and direct taxation, a very large sum of money. Second, the state sought to obtain spendable income from this larger collection. These were two different problems: the establishment of a given level of taxation and the ability to spend a given amount of revenue from that taxation.

The question of taxation in early seventeenth-century France appears particularly complicated because the clear-cut modern distinctions between taxation and loans, or between net and gross revenue, did not exist. The king often maintained the fiction that temporary expedients levied on the towns or even on entire provinces were "loans." Thus the Breton *fouage extraordinaire* of 1643–44 was officially titled "a loan in form of *fouage*." One need hardly point out that the loan was never repaid, even though the Estates and Sovereign Courts of Brittany specified the repayment schedule and included interest in their calculations! The general confusion between forced loan and direct tax was one that lasted throughout the sixteenth and seventeenth centuries.

This confusion was greatest when it applied to the officers, either in the form of *rentes* in the sixteenth century or *droits aliénés* in the seventeenth. The *rentes* and *droits* were borrowing through annuities: the king received an advance payment from an individual and repaid the purchaser through an annuity. The official rate of interest was 8.33 percent for *rentes* and 10 percent for *droits*. Yet the matter was not so simple. For example, the *droits* expanded when the direct tax levies went up; in effect, if direct taxation rose, the interest rate on the king's annuities went up with it. By the early 1630s, because of the *droits*, the king had to increase direct taxation by nearly twice the amount by which he wished to increase his revenue from direct taxation. If he had wanted to increase his revenue from direct taxation by 1 million l. in 1633, he would have had to levy about 1.8 million l. more in taxes.

The conversion of these *droits* into *rentes* had two financial consequences, one long-term and one short-term. As we have seen, the short-term consequence was a partial bankruptcy of some 12–15 million l., of which 10.5 million l. was paid by the officers of the direct tax system. The king increased his revenue (on paper) from direct taxation by 10.5 million l. with the stroke of a pen and without increasing taxes. The long-term financial consequence was that the interest rate on the *droits* remained fixed, so that interest no longer escalated with the taxes. When the king sold *droits* after 1634, he sold them in fixed sums per parish, so that they would not be tied to the escalating tax rates; in other words, he borrowed at a fixed rate of interest. The new rate of interest on the pre-1634 *droits* was approximately 4.17 percent, a major improvement on the 10 percent-plus the king had been paying.

The abolition of the *droits* thus provided a double financial bo-

nanza. As we have seen, however, the abolition had a much darker
side. The officers ceased to be concerned with the timely payment
of the taxes. Their indifference was the key factor in the enormous
nonpayment levels of the 1630s and 1640s. It led to the greater use
of the intendants, starting in 1634, and to the eventual grant of
power to apportion the taxes to the intendants, in August 1642.
While there were very important political reasons for the greater
use of the intendants—the aftermath of the Day of Dupes and the
various revolts of the *grands* and of provinces—one must not lose
sight of the extremely important financial changes of 1634 that
made the intendants essential from that perspective as well.

   If we understand the *droits* and *rentes* to have been a form of
floating the national debt, we can see that the two major expenses
of the French monarchy under Henry IV and Louis XIII were debt
service and military costs. The debt service on the *droits* created
after 1616 amounted to some 45 percent of the total collection of
direct taxation by 1633. There were also very heavy *droits* on the
gabelles. As for the *rentes*, they represented an enormous capital
by the end of the sixteenth century. The king had alienated vast
amounts of revenue between 1550 and 1600. For example, in Brittany *rentes* and alienations consumed about 25 percent of the direct
taxes, two-thirds of the regular wine tax, 60 percent of the export-
import duties (excluding those of Nantes), and nearly all of the
demesne in 1602. In France as a whole, the *aides* and *gabelles* were
particularly hard hit; half their respective products must have gone
to debt service in the form of *rentes,* alienations, and straight loans
(the Gondis and Sebastien Zamet, for example, had priority repayments of straight loans assigned to indirect tax receipts). The *décimes* of the clergy were almost wholly consumed by *rentes;* the
demesne was largely alienated.

   These enormous amounts for royal debt service hid yet another
huge sum: local borrowings. In Burgundy, when the intendant Bouchu oversaw the retirement of local debts in the 1660s, he found
that most of the debts dated from the League war of 1589–98. The
municipal debts of towns all over France, debts contracted to pay
for the upkeep of royal troops, were substantial. The debts dated
from the two periods of open war: 1589–98 and 1627–59. In a
sense these were municipal obligations, undertaken for local protection; however, the money went to the royal army. Were these
debts purely municipal, or were they the remnants of a certain form
of direct taxation?

If we come back to the problem of debt service as a whole, and return to Guéry's comments about the importance of debt service problems at the end of the Ancien Régime, we find that debt service was a crushing burden at various stages of the period 1589–1648. Under Henry IV, *rentes,* alienations, and loan repayments easily added up to 10–15 million l. per year (allowing for the half-payment of the *rentes*), or about 25–40 percent of the total collection (probably the latter). Regional and municipal debts were also very large; the *pays d'Etats* and many towns had six-figure debts, while the villages owed what, for them, were considerable sums.

Under Louis XIII, the debt service ran into the 10s of millions: the *droits* alone, as we have seen, some 12–15 million l.; the *rentes* perhaps 8 million more; alienations yet more millions; and straight loans and advances from the *traitants* millions, even 10s of millions more. All told, Louis XIII's debt service expenditure in the early 1630s must have been 30 million l. or more. This amount would have been about half his total revenues, excluding borrowing and quasi-borrowing through the sale of offices and *droits.* The partial bankruptcy of 1634 would have cut the debt service burden roughly in half, bringing Louis back down to a more comfortable level: perhaps 25 percent of gross revenue going for debt service.

Here we get back to our original dichotomy, because Louis had much more money to spend than he could raise through regular taxes. The extra money came from borrowing; the borrowing, in the form of *droits* and new offices, bore a strong resemblance to forced taxation. The lenders did get some return on their money— a major difference between these loans and regular taxes—but they did not get the return to which they were entitled. The difference was a form of direct taxation of the officers and other members of the bourgeoisie. If you had paid, say, 50,000 l. for a *droit* in 1633, and you got 2,083 l. instead of the 5,000 l. to which you were entitled in 1634, you would, in effect, have been taxed for the lost capital (29,170 l.). As the 1630s wore on, you would find that this assessment had gone up, because you would probably be receiving nothing at all by 1639 or 1640.

The history of royal debt service in this period was one of two periods of very high levels of debt (1589–1604 and 1630–48) interrupted by a period of lower debt service and even retirement of debt. Sully drastically cut debt service costs in the bankruptcy of 1604, and he further reduced the debt by his series of *traités* for debt retirement (most of which were signed between 1608 and

1610). In Brittany, for example, the debt retirement contracts of 1604–18 eliminated 6 or 7 million l. of debt. They eliminated liens on at least 500,000 l. of revenues, allowing Louis XIII the luxury of creating new alienations in Brittany after 1620. Sully signed similar contracts with *gabelle* farmers and with the Estates of Dauphiné, to cite only two of the many others. Again, the inroads into the debt made by these *traités* enabled Louis XIII to create new debts in the 1620s and after. Louis went a bit too far by 1633, so he reverted to Sully's old tactic: the partial bankruptcy. The technique worked so well that it was repeated again in 1648.

While these bankruptcies appear to us to have been the height of fiscal irresponsibility, they were, in large part, due to the unusual character of royal borrowing. The rather ambiguous nature of the *droits* made them prime targets for a rescheduling; the *rentes*, too, fit the mold of a tax/loan. In both cases, the chief lenders were the royal bureaucrats themselves. In the 1602–4 bankruptcy, Henry IV and Sully were able to offer something of positive value to the officers—the guaranteed return of 4.17 percent and the security of the *paulette*. The latter enabled the officers to make up, through the higher value of their offices, the loss they incurred on the *rentes*. In 1634, Louis XIII and Richelieu offered nothing in return for the loss. They turned their back on the officers and introduced, on a much larger scale than hitherto had been the case, the intendants. Not surprisingly, many officers turned their backs on the king and his minister.

The nature of royal debt service affected the nature and level of direct taxation. By selling so many new offices and *droits*, the king created a substantial new burden on the taxpayers. He got his money in the form of loans or advances; he paid the interest by increasing direct taxation or the *gabelles*, or by creating entirely new taxes. Insofar as it concerned the direct taxes, the royal borrowing policy more than doubled the burden on the country as a whole between 1620 and 1633. This increase, from some 16 million l. to about 33–35 million l., was not entirely unjustified from the perspective of keeping royal real direct tax revenue at the approximate level of the early sixteenth century. Given the inflation of the period between the 1520s and the 1620s, royal direct taxation did not reach its real level of the 1520s until the very end of the 1620s or even 1630. The level of 1630–34, in the low 30 millions, represented a very slight increase over the level of the 1520s, which can easily be explained by a larger population and a higher national output.

In the early and mid-1630s, three factors were at work in the relative stabilization of direct taxation at the 30–35 million l. level. First, any amount over 35 million l. would seem to have been too much to pay. Certainly the tax rolls of the early 1640s, with their enormous individual assessments (many peasants over 100 l. per year), were entirely unrealistic. This peasant inability to pay the tax increases was a direct consequence of the manner in which the tax burden was distributed. The direct tax base of seventeenth-century France was remarkably small. A very small group paid almost all of the taxes: as we have seen, the top quartile usually paid two-thirds or more of the taxes (save in privileged Brittany). In many cases the top 5 percent paid half the taxes. They were in no position to see their tax burden double, and the poorer peasants, those who controlled little or no land, could not pay much more than they did. Doubling the tax burden of a peasant who paid 1 or 2 pounds per year was not going to help the king's financial situation; he needed the greater sums only the top quartile of the peasantry could provide. As all of the local studies of seventeenth-century rural France have shown, this group was only slightly removed, in terms of assets, from the rural penury surrounding it.

Second, direct taxes became a much more serious threat to ground rents after 1625 or so. In many parts of France this increased royal pressure coincided with natural problems: the outbreaks of plague after 1624; economic stagnation or even recession in some areas in the 1630s and, far more broadly, in the 1640s. The higher taxes and the general dislocation of the war must bear some responsibility (varying according to area) for this latter factor. The wine trade of western France, for example, was virtually destroyed by the double burden of heavy internal taxes and difficulty of access to foreign markets (due to war).

Third, the officers lost interest in the regular payment of taxes. A surly, noncooperative bureaucracy was not a very effective tool for collecting ever-increasing taxes. These officers were also landlords, and their self-interest in protecting their ground rents was a strong incentive for laxity in tax collection.

The massive increase in the royal debt, further complicated by the inability of the king's suppliers and creditors to collect on their assignations in the early 1640s, had two possible consequences on the peasantry. In those areas in which the royal army did not often pass, the peasants simply kept on paying at the old rates (or they stopped paying altogether). It is most intriguing that the level of direct taxation in the early years of Colbert's administration was in the low 30 millions, precisely the level of the early 1630s (although in real terms, less). While it is hard to prove, one is tempted by the abundance of information about *non-valeurs* for the period 1634– 60 to say that the king rarely got more than 35 million l. or so from direct taxation in any given year between 1630 and 1660.

In those areas in which the royal army did pass, the situation was far more serious. The troops could be an unmitigated catastrophe: forced requisition of goods, forced payment of taxes, and general pillaging and disorder. The military reforms of Louis XIV were due, in no small measure, to the disastrous relationship between the army and the populace in the early part of the century.

Seventeenth-century French society was the scene of a bitter conflict between local elites and the central government for control of the country. There can be little question that the central government never achieved absolutism in any real sense of the term. The main reason for its failure to do so was that it could never raise enough money to pay for all it wanted to do. The king could not tax "à volonté." There were limits to how much he could raise, and those limits restricted his ability to extend his power in other ways.

Richelieu's analysis was right; without a surer financial base on which to build, the French state would never be able to overcome fully the power of local elites. The financial and taxation system of the Ancien Régime was both its inner weakness and its great strength. Its strength lay in its flexibility—its ability to adapt to differing local conditions. Its weakness was its inability to create a centralized, rationalized system. At each new crisis the system had to resort to expedients that mortgaged the future ever more heavily. When the crises were too close, the system broke down. It broke down in 1634, causing a collapse that lasted until the 1650s. The amazing aspect of the system in this period was that it functioned well enough to pay for French participation in the war against Spain.

The French government collapsed in the late 1640s; the Frondes were only one manifestation of the collapse. The financial and political collapses were intimately related, and the government's return to stability required, above all, sounder finances. It was the soundness of Colbert's fiscal system that enabled Louis XIV to achieve many political goals that his father was unable to attain.

The early seventeenth century was, in this way, a microcosm of the Ancien Régime. Political crises were a constant offshoot of the Ancien Régime's financial problems. The Revolution and the Fronde have this in common: the government could not raise enough money to pay for itself and this failure led to political agitation. The underlying financial problem was also quite similar in 1634, 1648, and 1789: crushing debt service because of loans taken out to pay for military expenses. That the monarchy could get away with two bankruptcies between 1634 and 1654, whereas bankruptcy seemed out of the question in 1788, says something both about the position of the monarchy within the respective societies and about the different mentalities of the two epochs.

The positive side of the tax system and, to a greater extent, in the 1640s, the financial system, was that it enabled the monarchy to survive. Between 1627 and 1661 the king survived two bankruptcies, constant warfare, a minority, a major internal political crisis and civil war, and serious economic decline. He emerged stronger than ever from this series of misfortunes. It was a truly remarkable achievement and it was possible because the financial system was strong enough to provide the king with resources unmatched by any ruler of his time.

The negative side of the tax system was that its inequities prevented the king from tapping the real wealth of his kingdom, except through rather dubious techniques such as the *droits aliénés*. France would remain partially hamstrung as long as its middle class and its nobility, as well as the clergy, remained outside the mainstream of the tax system. The local records show that the peasants had reached their limits in the 1630s; and they were not only incapable of doing more, they were unwilling to try.

The general lesson of the tax system is that the king of France faced real obstacles to the extension of his power, and that he was, to a large extent, unable to overcome them. While the peasants had little access to the formal political process, nonetheless they had a very great deal to say about what went on. Similarly, the local elites never allowed the king to cut them off completely from the surrounding population. The financial and tax system of seventeenth-century France was as much a compromise as its political system. Those compromises were a symbol of the king's weakness, as well as the source of his real power. If finances were indeed the sinews of the state, it is little wonder that the French Leviathan had so much trouble enforcing its will in provincial France.

Appendix A: *Elections* in France, 1583, 1620, 1640

1583	1620 (number of *élus*)	1640 (number of parishes)
Généralité *of Paris*		
Paris*	Paris (14)	Paris (430)
Beauvais*	Beauvais (13)	Beauvais (134)
Mantes*	Mantes (12)	Mantes (86)
Sens*	Sens (13)	Sens (122 or 137)
Senlis*	Senlis (13)	Senlis (81)
Meaux*	Meaux (14)	Meaux (107)
Melun*	Melun (14)	Melun (112)
Provins*	Provins (9)	Provins (57)
Vézélay*	Vézélay (9)	Vézélay (58)
Compiègne†	Compiègne (12)	Compiègne (36)
Montfort†	Montfort (11)	Montfort (58)
Etampes†	Etampes (10)	Etampes (41)
Tonnerre†	Tonnerre (11)	Tonnerre (127 or 130)
Dreux†	Dreux (8)	Dreux (70)
Nemours†	Nemours (9)	Nemours (129 or 133)
Nogent-s-Seine	Nogent-s-Seine (8)	Nogent-s-Seine (37 or 47)
St-Florentin	St-Florentin (9)	St-Florentin (35)
Coulommiers	Coulommiers (9)	Coulommiers (36 or 34)
	Joigny (10)	Joigny (88)

1583	1620 (number of élus)	1640 (number of parishes)
	Rozay-en-Brie (8)	Rozay-en-Brie (61 or 62)
Soissons*		
Clermont†		
Château-Thierry†		
Généralité of Soissons, created in 1595		
	Soissons (9)	Soissons (225 or 230)
	Clermont (9)	Clermont (109 or 114)
	Château-Thierry (8)	Château-Thierry (120 or 126)
	Laon (9)	Laon (336 or 485)
	Noyon (9)	Noyon (136 or 152)
	Crépy (9)	Crépy (92 or 86)
	Guise (6)	Guise (n.l.; 100)
Généralité of Amiens		
Amiens*	Amiens (10)	Amiens (294 or 296)
Montdidier*	Montdidier (11)	Montdidier (220)
Ponthieu*	Ponthieu (11)	Ponthieu (207 or 184)
St-Quentin*	St-Quentin (11)	St-Quentin (81 or 83)
Noyon*		
Péronne†	Péronne (10)	Péronne (209 or 211)
Doullens†	Doullens (9)	Doullens (240 or 215)
Généralité of Châlons		
Châlons*	Châlons (10)	Châlons (249 or 240)
Reims*	Reims (9)	Reims (444 or 410)
Troyes*	Troyes (11)	Troyes (344 or 264)
Rethel*	Rethel (7)	Rethel (262 or 225)

1583	1620 (number of *élus*)	1640 (number of parishes)
Langres*	Langres (9)	Langres (339 or 300)
Epernay	Epernay (7)	Epernay (80 or 86)
Laon*		
Chaumont	Chaumont (11)	Chaumont (269 or 153)
Sézanne	Sézanne (6)	Sézanne (71 or 74)
	Vitry-le-François (8)	Vitry-le-François (196 or 180)
		Bar-s-Aube† (n.l.; 200)
		Ste-Ménéhould (n.l.; 120)

Généralité *of Orléans*

Orléans*	Orléans (12)	Orléans (127)
Montargis*	Montargis (9)	Montargis (90 or 85)
Vendôme*	Vendôme (9)	Vendôme (94)
Châteaudun*	Châteaudun (10)	Châteaudun (138 or 157)
Chartres*	Chartres (11)	Chartres (206)
Blois*	Blois (11)	Blois (72)
Gien†	Gien (11)	Gien (87 or 81)
Clamecy	Clamecy (8)	Clamecy (64)
Dourdan	Dourdan (7)	Dourdan (65)
	Beaugency (8)	Beaugency (48)
	Pithiviers (7)	Pithiviers (80 or 81)
	Romorantin (7)	Romorantin (76)

Généralité *of Bourges*

Bourges*	Bourges (10)	Bourges (265 or 358)
Châteauroux (t)	Châteauroux (6)	Châteauroux (99 or 106)
La Châtre (t)		La Châtre (t) (61; n.l.)
	St-Amand (5)	St-Amand (n. l.; 110)

1583	1620 (number of élus)	1640 (number of parishes)
Généralité *of Riom*		
Riom	Riom (11)	Riom (131)
St-Flour*	St-Flour (9)	St-Flour (144)
	Issoire (2)	Issoire (138)
	Brioude (2)	Brioude (145)
		Clermont* (312)
		Orillac (Aurillac?) (96)
		Salers (149)
		Thiers (84)
Généralité *of Tours*		
Tours*	Tours (12)	Tours (487)
Chinon*	Chinon (9)	Chinon (79 or 61)
Loudun*	Loudun (10)	Loudun (57 or 49)
Saumur*	Saumur (6)	Saumur (76 or 82)
Angers*	Angers (12)	Angers (234 or 224)
Le Mans*	Le Mans (11	Le Mans (480 or 342)
Laval	Laval (8)	Laval (65)
Loches	Loches (8)	Loches (76)
Baugé	Baugé (9)	Baugé (80)
Château-Gontier	Château-Gontier (7)	Château-Gontier (67)
	Amboise (9)	Amboise (46)
	Mirabeau (8)	
	La Flèche (9)	La Flèche (100 or 106)
	Montreuil-Bellay (7)	Montreuil-Bellay (47 or 57)
		Richelieu (n.l.; 75)
		Château-du-Loir (n.l.; 81)
		Mayenne (n.l.; 65)

1583	1620 (number of *élus*)	1640 (number of parishes)
Généralité *of Moulins*		
Moulins*	Moulins (10)	Moulins (232 or 84)
Nevers*	Nevers (9)	Nevers (274 or 273)
Château-Chinon†	Château-Chinon (3)	Château-Chinon (42 or 43)
La Marche†	La Marche (9)	La Marche (256 or 298)
Franc-Alleu†(t)	Franc-Alleu (3)	Franc-Alleu (30 or 29)
	Gannat (10)	Gannat (224)
	Montluçon (4)	Montluçon (209 or 125)
		Combrailles† (56 or 55)
		La Charité-s-Loire† (n.l.; 100)
Généralité *of Lyon*		
Lyon*	Lyon (6)	Lyon (209 or 144)
Forez*	Forez (6)	Forez (415)
Beaujolais†	Beaujolais (9)	Beaujolais (123 or 126)
		Montbrison (n.l.; 221)
		Roanne (n.l.; 146)
		St-Chamond (n.l.; 126)
Généralité *of Poitiers*		
Poitiers*	Poitiers (11)	Poitiers (408 or 310)
La Rochelle	La Rochelle (9)	La Rochelle (407 or 85)
St-Maixent	St-Maixent (9)	St-Maixent (56 or 61)
Niort	Niort (10)	Niort (185; n.l.)

1583	1620 (number of élus)	1640 (number of parishes)
Fontenay	Fontenay (10)	Fontenay (182 or 162)
Thouars	Thouars (10)	Thouars (104)
Châtellerault	Châtellerault (9)	Châtellerault (56)
Blanc-en-Berry		
	Mauléon (8)	Mauléon (75 or 78)
	Sables-d'Olonne (9)	Sables-d'Olonne (96)
Généralité of Limoges		
Haut-Limousin*	Omitted from 1620 documents	Limoges (260 or 259)
Saintes		
Angoulême†		Angoulême (308 or 320)
St-Jeane-d'Angély		St-Jeane-d'Angély (198 or 200)
Bourganeuf		Bourganeuf (64 or 95)
Bas-Limousin†		
		Tulle (127 or 167)
		Brive (93 or 90)

Note: One document lists Blanc-en-Berry in 1640 with 83 parishes.

Généralité of Bordeaux

Bordeaux†	Bordeaux (0)	Bordeaux (n.l.; 456)
Périgord*	Périgord (8)	Périgord (441 or 470)
	Agenais (3)	Agenais (346 or 400)
	Les Lannes (0)	Les Lannes (288; n.l.)
	Condom (0)	Condom (60 or 156)
		Cognac (n.l.; 137)
		Sarlat (n.l.; 200)
		Saintes (301—in Limoges; 316)

1583	1620 (number of *élus*)	1640 (number of parishes)
		généralité of Mont-auban
	Armagnac (0)	Armagnac (60 or 330)
	Haut-Rouergue (0)	Rodez (458 or 274)
	Bas-Rouergue (0)	Villefranche (212 or 265)
	Rhodez (0)	Rhodez (206 or 289)
	Quercy (0)	Cahors (288 or 202)
	Montauban (0)	Montauban (83 or 200)
	Figéac (0)	Figéac (133 or 200)
	Rivière-Verdun (0)	Rivière-Verdun (133 or 134)
	Comminges (0)	Comminges (53 or 341)
Généralité *of Caen*		
Caen*	Caen (8)	Caen (244)
Avranches*	Avranches (7)	Avranches (87 or 97)
Bayeux*	Bayeux (8)	Bayeux (224)
Vire-et-Condé†	Vire-et-Condé (7)	Vire-et-Condé (126)
Falaise†	Falaise (8)	Falaise (237 or 337) (to Alençon)
Coutances†	Coutances (8)	Coutances (164)
Valognes	Valognes (6)	Valognes (190)
Mortain	Mortain (7)	Mortain (86 or 85)
Carentan-St-Lô	Carentan-St-Lô (9)	Carentan-St-Lô (112)
Généralité *of Rouen*		
Rouen*	Rouen (7)	Rouen (232)
Arques*	Arques (7)	Arques (284 or 274)
Montivilliers*	Montivilliers (8)	Montivilliers (157)
Caudebec*	Caudebec (8)	Caudebec (196)
Gisors*	Gisors (6)	Gisors (94)

1583	1620 (number of *élus*)	1640 (number of parishes)
Evreux*	Evreux (7)	Evreux (167; n.l.)
	Pont-de-l'Arche (5)	Pont-de-l'Arche (77 or 78)
	Pont-Audemer (7)	Pont-Audemer (160 or 156)
	Lyons (4)	Lyons (60)
	Neufchâtel (6)	Neufchâtel (118)
	Les Andélys (6)	Les Andélys (124 or 134)
	Conches (6)	Conches (164 or 163)
	Chaumont et Magny (7)	Chaumont et Magny (107 or 167)
		généralité of Alençon
Alençon*	Alençon (9)	Alençon (126 or 127)
Lisieux*	Lisieux (7)	Lisieux (146)
Bernay†	Bernay (6)	Bernay (131)
	Argentan (5)	Argentan (171)
	Dampfront (5)	Dampfront (46)
	Verneuil (7)	Verneuil (158 or 148)
	Mortagne-en-Perche (8)	Mortagne-en-Perche (n.l.; 160)

Sources:

1383   M. Rey, *Le domaine du roi sous Charles VI* (Paris, 1965), 180–81.
1500   G. Dupont-Ferrier, *Les élections et leur personnel* (Paris, 1930), map II.
1583   BN, Ms. Dupuy 233, fols. 12 and ff.
1620   BN, Ms. Fr. 16622, 16623, 16624.
1640   BN, Ms. Fr. 7736, Ms. Fr. 18481. The parish count listed first is from Ms. Fr. 18481, the second one from Ms. Fr. 7736

*   *Election* existed in 1383.
†   *Election* existed in 1500.
t   Tablier, or sub-élection.
n.l.   Not listed.

Appendix B: Total Revenues from Taxation, 1597–1647

Table B-1: *Direct Taxation in France, 1597–1647 (in 000 1.)*

Year	Pays d'élection	Pays d'Etats	Total
1597	18,789		
—			
1599	17,686		
1600	15,712	3,260	18,972
1601	16,159	2,551	18,710
1602	14,874	2,415	17,289
1603	15,421	2,386	17,807
1604	15,364	2,134	17,498
1605	15,314	2,306	17,620
1606	15,760	2,192	17,952
1607	15,364	2,493	17,857
1608	15,668	2,239	17,907
1609	15,730	2,267	17,997
1610	15,730	2,216	17,946
1611	16,264	2,200	18,464
1612	16,047	2,200	18,247
1613	15,730	2,200	17,930
1614	15,730	2,200	17,930
1615	15,894	2,360	18,254
1616	15,594	2,400	17,994
1617	15,730	2,286	18,016
1618	15,730	2,341	18,071
1619	15,730	2,200	17,930
1620	16,643	2,525	19,168
1621	18,997	2,255	21,252
1622	18,120	2,575	20,695
1623	18,749	2,435	21,184
1624	18,253	2,695	20,948
1625	18,253	2,555	20,808
1626	18,749	2,405	21,154
1627	19,605	2,505	22,110
1628	20,773	3,103	23,884
1629	21,730	3,048	24,778
1630	23,903	3,955	27,858

Table B-1. *(continued)*

Year	*Pays d'élection*	*Pays d'Etats*	Total
1631	19,213	3,945	23,158
1632	22,870	3,475	26,345
1633	26,064	4,605	30,669
1634	34,260	4,605	38,865
—			
1636			39,650
1637			40,838
1638			39,005
1639			43,725
1640	39,177	4,881	44,058
—			
1643	49,489	4,468	53,957
	(64,892)	(7,754)	(72,646)
—			
1647	50,539	5,945	56,484

Sources: Most of the figures are based on overall reconstruction, relying on two or more citations for individual provinces. For the period after 1634, the figures come from BN, Ms. Fr. 18490 (1636–40), and from BN, NAF 200 (1643). The figures in parentheses for 1643 and those of 1647 are from BN, Ms. Fr. 18510, fols. 7 and ff. There are many copies of these same documents in the Bibliothèque Nationale (Ms. Fr. 7736, to cite only one example). Figures from the *pays d'Etats* are a mixture of exact figures (always for Brittany, usually for Languedoc) and estimates (Provence, Dauphiné, Burgundy) based on isolated annual figures.

Notes: This table represents an estimate for direct taxation in all of France during the first half of the seventeenth century. The figures for the period up to 1634 are fairly accurate, taken largely from provincial archives and from central documents whose accuracy could be checked against local records. The figures for the period 1636–47 are from central records; they are, without question, pure fantasy. As has been explained in Chapters 3 and 4, the government simply could not collect these taxes. The actual collections were probably on the order of 50–60 percent of the amounts listed, and even this figure may be too high. The geographic distribution of the collection was also quite skewed, with certain areas—the Midi and the Cotentin—paying far less than half of their assessments.

All these figures leave out one of the most onerous of tax burdens, paying for the upkeep of the troops in the field. The basic cost was 5 shillings a day per soldier, plus the higher allowance for officers and the costs of subsidiary special services—wood for beds, candles, and so on. The king tried to regularize the winter costs of the troops in the 1640s with a levy known as the *quartier d'hiver:* in 1646, he envisaged 18.5 million l. for this tax. In earlier years there are documents for the *étapes* levied in various parishes or even entire *élections* (bishoprics in Brittany). The known military activity of the period 1600–1634 coincides with those periods for which we have evidence of *étapes:* 1614–17, 1621–22, and 1627–28. For Dauphiné and Provence, one would have to add the early 1630s.

During peacetime the cost of feeding the French army must have been about 1.8–2.0 million l. a year until the late 1620s (based on an army of 20,000 men). Every time the army grew in size, this feeding cost also rose. It includes the basics of food and lodging, and thus does not count stocking fortresses and other expenses. In 1630, for example, the king raised 22,990 l. in Brittany to help pay for 20,000 uniforms for the army being sent to Italy. In 1637, when the duke of Brissac stocked Port Louis, he ordered 8 tons of wheat (at 105 l. per ton); 66 quintals of biscuit (6 l. each); 290 *minots* of salt (at 12 shillings each); 69 pipes of Angevin wine (at 31.5 l. a pipe); 25,822 lb. of lead; 30,000 lb. of powder; nearly 4,000 cannon balls; 238 muskets; and 156 pikes. Such supplies were paid for by the local population by means of a special surtax.

The documents miss other levies as well. In the 1643 listing, for example, the documents in question ignore an extraordinary *fouage* in Brittany of some 400,000 l. The most important problem, other than that of *étapes*, is that the *pays d'Etats* had highly individualistic tax systems. In Provence the communities raised their general contributions as they saw fit; in Brittany the Estates made their grant to the king through wine tax revenues (whereas in Languedoc the Estates used direct taxes, thus making it appear that Languedoc paid heavier taxes than Brittany); in Burgundy the extra money often came from salt surtaxes; in Dauphiné, Burgundy, and Provence, levies for troops in the field may well have formed the largest single segment of taxation, and such levies are excluded from the table. These areas also levied substantial sums to pay for debts, which were contracted to pay the royal army. Marseille, for example, levied almost 1.1 million l. in taxes from 1610 to 1617: how much was levied in Provence as a whole for such purposes?

The best that can be said of the figures is that the king of France levied 18–20 million l. a year in direct taxes from 1600 to 1620, with short, rapid increases in 1601, 1610, and 1614–17. In the 1620s, direct taxation rose steadily, to perhaps 28 or 30 million l. in 1627 and 1628 (counting military levies). In the early 1630s, direct taxes were on the order of 30–35 million l. It is likely that, despite central figures to the contrary, direct taxation did not rise substantially above this level in the late 1630s and 1640s.

Table B-2: *Direct Taxes and Payments for the* Droits Aliénés, *1616–34* (Pays d'Election *only*)

Year	Direct Taxes	Payments for Droits Aliénés	Total
1616	15,594	2,408	18,002
1617	15,730		15,730
1618	15,730	7,150	22,830
1619	15,730		15,730
1620	16,643	486	17,129
1621	18,997	6,590	25,587
1622	18,120	7,400	25,520
1623	18,749	7,700	26,449
1624	18,253		18,253
1625	18,253		18,253
1626	18,749		18,749
1627	19,605	4,800	24,405
1628	20,773		20,773
1629	21,730	14,000	35,830
1630	23,903		23,903
1631	19,213	3,900	23,113
1632	22,870	31,700	54,570
1633	26,064	10,400	36,465
1634	34,260	8,400	42,660

Note: The receipts for *traités* involving the *droits aliénés* on the direct taxes are listed in the year of their creation. Actual payment would have been spread out over several years and would have entailed a *remise* of one-sixth to the *traitant*. Nonetheless, the king could (and did) assign expenses to the expected receipts of the *traité* as soon as it was signed, so that one can, in a certain legitimate sense, list the revenue in the year of creation. Note that these figures do not include sales of offices or sales of *droits* on nondirect taxes (such as the *gabelle*).

Table B-3: *Taxation in France, 1607, 1620, 1634, 1640*

	1607 in 000 l.	(%)	1620 in 000 l.	(%)	1634 in 000 l.	(%)	1640 in 000 l.	(%)
Direct taxes	17,857	58.8	19,168	56.9	38,865	61.5	44,058	56.6
Salt taxes	6,687	22.0	7,775	23.1	14,335	22.7	19,483	25.0
Sales taxes	3,814	12.6	4,194	12.4	5,556	8.8	7,495	9.6
Transit taxes	2,013	6.6	2,568	7.6	4,423	7.0	6,747	8.7
Total	30,371		33,705		63,179		77,783	

Note: The direct taxes were not fully paid in 1640 and may not have been fully paid in 1634. Most tax farms also carried substantial rebates by 1640, so that most forms of revenue actually produced less than the figures cited would indicate. The direct taxes may have produced 30 million l. or even less, the indirect ones perhaps 80 percent of the cited figures. This amount would give overall tax revenues of some 60 million l. in 1640. One also has to adjust the 1640 figure for the devaluation of 1636, which was just under 21 percent.

Glossary of French Terms

aides	Originally, the taxes levied to pay the ransom of King John (1360). Here, the later meaning, a group of indirect taxes, chiefly on wine.
bordage	Tiny holding, leased by a *bordier;* this term is common in western France.
bordereau de l'Epargne	Account statement of the Central Treasury.
bureau des finances	Collective group of treasurers of France in each *généralité* except that of Brittany.
commissaire des tailles	Parish official charged with drawing up the tax roll after 1616.
comptants ès mains du roi	Cash spent by the king without use of normal written authorizations.
crue	Surtax. In most cases the reference here is to the *grande crue* or garrison tax, created by Henry IV.
denier	Pence. The rate of interest was expressed by such phrases as the *denier 12,* meaning the twelfth penny (8.33 percent).
droits aliénés	Alienated rights. The officer would purchase the right to a surtax, expressed in pennies per pound, levied within his jurisdiction. The cost to the officer was ten times the annual value of the *droit.*
élection	Local financial district, first created in the fourteenth century, often along diocesan lines. It took its name from its chief administrative officer, the *élu.*
Epargne	Central Treasury. Thus, the *trésorier de l'Epargne,* the Central Treasurer.

état au vrai	Final account for a given officer or jurisdiction.
état du roi	Preliminary account of a given officer or jurisdiction.
étapes	Money raised to feed and supply troops in the field. Troops took the necessary supplies, and the money to pay for them was later raised in an indeterminate area.
gabelle	Salt tax. Often used as a generic term for unpopular taxes or, more commonly, in a slight variation, *gabeleurs,* for tax agents. The *gabelle* was farmed; its chief administrative officer was the head of the salt warehouse, the *grenetier.*
gages	Annuity paid in the guise of a salary or wages. The most common rate was 10 percent of the official value of the office.
généralité	Regional financial district, so called after its chief administrative officer, the *général* (after 1577, known as a treasurer of France).
laboureur	Well-off peasant, usually owner of a plough team.
mandement de l'Epargne	Order to pay from the Central Treasury.
métayer	Literally, sharecropper; here, the western French meaning of lessee of a substantial holding, on terms of equal division.
non-valeurs	Shortfall in tax collection.
pancarte	Tax of 5 percent on sale in towns, created by Henry IV, abolished in 1602 in return for an addition to the *crue.*
pays d'Etats	Area with Estates. In 1600, Brittany, Burgundy, Languedoc, Provence, Dauphiné, and the Southwest.
pays d'élection	Area with *élections;* essentially the North and part of the center. Dauphiné and the Southwest were added to this area in the early seventeenth century.

rente   Annuity. The largest single group of royal *rentes* were the *rentes sur l'Hôtel de Ville de Paris*, annuities guaranteed by the income of the city of Paris (later supplemented by giving Paris liens on certain royal tax revenues).

taille   Main direct tax, created by Charles VII to pay the men-at-arms. In the North it was known as the *taille personnelle* because it was based on the status of the person; in much of the South—Languedoc, Dauphiné, and part of the *généralité* of Guyenne—it was the *taille réelle*, based on the status of the land. Here the term *tailles* is used for the direct taxes as a group.

traité   An agreement with a farmer to lease a royal tax or to provide a service. The contract was a *traité*, the lessee was a *traitant*. If the lessee himself thought up the idea of the tax, it was called a *parti*, and he was thus a *partisan*.

Selected Bibliography

The following is not a list of all works consulted in the preparation of this manuscript; rather it is a list of the most relevant materials. The interested reader can find a more comprehensive bibliography in J. Collins, "Taxation in Bretagne, 1598–1648" (Ph.D. dissertation, Columbia University, 1978) and R. Mousnier, *La Vénalité des Offices* (Paris, 1971).

Archival Sources

At the Archives Nationales, the most important materials are the papers of Sully, series 120 AP; the papers of the Council of State and of Finances, series E; and the papers of the Chamber of Accounts of Paris, series P. At the Bibliothèque Nationale, I used four collections: Cinq Cents Colbert (16, 41, 106, 256, 289, 455, and 491); the Manuscrits Dupuy (41, 233, 824, 848); the Manuscrits Français (3127, 3411, 3558, 7736, 10839, 16622–16624, 16626, 16627, 16905, 17321, 18205, 18479, 18490, 18510, 21479, 22311, 22330, 22342); and the Nouvelles Acquisitions Françaises (172, 200, 21878).

Most of the research was done outside of Paris, in the departmental archives of: Calvados (series 4 C); Cher (series C, notably 714, 744–46, 972–75, and 982–86); Côtes-du-Nord; Deux-Sèvres; Eure; Finistère; Gironde (series C, papers of the *bureau des finances* of Bordeaux); Haute-Vienne (C 145, 146, 400, 550–52); Ille-et-Vilaine (notably series C, papers of the Estates of Brittany); Loire-Atlantique (especially series C, papers of the Chamber of Accounts of Nantes); Marne (series C, papers of the *bureau des finances* of Châlons, C 2489–2500 and 2530); Morbihan; Rhône (papers of the *bureau des finances* of Lyon, notably subseries 3 C and 8 C); Somme; and Seine-Maritime (papers of the *bureau des finances* of Rouen and of the *Cour des Aides* of Rouen). At Nantes I also used extensively the municipal archives, series AA, CC, and FF.

Printed Sources

De Beaurepaire, C. de Robillard. *Cahiers des Etats de Normandie.* Rouen, 1873–89.

De Calan, C. de la Lande. *Documents inédits relatifs aux Etats de Bretagne de 1491 à 1589.* Rennes, 1908. (Note: This material was also consulted in the archival originals.)

Durand, Y. *Cahiers de doléances de la noblesse des gouvernements d'Orléannais, de Normandie et de Bretagne.* Nantes, n.d.

———. *Cahiers de doléances des paroisses du bailliage de Troyes.* Paris, 1966.

———, Mousnier, R., and Labatut, J. *Deux cahiers de la noblesse pour les Etats Généraux de 1649.* Paris, 1965.

Fontanon, A. *Les édicts et ordonnances des rois de France.* 3 vols. Paris, 1611.

Forbonnais, F. *Recherches et considérations sur les finances de France depuis l'année 1595 jusqu'à l'année 1721.* Liège, 1758.

Grillon, P., ed. *Papiers d'Etat de Richelieu.* 4 vols. Paris, 1975–80.

L'estoile, P. de. *Journal pour le règne de Henri IV.* Paris, 1948.

Loyseau, C. *Cinq livres du droit des offices.* Paris, 1613, 1644.

Mallet, J. R. *Comptes rendus de l'administration des finances de la France....* London and Paris, 1789.

Mousnier, R., ed. *Lettres et mémoires adressés au Chancelier Séguier (1633–1649).* 2 vols. Paris, 1964.

Ordonnances des rois de France de la troisième race. 14 vols. Paris, 1722–1848.

Règlements rendus sur le fait des tailles. Rouen, 1710.

Romier, L. *Lettres et chêvauchées du bureau des finances de Caen sous Henri IV.* Rouen, 1910.

Sully, M. de Béthune. *Les économies royales de Sully.* Edited by B. Barbiche and D. Buisseret. Paris, 1970.

———. *Mémoires des sages et royales oeconomies d'estat....* Edited by J. F. Michaud and J. J. F. Poujoulat, 2d series, vols. ii and iii. Paris, 1837.

Varin, P. *Archives administratives de la ville de Reims.* 3 vols. Paris, 1848.

Voysin de la Noiraye, J.-B. *Mémoire sur la généralité de Rouen en 1665.* Edited by E. Esmonin. Paris, 1913.

Secondary Sources

Antoine, M. "L'administration centrale des finances en France du XVIe au XVIIIe siècles." *Histoire comparée de l'administration (IVe–XVIIIe siècles).* Munich, 1980.

———. "Le régalement des tailles en 1624–1626." *Revue Historique* 259 (1981): 27–63.

Barbiche, B. "Les commissaires députés pour le régalement des tailles en 1598–1599." *Bibliothèque de l'Ecole des Chartes* 118 (1960): 58–96.

———. *Sully*. Paris, 1981.

Bayard, F. "Fermes et Traités dans la première moitié du XVIIe siècle." *Bulletin du Centre d'histoire économique et sociale de la région lyonnaise* 4 (1975): 45–80.

———. "Le Secret du roi, étude des comptants ès mains du roi, sous Henry IV." *Bulletin du Centre d'histoire économique et sociale de la région lyonnaise* 3 (1974): 1–27.

Beik, W. *Absolutism and Society in Seventeenth-Century France. State Power and Provincial Aristocracy in Languedoc*. Cambridge, England, 1985.

Bercé, Y.-M. *Histoire des Croquants*. Geneva, 1974.

———. "La bourgeoisie bordelaise et le fisc sous Louis XIII." *Revue Historique de Bordeaux* 13 (1964): 41–65.

Boislisle, A. de. "Semblançay et la Surintendance des Finances." *Annuaire-Bulletin de la Société de l'Histoire de France* 18 (1881): 225–74.

Bonney, R. *The King's Debts*. Oxford, 1981.

———. *Political Change in France under Richelieu and Mazarin, 1624–1661*. Oxford, 1978.

———. "The Secret Expenses of Richelieu and Mazarin, 1624–1661." *English Historical Review* 91 (1976): 825–36.

Bosher, J. "*Chambres de justice* in the French monarchy." In *French Government and Society, 1500–1850. Essays in Memory of Alfred Cobban.*, edited by Bosher 19–40. London, 1973.

Brown, E. A. R. "Cessante Causa and the Taxes of the Last Capetians: The Political Applications of a Philosophical Maxim." *Studia Gratiana* 15 (1972): 565–87.

———. "Philip the Fair, Plena Potestas and the Aide pur fille Marier." *Studies Presented to the International Commission for the History of Representative and Parliamentary Institutions* 39 (1970): 1–28.

Caillard, M. "Recherches sur les soulèvements populaires en Basse-Normandie (1620–1640)." *Cahiers des Annales de Normandie* 3 (1963): 23–153.

Charmeil, J.-P. *Les trésoriers de France à l'époque de la Fronde*. Paris, 1963.

Collins, J. B. "Les impôts et le commerce du vin en Bretagne au XVIIe siècle." *Actes du 107e Congrès National des Sociétés Savantes* 1 (1982): 155–68.

————. "Sur l'histoire fiscale du XVIIe siècle: Les impôts directs en Champagne entre 1595 et 1635." *Annales E.S.C.* 34 (1979): 325–47.

————. "Taxation and Peasant Revolts in Sixteenth- and Seventeenth-Century France." *Proceedings of the Tenth Western Conference for French History* 10 (1982): 155–68.

————. "Taxation in Bretagne, 1598–1648." Ph.D. diss., Columbia University, 1978.

Contamine, P. *Guerre, Etat et Société à la fin du Moyen Age.* Paris, 1972.

Coville, A. *Les Etats de Normandie au XIVe siècle.* Paris, 1894.

Dent, J. *Crisis in Finance: Crown, Financiers and Society in Seventeenth-Century France.* New York, 1973.

Dessert, D. *Argent, pouvoir et société au Grand Siècle.* Paris, 1984.

————. "Finances et société au XVIIe siècle: à propos de la Chambre de Justice de 1661." *Annales E.S.C.* 29 (1974): 847–81.

Devic, Dom Claude, and Vaissete, Dom J. *Histoire générale de Languedoc.* 14 vols., new ed. Toulouse, 1876–89.

Dewald, J. *The Formation of a Provincial Nobility: The Magistrates of the Parlement of Rouen, 1499–1610.* Princeton, 1980.

Doucet, R. "L'état des finances de 1523." *Bulletin philologique et historique* (1920): 5–123 and introduction.

————. "L'état des finances de 1567." *Bulletin philologique et historique* (1926–27): 3–32.

————. "Les finances de France en 1614." *Revue d'Histoire Economique et Sociale* 18 (1930): 133–63.

————. "Le grand parti de Lyon." *Revue Historique* 171 (1933): 470–505 and 172 (1934): 1–41.

————. *Les institutions de la France au XVIe siècle.* Paris, 1948.

Drouot, H. *Mayenne et la Bourgogne.* Paris, 1935.

Dupont-Ferrier, G. *Etudes sur les institutions financières de la France à la fin du Moyen Age.* Vol. 1. *Les élections et leur personnel.* Paris, 1930. Vol. 2. *Les finances extraordinaires et leur mécanisme.* Paris, 1932.

————. *Nouvelles études sur les institutions financières de la France à la fin du Moyen Age.* Paris, 1933.

Esmonin, E. *La taille en Normandie au temps de Colbert.* Paris, 1913.

Foisil, M. *La révolte des Nu-Pieds.* Paris, 1970.

Frêche, G. "Compoix, propriété foncière, fiscalité et démographie." *Revue d'Histoire Moderne et Contemporaine* 18 (1971): 321–53.

Goubert, P. *Beauvais et le Beauvaisis de 1600 à 1715.* Paris, 1960.

Guéry, A. "Les finances de la monarchie française sous l'Ancien Régime." *Annales E.S.C.* 33 (1978): 216–39.

Harding, R. *Anatomy of a Power Elite: The Provincial Governors of Early Modern France.* New Haven, 1978.

Hayden, J. M. *France and the Estates General of 1614.* Cambridge, 1974.

Hennemann, J. B. *The Captivity and Ransom of John II.* Princeton, 1976.

———. *Royal Taxation in Fourteenth-Century France.* Princeton, 1971.

Heumann, P. "Un traitant sous Louis XIII: Antoine Feydeau." *Revue d'Histoire Moderne* 10 (1938): 5–45.

Huppert, G. *Les bourgeois gentilshommes.* Chicago, 1977.

Jacquart, J. *La crise rurale en Ile-de-France, 1550–1670.* Paris, 1974.

Karcher, A. "L'Assemblée des notables de St-Germain-en-Laye (1583)." *Bibliothèque de l'Ecole des Chartes* 94 (1956): 115–62.

Kettering, S. *Judicial Politics and Urban Revolt: The Parlement of Aix, 1629–1659.* Princeton, 1978.

Lefebvre, A., and Triboullard, F. "L'élection de Valognes de 1540 à 1660." *Annales de Normandie* 21 (1973): 208–33.

Le Roy Ladurie, E. *Les Paysans de Languedoc.* Paris, 1966.

———, and Recurrat, J. "Etat des ventes du sel vers 1625." *Annales E.S.C.* 24 (1969): 999–1010.

———, and ———. "Sur les fluctuations de la consommation taxée du sel dans la France du nord aux XVIIe et XVIIIe siècles." *Revue du Nord* 54 (1972): 385–98.

Ligueron, L. "Les dettes des Communautés du bailliage de Dijon au XVIIe siècle." *Annales de Bourgogne* 53 (1981): 65–79.

Major, J. R. "Bellièvre, Sully and the Assembly of Notables of 1596." *Transactions of the American Philosophical Society,* new ser. 64 (1974): 3–31.

Mandrou, R. *Introduction to Modern France.* New York, 1975.

Meuvret, J. "Comment les Français du XVIIe siècle voyaient l'impôt." *XVIIe Siècle* 25–26 (1955): 59–82.

———. *Etudes d'Histoire Economique.* Paris, 1971.

———. *Le problème des subsistances à l'époque de Louis XIV.* Paris, 1979.

Michaud, H. "L'ordonnancement des dépenses et le budget de la monarchie, 1587–1589." *Annuaire-Bulletin de la Société de l'Histoire de France* (1972): 87–150.

Miskimin, H. *Money and Power in Fifteenth-Century France*. New Haven, 1984.

Mousnier, R. *Fureurs Paysans*. Paris, 1967.

———. "Monarchie contre aristocratie dans la France du XVIIe siecle," *XVIIe Siècle* 31 (1956): 377–81.

———. *La Plume, La Faucille et Le Marteau*. Paris, 1970.

———. "Sully et le conseil d'Etat et des finances: La lutte entre Bellièvre et Sully." *Revue Historique* 192 (1941): 68–86.

———. *La Vénalité des Offices*. Rouen and Paris, 1945, 1970.

———, and Hartung, F. "Quelques problèmes concernant la monarchie absolue." *Relazione del X Congresso Internationale de Scienzi Storiche* (Florence, 1955).

Pagès, G. "Autour du 'grand orage': Richelieu et Marillac. Deux politiques." *Revue Historique* 179 (1937): 63–97.

———. "Le conseil du roi et la vénalité des offices pendant les premières années du ministère de Richelieu." *Revue Historique* 182 (1938): 245–82. (If one were to single out one of Pagès's articles on this subject, this would be it.)

———. "Le conseil du roi sous Louis XIII." *Revue d'Histoire Moderne* 9 (1937): 7–38.

———. "Essai sur l'évolution des institutions administratives en France du commencement du XVIe à la fin du XVIIe siècle." *Revue d'Histoire Moderne* 7 (1935): 8–57; 113–38.

———. "La vénalité des offices dans l'ancienne France." *Revue Historique* 169 (1932): 477–95.

Permézel, J. *La politique financière de Sully dans la généralité de Lyon*. Paris, 1935.

Pillorget, R. "Les Cascaveoux: l'insurrection aixoise de l'automne 1630." *XVIIe Siècle* (1964): 3–30.

———. *Les mouvements insurrectionnels en Provence de 1595 à 1715*. Paris, 1975.

Porshnev, B. *Les soulèvements populaires en France avant la Fronde*. Paris, 1963.

Prentout, H. *Les Etats de Normandie*. 3 vols. Rouen, 1925.

Radding, C. M. "The Administration of the Aids in Normandy, 1360–1380." In *Order and Innovation in the Middle Ages: Essays in Honor of Joseph R. Strayer*, edited by W. Jordan, B. McNab, and T. Ruiz, 41–53. Princeton, 1976.

———. "The Estates of Normandy and the Revolts in the Towns at the Beginning of the Reign of Charles VI." *Speculum* (197): 79–90.

Ranum, O. *Richelieu and the Councillors of Louis XIII.* Oxford, 1963.

Revue Henri IV. (This short-lived review, 1904–9, published at Châlons-s-Marne, featured the work of the great financial historian Albert Chamberland. It also published many documents from the reign of Henry IV. I cite it here once, rather than listing the many articles.)

Rey, M. *Le domaine du roi sous Charles VI.* Paris, 1965.

———. *Les finances royales sous Charles VI: les causes du déficit, 1388–1413.* Paris, 1965.

Roupnel, *La ville et la campagne dijonnaise.* Paris, 1955.

Solon, P. "Popular Response to Standing Military Forces in Fifteenth-Century France." *Studies in the Renaissance* 19 (1972): 78–111.

Spooner, F. *L'économie mondiale et les frappes monétaires en France, 1493–1680.* Paris, 1956.

Van Doren, L. S. "The Royal *Taille* in Dauphiné, 1560–1610." *Proceedings of the Third Western Conference for French History* 3 (1975): 35–53.

———. "War Taxation, Institutional Change, and Social Conflict in Provincial France—The Royal *Taille* in Dauphiné, 1494–1559." *Proceedings of the American Philosophical Society* 121 (1977): 71–96.

Wolfe, M. *The Fiscal System of Renaissance France.* New Haven, 1972.

Index

Absolutism, limits of, 2, 3, 214

Aides, 4, 47, 200; Assembly of Notables' (1596) attitude toward, 77; centralization of, 38, 44; creation of, 24; *équivalent* of, 28, 46, 47, 90, 92–93, 168*n*; farm of, 79; income from, 49 (1523), 50–51 (1549); liens and *rentes* on, 59, 60–61, 64, 72–73, 216

Aix-en-Provence: number of treasurers in, 93; revolt in, 66; as seat of *recette générale,* 34; town debts of, 74*n*23

Alençon: creation of *généralité* of, 94; list of *élections* in, 230; revenue of, in 1630s and 1640s, 153

Amiens: Estates General of Languedoil meeting at (1363), 23–25; as seat of *recette générale,* 34, 47; siege of (1597), 77; town debts of, 74*n*23, 75*n*26

Amiens, *généralité* of: *élus* per *élection* in, 117; exemption of, from garrison tax, 48, 93; high regional costs of, 117; list of *élections* in, 224; number of *élections* in, 124; revenue of, in 1597, 159–60

Army, 24, 28, 101–3; garrisons, 3, 77, 109, 117, 120, 132; use of, to collect taxes, 163, 202, 203, 216, 220. See also *Etapes;* Garrison tax; Military

Assembly of Notables of 1583, 42–44; documents drawn up for, 50, 53, 62

Assembly of Notables of 1596, 6, 148; and the royal debt, 67–70; king's proposals to, 75–76; reply to proposals and its effect, 76–77, 78–81, 87

Asserac, hamlet of: taxes in, 179, 188

Assignations: irregular, 110, 116; regular, 109–10, 131–35, 150

Audierne: disappearances from tax rolls of, 184–85, 186, 190; tax distribution of, 179, 188; women taxpayers in, 182

Augé, parish of: tax distribution of, 175, 178; taxes in, 174, 175–76, 179, 186

Aveize, parish of: tax distribution of, 178; taxes in, 174, 177

Bankruptcy, 12, 17; of 1648, 142, 218; of 1634, 8, 100, 104, 105, 142, 145, 218; of 1602, 64, 66, 76

Bordeaux: *Convoi* of, 133; creation of *recette générale* at, 34; route to Lyon from, 128; town debts of, 74

Bordeaux: *généralité* of, 12, 48; army seizure of money in, 203; *élections* created in, 123, 125; *élus* per *élection* in, 117; list of *élections* in, 228–29; *non-valeurs* in, 163; public works levy in, 126; receiver general of, fined, 164; revenues of, 155–58. *See also* Guyenne

Bordiers (bordages), 208, 212; prominent among disappeared group, 14, 184, 186

Bourgeoisie: purchase of offices and Crown liens by, 5, 6–8, 17, 36, 59, 62, 64, 68, 85, 90, 97, 105–6; relationship of, with the Crown, 3, 19, 36, 209; tax exemptions of, 97; taxation of, 17, 97, 105–6. *See also* Local elites; Officers

Bourges: *généralité* of, 12; creation of,

247

Compositor:	Graphic Composition
Printer:	McNaughton and Gunn
Binder:	John H. Dekker
Text:	10/12 Sabon
Display:	Sabon